The Political Theory
of
The Federalist

The Political Theory
of
The Federalist

David F. Epstein

The University of Chicago Press
Chicago and London

The University of Chicago Press, Chicago 60637
The University of Chicago Press, Ltd., London

ISBN-13: 978-0-226-21299-9 (cloth)
ISBN-13: 978-0-226-21300-2 (paper)
ISBN-10: 0-226-21299-8 (cloth)
ISBN-10: 0-226-21300-5 (paper)

Library of Congress Cataloging-in-Publication Data

Epstein, David F.
  The political theory of the Federalist.
  Includes bibliographical references and index.
  1. Federalist.   2. Political science—United States—
History.   I. Title.
JK155.E64   1984   342.73′029   83-17858
ISBN 0-226-21299-8   347.30229
ISBN 0-226-21300-5 (paper)

To Ruth

Contents

CONTENTS

Acknowledgments

I am most grateful to Harvey C. Mansfield, Jr., and Nathan Tarcov, whose care and discernment in reading earlier versions of this book encouraged and enabled me to improve it. Judith Shklar and two anonymous referees for the University of Chicago Press also deserve thanks for a number of very helpful suggestions. The late Martin Diamond would have improved this book by his counsel; I wish to acknowledge my reliance on his writings and his example.

Introduction

The Federalist was written in some haste, published first in newspapers, and openly devoted to a concrete task: the ratification of the newly proposed Constitution for the United States. That a practical book tied to a particular occasion could be judged by Thomas Jefferson "the best commentary on the principles of government, which ever was written"[1] suggests that its argument was of impressive quality and wide applicability. Because *The Federalist* recommended a form of government intended to endure, it could not confine its analysis to the circumstances of 1787; and insofar as that form of government was offered as an example for mankind, *The Federalist* did not confine its analysis to America.

> [W]e must bear in mind that we are not to confine our view to the present period, but to look forward to remote futurity. Constitutions of civil government are not to be framed upon a calculation of existing exigencies, but upon a combination of these with the probable exigencies of ages, according to the natural and tried course of human affairs. (34, p. 207)[2]

The "tried course of human affairs" is history, or "experience," which ought to be consulted "whenever it can be found" (52, p. 327). Experience can be understood and calculated upon only if "tried" events reveal that there is a "natural" course of events from which one can reason. *The Federalist*'s own standards suggest that its argument must be judged not only for its appropriateness to the circumstances of 1787, but in light of political history and human nature generally. To recommend a form of government for America's "remote futurity," and even for the "esteem and adoption of mankind" (10, p. 81) is to engage in an argument about political theory of continuing relevance to those who have lived with that government, and to mankind in general.

While *The Federalist*'s practical occasion posed theoretical questions, it might be thought that the depth and coherence of *The Federalist*'s answers were limited by its rapid composition, serial publication, and plural authorship. But the work was written with more care and precision than is often assumed. The authors (Alexander Hamilton, James Madison, and John Jay)[3] were aided by many years' experience of and reflection on their subjects, so that they did not begin from scratch when facing each deadline.[4] The compatibility of the three authors is suggested by the fact that the solicited contributions of a fourth writer were rejected.[5] While Madison's disclaimer that the authors are not "mutually answerable for all the ideas of each other"[6] has often been quoted, it should be noted that Madison and Hamilton wrote their essays while both were in New York and could discuss matters with one another. In a letter Hamilton wrote to Madison immediately after the latter departed for Virginia, Hamilton refers to "the *principles we have talked of*, in respect to the legislative authorities."[7] I do not insist that the authors are indistinguishable, and will note some occasions on which there is a conflict.[8] But reports of inconsistency have been greatly exaggerated.[9]

Many parts of *The Federalist*'s text suggest purposes other than the hurried production of effective campaign literature. For example, *Federalist* 10 looks to "the nature of man" to explain the "causes" of faction—even though it suggests that the cure will attack faction's effects (which are widely known) and not its causes. And *Federalist* 37's discussion of what would now be called epistemology is surely much more elaborate than was necessary or even useful for the book's immediate purpose. The authors probably hoped the book would be studied by future generations.[10] Even if arguments for conclusions an audience already accepts appear "superfluous" at the time, they may be important later if different assumptions become prevalent (1, pp. 36–37). Because an unsound "popular creed" about politics (26, p. 169) might frustrate the Constitution's ultimate success even if it did not prevent its immediate ratification, *The Federalist* may have intended to "fortify opinion" in the future (49, p. 315). It also seems likely that in some cases the authors simply presented the results of their own thinking about the issues under consideration, without precisely calculating whether each particular point was essential to these practical purposes. The book's preface announces a wish to "promote the cause of truth" as well as to "lead to a right judgment of the true interests of the community."[11]

Furthermore, the somewhat hurried and particular circumstances of composition are an additional justification for careful study of the book. Since *The Federalist* is not a formal treatise in political theory, but a series of essays in service of a specific political cause, one cannot expect every important word to be explicitly defined, or every premise to be fully defended. That does not mean that *The Federalist*'s authors used words imprecisely or failed to think through their premises. The reader must attempt to understand the meaning of arguments which are sometimes tersely stated. The present study does not attempt only to learn what truths *The Federalist* "intended to be inculcated" (15, p. 105) with its newspaper readers, but to illuminate the *understanding* of politics which informs and supports the book's practical argument. For this purpose it is not inappropriate to read the book more carefully than a typical reader then or since was likely to.

Because of *The Federalist*'s association with an American Constitution which, with some changes, has remained authoritative, it has been "justly supposed to be entitled to great respect" by those engaged in "expounding the constitution."[12] More general characterizations or judgments of the American political order have also invoked *The Federalist*. Depending on the degrees of wisdom and influence attributed to *The Federalist* and the Constitution, the book has been available for patriotic appreciation of the American regime's fundamental principles, for critical revelation of the regime's essential deficiencies, or for melancholy or satisfied contemplation of the subsequent degradation or improvement of that regime. A once common view held that *The Federalist* and the Constitution manifest an undemocratic beginning to American liberal democracy, a beginning later corrected by progress visible in Jeffersonian, Jacksonian, and Rooseveltian revolutions but perhaps not fully corrected yet.[13] A more recent and sophisticated view holds that *The Federalist* reveals the liberal beginnings of American liberal democracy, a liberalism which displaced an earlier tradition of "republicanism" or "civic humanism."

This reported shift away from the republican tradition had gone unnoticed by earlier historians who believed that American thought consists of a continuous and generally unchallenged liberal tradition derived from or stated most clearly in the philosophy of John Locke. Liberal thought treats government as a device by which individual men can protect their own life, liberty, and property. Governments are instituted by popular consent for this purpose, and are limited to this purpose by arrangements such as separation of powers and representation, and by the right of revolution. Men living under a liberal regime may safely engage in the pursuit of economic gain, and their attachment, such as it is, to the community as a whole can be merely instrumental to their selfish ends. But recent historians have turned away from Locke and located a distinct tradition of "republican" thought, imported from the radical opposition party of England and influential in the American revolution. Bernard Bailyn and Gordon S. Wood have argued the importance of this view in early America, and J. G. A. Pocock has traced this tradition of republicanism or "civic humanism" through a series of political writers stretching from ancient Greece to the American Revolution and beyond.[14] This tradition emphasizes man's political nature and his capacity for attaining a "civic virtue" in which his own personality is fulfilled in his patriotic contribution to the common good. This tradition presents a clear alternative to Lockean liberalism, according to which men's personalities are by nature devoted to their private and chiefly economic good.

Wood suggests that the era of *The Federalist* was characterized by a rejection of this "classical" republican tradition. Pocock reports the survival of the republican tradition past 1787, but largely as a source of criticism of the principles which eclipsed it. The crucial departure was the abandonment of the "paradigm" of "virtue":

> As Federalist thought took shape, and the people were less and less seen as possessing virtue in the classical sense, it is not surprising to find, in Madison's writings and those of others—the tenth issue of *The Federalist* is the *locus classicus*—an increasing recognition of the importance, and the legitimacy, in human affairs of the faction pursuing a collective but particular interest, which in older Country and republican theory had figured as one of the most deadly means to the corruption of virtue by passion. Interest and faction are the modes in which the decreasingly virtuous people discern and pursue their activities in politics. . . .[15]

Thus *The Federalist* occupies an important position in this account of the rejection of republicanism. Precisely in the thought of this era, it is said, one finds the hopes for civic spirit fading under the weight of events or perhaps only their perceived weight. Thus *The Federalist* can be seen as either a brilliant but depressing explanation of the discovery that human vice makes civic humanism impossible, or an unduly pessimistic book whose influential rhetoric helped create political arrangements which made civic humanism come to appear impossible.

According to this view, *The Federalist* crystallizes or epitomizes the adoption of a new "paradigm" about politics, according to which government is a limited instrument for the protection of peace and commerce, whose purposes are served only by social circumstances or institutional arrangements which counterbalance, but do not improve upon, men's private-spirited aims. While this "new science of politics" has sometimes been identified with twentieth-century political scientists' diagnosis of a "pluralism" among competitive interest groups, historians have noted respects in which *The Federalist* is not so "recognizably modern."[16] *The Federalist* appears to share with John Locke such old-fashioned views as that men have "rights" and not merely "interests," and that government should be instituted by a people's formal consent and not merely accepted by its informal consensus. *The Federalist*'s Lockean liberalism thus appears distinctive in comparison with both the republican tradition which preceded it and the later "pluralist" analysis of American politics.

But there is one formidable difficulty with the view that *The Federalist* rejected a classical republican tradition in favor of Lockean liberalism. That is *The Federalist*'s repeated and very emphatic insistence on a "strictly republican" or "wholly popular" form of government.[17] The limited monarchy of England defended by Locke[18] is not "defensible," according to *The Federalist* (39, p. 240)—despite the fact that it is a "free government" with a long record of success. A government with only "one republican branch" is indefensible; *The Federalist* requires all officials to be directly or indirectly elected by the people. Those who have found *The Federalist* tainted by "undemocratic" principles have pointed not so much to the institutions it defends as to certain of its arguments which manifest doubts about popular wisdom, doubts about the majority's commitment to justice, and elitist hopes for "fit characters" who can contribute their unequal talents to government. Whether or not later democrats have so far and so successfully freed themselves from those concerns as to justify calling *The Federalist* but not themselves "undemocratic," *The Federalist*'s defense of a "wholly popular" government in spite of those concerns is remarkable. If one compares *The Federalist* not with more recent opinion but with the most respectable theoretical sources of its time (Locke and Montesquieu) and compares the regime it defended with the most respectable actual regime of its time (Great Britain's), one would have cause to wonder not at the doubts expressed about or refinements proposed for popular government, but at the fact that a wholly popular government was insisted upon at all. *The Federalist* admits that popular government has a bad reputation which it has fully earned by its history of instability, injustice, and failure (10, pp. 77, 81); the history of Greek and Italian republics shows that their forms of government are "indefensible" (9, p. 72). Paradoxically, however, *The Federalist* asserts that only a "strictly republican" form can make the new Constitution "defensible" (39, p. 240).

How, then, does *The Federalist* defend republican government? Most obviously, it does so by explaining a "more perfect structure" than the ancient republics had, so that "the excellencies of republican government may be retained and its imperfections lessened or avoided" (9, pp. 72–73). The republican form can be vindicated if it can be made consistent with the order of society and with the protection of men's rights, i.e., if it can be reconciled with liberal ends. More fundamentally, however, one must consider why *The Federalist* tries to improve the republican form rather than abandons it, why one should seek only a *republican* remedy to republican diseases (10, p. 84); in short, what are the "excellencies of republican government" which deserve to be retained?

The fact that *The Federalist* does not say very much about why it insists on popular government is surely related to the predispositions of its audience—just as the later scholarly silence on this question is related to the predispositions of the later audience. While it has been suggested that *The Federalist*'s commitment to a "strictly" popular government is an unexamined premise or a concession to its readers' prejudices, I suggest that *The Federalist* does offer an argument for wholly popular government.

That argument is based on a psychology which understands the specifically political, rather than economic, impulses of men. These political impulses range from the "love of fame" which is the "ruling passion of the noblest minds" (72, p. 437), to the more common love of power, or "ambition," of political men, to the "passion" of opinionated partisans (10, p. 78). Both the economic view of self-interest which has come to be associated with liberalism, and the political hopes for self-abnegation which were once associated with republicanism, obstruct an appreciation of this important aspect of man's nature, which is neither economic nor altruistic but is selfish and political. Human selfishness takes the form not only of self-indulgence and exertion in the pursuit of self-indulgence, but also of self-assertion. For this reason politics cannot be fully understood as either simply an arena for the practice of virtue or simply a realm for the competition or aggregation of interests.

Early liberals like Hobbes and Locke clearly recognized the force of man's political impulses, even while asserting man's natural freedom from political authority and denying that he should be considered by nature a "political animal." Hobbes appears to have hoped that a political order with limited and uncontroversial ends, and an acknowledgedly legitimate beginning, could generally soothe or repress men's political impulses and encourage them to enjoy the *"Liberty* of *Subjects"* to live private, economic lives.[19] While similarly emphasizing government's purpose of securing public safety and private rights, *The Federalist* seems to doubt the feasibility and even the desirability of quieting men's political impulses. *The Federalist* rejects Hobbesian absolute monarchy, but it also departs from other liberal predecessors who defended limited or mixed monarchy. Even if Locke and Montesquieu were correct in thinking that a mixed government like England's could secure men's safety and protect men's interests, such a government offends the spirit of political self-assertion which *The Federalist* recognizes and even admires.[20] *The Federalist*'s attachment to "wholly popular" government, even if a bow to prejudice, is a theoretically self-conscious bow; that is, the popular prejudice for popular government is not a circumstance which prevents action according to theory, but is a manifestation of a fact of political life which theory can understand.

Both why and how *The Federalist* proposes to combine liberalism with a "strictly republican" form of government are the broad subjects of this study. The length of *The Federalist* makes it impractical to offer a commentary on the entire work, but makes it unconvincing to extract "thematic" statements which buttress a particular interpretation. Insofar as possible, therefore, this study elaborates *The Federalist*'s theoretical themes by attending to the contexts in which they are developed, and is organized roughly in accordance with the organization of *The Federalist*.

The Federalist consists of 85 essays divided into two volumes. *Federalist* 1 introduces the work, and concludes with an outline of topics to be discussed. The first three topics form a logical whole and compose volume 1:

> —*The utility of the UNION to your political prosperity* [nos. 2–14]
> —*The insufficiency of the present Confederation to preserve that Union* [nos. 15–22]
> —*The necessity of a government at least equally energetic with the one proposed, to the attainment of this object* [nos. 23–36] (1, p. 36)

This argument resembles in its structure and some of its details the arguments of Hobbes and Locke, according to which government is a means to an end, an instrument which men institute by their voluntary consent so as to secure themselves a "more contented" life than is possible without government.[21] According to *The Federalist*, "energetic government," by preserving the Union, will serve the people's "political prosperity"; it is the kind of government a people would be well advised to institute. But even while advising a people about its choice of government, *The Federalist* almost begins by suggesting that the ability of the people to choose their own "good government" is a "question":

> It has been frequently remarked that it seems to have been reserved to the people of this country, by their conduct and example, to decide the important question, whether societies of men are really capable or not of establishing good government from reflection and choice, or whether they are forever destined to de-

pend for their political constitutions on accident and force. (1, p. 33)

The major theoretical themes of volume 1 are fundamental issues of liberalism. First, are men's circumstances and abilities such that they are "really capable" of exercising their right to choose their own government? *Federalist* numbers 2–14 suggest both the ends which (it is hoped) can unite and attract men's voluntary choice of government, and the obstacles posed by "accident and force" (chapter 1 of the present study). Second, what kind of government can successfully secure the ends men seek when they institute government? *Federalist* numbers 15–36 give the general answer "energetic government"; but explain that government must also be "modeled" in such a manner that the very energy which secures the people's safety will not endanger their safety (chapter 2).

Volume 2 applies these principles to a detailed analysis of the proposed Constitution, showing how it creates a government which is energetic and safe, as well as possessed of other qualities (for example, "stability") which are useful to political prosperity even if not clearly "necessary" to preserve the Union. Thus volume 2 more fully elaborates the principles of "good government," and shows how the proposed Constitution conforms to those principles. However, the announced topic of volume 2 suggests a narrower or different focus: "—*The conformity of the proposed Constitution to the true principles of republican government*" (1, p. 36).[22] And this standard of "republican government" is at odds with some essential ingredients of "good government."[23] In the introduction to the second volume, Madison explains how difficult it is to combine "the requisite stability and energy in government with the inviolable attention due to liberty and to the republican form" (37, p. 226). The true principles of republican government, the nature of good government, and the connection between them are the themes of volume 2's explanation of the proposed Constitution.

Before turning to volume 2, however, I will (in chapter 3) give close consideration to an early essay which develops all of these themes: the famous *Federalist* 10. That essay discusses a particularly important contribution of the Union to political prosperity, its cure for "faction." *Federalist* 10 shows how the Union can "secure the public good and private rights against the danger" of faction, and thereby rescue popular government "from the opprobrium under which it has so long labored" (pp. 80–81). While the essays surrounding *Federalist* 10 describe various particular elements of "your political prosperity"—safety from foreign and interstate wars (nos. 2–7), avoidance of despotism and insurrection (nos. 8–9), commercial prosperity (no. 11), lower taxes and more economical government (nos. 12–13)—*Federalist* 10's formulation, "the public good and private rights," appears to be a comprehensive statement of the political prosperity which good government should secure. The "public good and private rights" are the central concerns of, respectively, republican and liberal political thought. I will consider the meaning of and relation between these two fundamental objects of government, as well as the means by which *Federalist* 10 suggests they can be secured. *Federalist* 10's insistence on a "republican remedy"—so as to rescue popular government from "opprobrium"—manifests its determination to secure the objects of good government by means of a republican form. I will consider both how and why it proposes to do so. In addition, *Federalist* 10's explanation that the seeds of faction are sown in the "nature of man"—in man's impulses of "passion" and "interest"—lays a groundwork for understanding *The Federalist*'s account of how human impulses can be put to work in the operation of a good government.

Volume 2 (nos. 37–85) is divided into sections which are announced in the course of the book.[24] It may be outlined as follows:

Conformity of the proposed Constitution to republican principles (nos. 37–84)
   Introduction (37–38)
   General form of the proposed Constitution (39–40)
   Powers vested in the government (41–46)
   Particular structure of the government (47–83)
      Separation of powers (47–51)
      House of Representatives (52–61)
      Senate (62–66)
      Executive (67–77)
      Judiciary (78–83)
   Answers to objections (84)
Conclusion (85)

The section on the "general form" of the proposed Constitution (nos. 39–40) gives the book's clearest argument for a "strictly republican" form; it is preceded by an introduction (nos. 37–38) admitting both the limits of human reason and the tensions between republicanism, energy, and stability. Chapter 4 will discuss these sections, and explain how *The Federalist* finds in man's passionate sense of honor a foundation for popular government which man's limited powers of reasoning cannot fully supply.

Having anticipated the section on the "powers" of government (nos.41–46) while discussing the necessity of energy (as indeed *The Federalist* itself did, leading to the only major "repetitions of ideas" which might "displease a critical reader"),[25] I turn in the final three chapters to the "particular structure" of the government. *The Federalist*'s explanation of structure is famous for showing how government can be made "safe" to the governed. Separation of powers (nos. 47–51, chapter 5), and representation (nos. 52–61, chapter 6) are two devices directed primarily to that end. Less familiar are the book's explanations of how the proposed structure creates a "good government" which usefully serves the public good rather than only refraining from doing the public harm. Part of the explanation of representation (chapter 6, second section), and particularly the discussion of the government's "more permanent branches" which provide qualities like energy and stability (nos. 62–83, chapter 7) develop this argument.

Because *The Federalist* was the first book to recommend a "wholly elective" (65, p. 396) form of government, it did not take for granted that such a regime was justified, possible, or certain to succeed. Those who take all of those things for granted may celebrate *The Federalist* without studying it; those who for various reasons find any or all of those propositions open to doubt can learn from the analysis offered by *The Federalist* in defense of this novel regime.

·[ONE]·

Government by Choice

After an unequivocal experience of the inefficacy of the subsisting federal government, you are called upon to deliberate on a new Constitution for the United States of America. (1, p. 33)

The Federalist was written by men who favored a new Constitution for the United States and addressed to those with the authority to decide on a new Constitution. The procedure of a ratification by the people through their specially elected representatives was not a necessary or even a strictly legal part of the revision of the Articles of Confederation undertaken by the Philadelphia convention. The convention decided on this procedure both out of optimism about its likely results and because a popular ratification was justified and required by theoretical principles of considerable weight.

The fabric of American empire ought to rest on the solid basis of THE CONSENT OF THE PEOPLE. The streams of national power ought to flow immediately from that pure, original fountain of all legitimate authority. (22, p. 152; see 49, p. 313)

The view that governments derive "their just powers from the consent of the governed" and that therefore "it is the Right of the People . . . to institute new Government" is asserted by the Declaration of Independence and argued by, most notably, John Locke. According to the Declaration, the people have a right "to institute new Government, laying its foundation on such principles and organizing its powers in such form, as to them shall seem most likely to effect their Safety and Happiness."

But the appearance that the Americans of 1787 are merely exercising in practice a right previously demonstrated by theorists is immediately complicated by Hamilton's suggestion that American practice could affect that theory:

> It has been frequently remarked that it seems to have been reserved to the people of this country, by their conduct and example, to decide the important question, whether societies of men are really capable or not of establishing good government from reflection and choice, or whether they are forever destined to depend for their political constitutions on accident and force. (1, p. 33)

What the Americans do may decide an important question about societies of men everywhere. If it should turn out to be true that societies are "forever destined to depend for their political constitutions on accident and force," then a "new Government" would never be instituted by a popular "consent" or "choice"; it could not possess the "legitimate authority" that can only flow from that "pure, original fountain." Even if one supposes that popular consent can confer legitimacy not only by originating government ("fountain") but also by acquiescing to a government originated in some other way,[1] such tacit consent is only meaningful if it can be withdrawn, and it cannot usefully be withdrawn if the people are unable to institute a new government to replace the one they find oppressive. If governments cannot be instituted by "THE CONSENT OF THE PEOPLE," and cannot be replaced by the people when they lose that consent, then all government is illegitimate or potentially illegitimate; or else insistence on consent sets too strict a standard of legitimacy. What the Declaration of Independence calls a "self-evident" truth—that new governments are instituted by popular consent—is treated by *Federalist* 1 as an "important question." What is self-evident is the importance of America's deliberation (it "speaks its own importance" [1, p. 33]), because the result of that deliberation could confirm or refute the Declaration's assertion.

According to Hamilton's statement, the alternative to a society instituting government by "reflection and choice" is its receiving government by "accident and force." *Some* government seems unavoidable, as *Federalist* 2 confirms: "Nothing is more certain than the indispensable necessity of government," regardless of "whenever and however it is instituted" (p. 37). Hamilton's presentation of the alternatives omits the possibility of a man or men being natural rulers of society; perhaps he agrees with Socrates' remark in Plato's *Republic* that rule by those naturally qualified would only occur in the event of some "divine chance," i.e., accident; perhaps he agrees with Hobbes that those Aristotle thought "by Nature . . . more worthy to Command" could in fact command others (if at all) only by "force."[2] Hamilton also does not speak of a divinely appointed ruler, perhaps accepting Locke's claim to have shown the absurdity of such a view in his *First Treatise*. Locke himself offered his doctrine of "consent" as the only alternative to basing government on "Force and Violence." Because Sir Robert Filmer's argument that government derives from *"Adam's Private Dominion and Paternal Jurisdiction"* is untenable, Locke says,

> he that will not give just occasion, to think that all Government in the World is the product only of Force and Violence, and that Men live together by no other Rules but that of Beasts, where the strongest carries it, and so lay a Foundation for perpetual Disorder and Mischief, Tumult, Sedition and Rebellion, . . . must of necessity find out another rise of Government, another Original of Political Power, and another way of designing and knowing the Persons that have it, then what Sir *Robert F.* hath taught us.[3]

A government founded only on force invites attempts to replace it by force. Men cannot live in peace unless there is some more decisive "Original of Political Power"—which Locke finds in the principle of popular consent.

But are "societies of men" "really capable" of instituting government in the way Locke describes? Locke did not make perfectly clear whether men's actual "conduct and example" were necessary to prove his theory.[4] David Hume, "a writer equally solid and ingenious" (84, p. 526), regarded the matter of "fact and reality" as a decisive objection to Locke's "philosophical notions." For one thing,

> Almost all the governments which exist at present, or of which there remains any record in story, have been founded originally, either on usurpation or conquest, or both, without any pretence of a fair consent or voluntary subjection of the people.[5]

The success of conquest or usurpation leaves no occasion for a popular choice. And Hume goes further; if, rarely, a situation arises where the institution of government would depend on the decision of a large number of men,

> Every wise man then wishes to see, at the head of a powerful and obedient army, a general who may speedily seize the prize, and give to the people a master which they are so unfit to choose for

themselves; so little correspondent is fact and reality to those [i.e., Locke's[6]] philosophical notions.[7]

According to Hume, the people are "unfit" to institute government by their own choice even when circumstances might permit.

In this chapter I will consider *The Federalist*'s response to these two Humean objections: first, the degree to which force and accident preempt any occasion for the people to choose their government; second, the intrinsic fitness or unfitness of the people for the task. *The Federalist*'s concern with whether and how the principle of consent can be put into practice may seem unimportant to those later writers who treat consent as hypothetical and who deduce a theory of justice from what men presumably would consent to under proper conditions.[8] But, among other problems, that approach leaves unclear how what deserves consent can be put into practice. If justice deserves consent but is not really capable of winning it, there is no "solid basis" for government in "THE CONSENT OF THE PEOPLE," but only the accidental or forceful rule of those who understand justice, vulnerable of course to the accidental success or forceful assaults of those who understand it differently. Precisely if it is to be a "solid basis" for government, "THE CONSENT OF THE PEOPLE" must be more than hypothetical.

Force and Accident

A society's intrinsic ability to reflect and choose would be irrelevant if some native or foreign men in command of sufficient force chose to obstruct or reverse the society's choice. The view that right is distinguished from might does not settle the important question of whether societies are really capable of acting in accordance with their alleged rights. In *Federalist* 11, Hamilton seems to agree with Hume's view of the historical record of usurpation and conquest:

> The world may politically, as well as geographically, be divided
> into four parts, each having a distinct set of interests. Unhappily
> for the other three, Europe, by her arms and by her negotiations,
> by force and by fraud, has in different degrees extended her do-
> minion over them all. Africa, Asia, and America have successively
> felt her domination. (11, p. 90)

The victories by "force" and "fraud" show the reign of what *Federalist* 1 calls "force" and "accident," since, from the point of view of the defrauded, successful domination without force is a kind of accident.[9] Europe's successful domination suggests a disagreeable answer to *Federalist*

1's question; the "societies of men" ruled by Europe cannot choose their own governments.

> The superiority she [Europe] has long maintained has tempted her to plume herself as the mistress of the world, and to consider the rest of mankind as created for her benefit. Men admired as profound philosophers have in direct terms attributed to her inhabitants a physical superiority and have gravely asserted that all animals, and with them the human species, degenerate in America—that even dogs cease to bark after having breathed awhile in our atmosphere. . . . Facts have too long supported these arrogant pretensions of the European. (11, pp. 90–91)

The view that "all men are created equal" in their "unalienable Rights" to "Life, Liberty, and the pursuit of Happiness" is incompatible with the claim that European humans have a physical superiority and that the rest of mankind is created for Europe's benefit. As in *Federalist* 1, the rights of men asserted by Locke and America's Declaration of Independence are inseparable from a view of what men are "really capable of." If European superiority permits her to dominate all other men according to Europe's own interest, then the alleged origin of legitimate government in the choice of the governed is untenable. Leaving aside the internal politics of Europe itself, one could safely conclude that the rest of mankind will receive government by "force and accident." Even after citing what seems to be a preposterous insult to the dogs of America, Hamilton concedes much: "Facts have too long supported these arrogant pretensions of the European." The theory of Europe's superiority cannot be refuted without a change in the facts:

> It belongs to us to vindicate the honor of the human race, and to teach that assuming brother moderation. Union will enable us to do it. (11, p. 91)

Americans who establish their own "great American system" can avoid serving as the "instruments of European greatness." While this might seem to vindicate American honor, Hamilton says it will vindicate the honor of the "human race."

This is one of several important passages in which *The Federalist* invokes human "honor."[10] According to Hume,

> When we assert that all lawful government arises from the consent of the people, we certainly do them a great deal more honour than they deserve, or even expect and desire from us.[11]

But *The Federalist* treats a society's choice of government precisely as a point of honor—rather than as, say, a matter of interest. A society ruled by force may also have its interests injured, but *The Federalist* most emphatically insists on the affront to men's honorable wish to choose for themselves.[12] The human race is dishonored if it is ruled by force and accident. If the human desire to choose is utterly inefficacious, human beings are like dogs who cannot bark. We are ruled by the force of "physical superiority." If America can show the efficacy of choice as against force and accident, human honor will be vindicated.

But this requires that America choose to be forceful—hardly an unqualified victory for choice over force. Nonetheless, men are not simply ruled by force if force can be chosen. We are not destined to be ruled by whoever happens to be forceful now. By organizing its own force, a society of men asserts its choice even as it accepts the power of force. America can organize such a force by choosing to be united: "Union will enable us to do it."

The fact that a society's choice of government must include a choice to be forceful enough to defend that choice was illustrated in the American Revolution. Americans won their independence "fighting side by side throughout a long and bloody war," making use of their "joint counsels, arms, and efforts" (2, p. 38); counsels, i.e., reflection and choice, would not have been enough. Similarly, while the wiser choices of a new national government can avoid provoking just wars (3, pp. 42–45), the nation's own force must be marshalled to defeat the unjust attacks from nations which "in general will make war whenever they have a prospect of getting anything by it" (4, p. 46).[13]

But a society's choice to organize its force is problematic. Victory in battle cannot "be calculated by the rules which prevail in a census of the inhabitants, or which determine the event of an election" (43, p. 277). And military operations are best led by a single hand (70, p. 427). Can societies of men keep control of their own force when they choose to exert it, or—as Hobbes suggests—is the choice of a sufficiently forceful government the choice to end all choice?[14] If the American Union were dissolved, Hamilton argues, the separate states would face precisely this Hobbesian choice:

> Safety from external danger is the most powerful director of national conduct. Even the ardent love of liberty will, after a time, give way to its dictates. The violent destruction of life and property incident to war, the continual effort and alarm attendant on a state of continual danger, will compel nations the most attached to liberty to resort for repose and security to institutions which have a tendency to destroy their civil and political rights. To be more safe, they at length become willing to run the risk of being less free. (8, p. 67)

Because wars without standing armies and fortifications bring great "PLUNDER and devastation" and "continual effort and alarm," men are driven to prefer the standing armies and stronger executives which can bring peace.

> Thus we should, in a little time, see established in every part of this country the same engines of despotism which have been the scourge of the old world. This, at least, would be the natural course of things; and our reasonings will be the more likely to be just in proportion as they are accommodated to this standard. (8, p. 68)

Hamilton's reasoning from the "natural course of things" precisely parallels Hobbes's reasoning from the "natural condition" of man. For the sake of their safety, men choose a government forceful enough to repel the force of others; but this seems to be only an anticipatory surrender of choice to force. If the natural course of things leads from war to standing armies to despotism, men's choice of government does not amount to much.

But Hamilton claims that a united America can avoid this bleak prospect. He prefaces that claim with examples of two peoples for whom the force required by war did not extinguish choice: the "ancient republics of Greece," which had war but not standing armies, and the "kingdom of Great Britain," which has standing armies but not despotism. Both examples are relevant precedents for America.

Regarding ancient Greece:

> It may, perhaps, be asked . . . why did not standing armies spring up out of the contentions which so often distracted the ancient republics of Greece? Different answers, equally satisfactory, may be given to this question. The industrious habits of the people of the present day, absorbed in the pursuits of gain and devoted to the improvements of agriculture and commerce, are incompatible with the condition of a nation of soldiers, which was the true condition of the people of those republics. The means of revenue, which have been so greatly multiplied by the increase of gold and silver and of the arts of industry, and the science of finance, which is the offspring of modern times, concurring with the habits of nations, have produced an entire revolution in the system of war, and have rendered disciplined armies, distinct from the body of the citizens, the inseparable companion of frequent hostility. (8, pp. 68–69)

Modern peoples are too busy to be soldiers, and modern warfare is too difficult for amateurs. These "equally satisfactory" answers both refer to the greater wealth which industrious modern men produce and which modern war makes use of. The industrious pursuit of "gain" changes the "habits of the people," while the wealth they produce can serve the unchanged "habits of nations." Thus the transformation visible in modern times may be attributed to the people's own attraction to the prosperity of a peaceful, industrious life, or to the necessity nations habitually feel to improve their "system of war" however they can.

For either or both of these reasons, modern policy stimulates wealth by promoting commerce. Commerce is a recent development in the "prevailing system of nations" (6, pp. 56–57; see 42, p. 266, describing commerce in slaves as the "barbarism of modern policy"), and commerce has impressive effects:

> By multiplying the means of gratification, by promoting the introduction and circulation of the precious metals, those darling objects of human avarice and enterprise, it serves to vivify and invigorate all the channels of industry and to make them flow with greater activity and copiousness. (12, p. 91)

But *Federalist* 8 suggests that modern affluence is not altogether beneficial. The riches that industrious modern men produce are available for nations to use in obtaining greater and greater forces. Industrious men cannot be soldiers, and their industry raises the standards of war to a level which requires professionals. When one nation uses its wealth to create a disciplined standing army, such armies become necessary for all nations. But where there is an army separate from the citizens, the "military state becomes elevated above the civil," and the "condition of the citizen" is degraded by the soldier's importance (8, p. 70). In modern times men are governed by "despotism"; they do not live in republics. Ancient times were not characterized by the victory of force over choice because citizen-soldiers could enforce their own choices. Hamilton's immediate point is that this solution is not available to modern Americans, but I will consider later how America might modify it (see chapter 2, below).

Great Britain is an exception to the natural course of modern times. This is because her "situation," i.e., location, leaves her "seldom exposed" to "internal invasions." As a result, the standing army is relatively small compared to the people's "natural strength" and the people do not love or fear it (8, p. 69). Britain's "insular situation, and a powerful marine" protect her.

> This peculiar felicity of situation has, in a great degree, contributed to preserve the liberty which that country to this day enjoys, in spite of the prevalent venality and corruption. If, on the con-

trary, Britain had been situated on the continent, and had been compelled, as she would have been, by that situation, to make her military establishments at home coextensive with those of the other great powers of Europe, she, like them, would in all probability be, at this day, a victim to the absolute power of a single man. (8, p. 70)

In short, Britain is lucky. To be relatively out of reach of the force of neighboring enemies is an exception to the natural course of things. Hamilton emphasizes that a united America may "for ages" enjoy a similar advantage, due to the distance of Europe and the weakness of European colonies nearby. Without unity, of course, Americans would be enemies to each other and thereby resemble continental Europe rather than England.

Thus the practical subject of the first part of *The Federalist*—"*The utility of the UNION to your political prosperity*" (1, p. 36)—is linked to the important question posed in *Federalist* 1. By choosing union, Americans can choose a sufficient force to defend themselves against the force of others, but need not choose the despotic force which would be necessary for that purpose in a smaller and more vulnerable country. But the fact that America, like Britain, enjoys a "peculiar felicity of situation" recalls another term of *Federalist* 1's question: "accident." Is union really a choice by which societies of men can overcome their vulnerability to force, or is it only the good fortune of America? *Federalist* 2 suggests that the American Union might be a gift of Providence:

It has often given me pleasure to observe that independent America was not composed of detached and distant territories, but that one connected, fertile, widespreading country was the portion of our western sons of liberty. Providence has in a particular manner blessed it with a variety of soils and productions and watered it with innumerable streams for the delight and accommodation of its inhabitants. A succession of navigable waters forms a kind of chain round its borders, as if to bind it together; while the most noble rivers in the world, running at convenient distances, present them with highways for the easy communication of friendly aids and the mutual transportation and exchange of their various commodities.

With equal pleasure I have as often taken notice that Providence has been pleased to give this one connected country to one united people. . . . (2, p. 38)

Providence's "particular manner" with independent America gives us blessings which other societies of men lack. If our unity is a providential gift, it is not really a choice, or at least not purely a choice. But Jay does not seem entirely guided by what he describes as Providence's intentions. He observes with "pleasure" America's gifts, as if he himself judges them to be good and does not simply accept them as good because they are providential. One could also say that Providence's intention regarding rivers is ambiguous; some of them provide "easy communication" within the country, while others are part of the "chain" which defines its borders. A future political decision could reclassify, say, the Mississippi River. And Jay's "pleasure" in observing that America contains "one united people" requires that he ignore the presence of the Indians who are visible in *Federalist* 3 (p. 44).

Furthermore, in the papers immediately following Jay's providential meditations, *The Federalist* indicates the great danger of war between the states. Unity is not guaranteed by geographical or ethnic contiguity; on the contrary, it is a "sort of axiom in politics that vicinity, or nearness of situation, constitutes nations natural enemies" (6, p. 59); and sentimental attachments among Americans will only aggravate their indignation against one another when conflicts arise (see 7, p. 63). Only by choosing an effective national government can the Union be secured; the "profound peace" (85, p. 527) Americans enjoy in 1787 cannot last long because it is contrary to the "natural and necessary progress of human affairs" (8, p. 68).

Not only a consideration of future probabilities but a remembrance of past events indicates that "Union" is not a given. In *Federalist* 14 Madison appeals to the "kindred blood" of the Americans, and to its having been "mingled" when shed in the Revolutionary War, when he urges his readers to "[h]earken not to the unnatural voice" which would divide up the American "family" (pp. 103–4). Disunion would be a more alarming novelty than the admittedly novel extended republic proposed by *The Federalist*. However, Madison does not rely on this appeal for conservation, but proceeds to defend "novelty" altogether as congenial to the glorious spirit of America. He notes that America's revolutionaries did not shrink from novelty—thus reminding us that the argument for conservation of the "family," of the united "great, respectable, and flourishing empire" could have been applied to the British Empire before America hearkened to an "unnatural voice" and chose the novelty of independence. Not inherited or sentimental or blood ties but the political choice of 1776 explains the unity of the American rather than the Anglo-American family; and only further political choice, *The Federalist* argues, can preserve the Union. Madison calls men choosing their own, new ways rather than accepting natural, traditional ways "noble," glorious, and "manly"—again suggesting the connection between choice and human honor.

But while Providence, or accident, does not make our choice of Union unnecessary, it may make it possible. For one thing, 1787 is a time of "profound peace" (85, p. 527) in which Americans can conduct "those calm and mature inquiries and reflections which must ever precede the formation of a wise and well-balanced government for a free people" (2, p. 39). This leisure was lacking in 1776, which is why the choices made then need amendment. Americans living under defective governments hurriedly chosen in 1776 enjoy a leisure in 1787 which can be attributed not to any "capacity of the existing government," but to "causes that are fugitive and fallacious," or, more simply, to "good fortune" (41, p. 261). Our coastal residents "sleep quietly in their beds," but not because the government can protect them; the states are at peace with each other, but not because the government secures their union. Our situation contradicts the natural fact that independent neighbors are enemies, and that situation cannot last long. Good fortune provides an opportunity for us to choose measures which can assure our security when our luck runs out.

Furthermore, America seems potentially united or potentially unitable, a choice which Providence or luck makes more easily available to us than to, say, Europe. Our "felicity of situation" makes defense possible, and particularly makes possible a defense which does not depend on despotic government. But this too is a temporary gift. By choosing union, we may "for ages" enjoy our geographically given exemption from the need for large standing armies. But the exemption is not forever. *The Federalist* argues that we may some day need a standing army, and even a sizable standing army; we cannot therefore choose a constitution which flatly bans standing armies, much as the people might wish that. The possibility of a society successfully retaining its choice of government, under modern conditions, depends on whether the standing army can be made compatible with liberty, a subject given considerable attention by *The Federalist* and to which I will return in the next chapter.

America's accidental advantages in choosing her own government suggest that America can decide what societies of men are "really capable" of in only a limited way. If we fail despite our very favorable circumstances, the conclusion must be that men cannot establish government by reflection and choice. If we succeed, our reliance on lucky accidents suggests that a similar choice will not always or often be available to other societies of men.

Fitness for Choice

Thus America's circumstances permit her to choose a union which will secure her against domination by force. But will the people in fact choose that union? Given the opportunity to choose, will a society of men choose well? Hamilton's important question in *Federalist* 1 was whether men could institute "good government" by reflection and choice; the "political constitutions" men might receive from accident and force were not called "good," presumably because it would be simply an accident if those with most force or those who accidentally ruled despite inferior force ruled for the good of the people. Furthermore, a people's inadvertent choice of a bad government would be a kind of accident; Hamilton speaks of a "wrong election" by Americans as a "misfortune" for mankind (1, p. 33). If the people chose a hateful tyranny or an impotent government which could easily be conquered by a hateful tyranny, their "choice" would be absurd. According to the Declaration of Independence, the people are entitled to choose whatever government seems to them "most likely to effect their Safety and Happiness"; and if they choose poorly, they are entitled to alter or abolish their government and try again. Prudence dictates that this not be done too frequently; and unless men are "really capable" of choosing well at least sometimes it is hard to see why it should be done at all.

Men would be most capable of choosing well if both their "head[s]" and their "heart[s]" were in the right place (1, p. 35), i.e., if they were both "considerate" and "good":

Happy will it be if our choice should be directed by a judicious estimate of our true interests, unperplexed and unbiased by considerations not connected with the public good. (1, p. 33)

A "considerate" man is one who is thoughtful, who can make a "judicious estimate." A "good" man is moved by the "inducements . . . of patriotism" (and perhaps philanthropy) to care for "our true interests," that is, "the public good." Almost the same thought is expressed at the end of volume 1:

Happy will it be for ourselves, and most honorable for human nature, if we have wisdom and virtue enough to set so glorious an example to mankind! (36, p. 224)

Here again *The Federalist* connects the choice of a good government by Americans with the "honor" of human nature.

A happy choice of government would be directed by considerateness and goodness, i.e., by wisdom and virtue—or more precisely by "wisdom and virtue enough," since men "are yet remote from the happy empire of perfect wisdom and perfect virtue" (6, p. 59). But how much wisdom and virtue is enough, and how much is available? Hamilton's argument in *Federalist* 1 immediately admits that a judicious and unbiased choice "is a thing more ardently to be wished than seriously to be expected."

> The plan offered to our deliberations affects too many particular interests, innovates upon too many local institutions, not to involve in its discussion a variety of objects foreign to its merits, and of views, passions, and prejudices little favorable to the discovery of truth. (1, p. 33)

The existence of "particular interests" and "local institutions" means that the society of men which is supposed to reflect on and choose a government is not homogeneous in either its motives or its thoughts. Existing interests and institutions have given some men "objects" of their own. From the point of view of "patriotism," those objects create a "bias," a "fault of the . . . heart." In addition, the existing interests and institutions are responsible for certain "views, passions, and prejudices little favorable to the discovery of truth." These entrenched thoughts lead men to be defective in judiciousness or considerateness, which is a "fault of the head."

Two classes of men have their hearts on objects other than the "public good." These are state officers, whose "obvious interest" is to cling to the power and salary they already have; and men of "perverted ambition," a category which includes both petty men who think subdivided confederacies would increase their chances of "elevation" and tyrannical men who think "confusions" would favor their aggrandizement.

> It is not, however, my design to dwell upon observations of this nature. I am well aware that it would be disingenuous to resolve indiscriminately the opposition of any set of men (merely because their situations might subject them to suspicion) into interested or ambitious views. (1, p. 34)[15]

"[O]bservations of this nature" means imputations about the motives of the Constitution's opponents. It is true that *The Federalist* does not "dwell on" such observations, but it does briefly recur to them from time to time.[16] The men whose situations "might subject them to suspicion" of bad motives are officeholders and nonofficeholders, who may be suspected of interested and ambitious views, respectively. All men are in a situation which subjects them to suspicion; their attachment to themselves makes them want to keep what they have or obtain what they do not have—for themselves. In either case, they may be suspected of not being moved purely by "patriotism."

Neither side should attack the other's motives, Hamilton says, because neither side's partisans are entirely virtuous in their own motives; that is, the attacks are imprudent but true, or rather imprudent because true.

> [W]e are not always sure that those who advocate the truth are influenced by purer principles than their antagonists. Ambition, avarice, personal animosity, party opposition, and many other motives not more laudable than these, are apt to operate as well upon those who support as those who oppose the right side of a question. (1, p. 34)

But while men's private motives may detract from the "virtue" which would choose good government, Hamilton asserts that his own motives are good and admits that some of his opponents have good motives.

> [I]t cannot be doubted that much of the opposition which has made its appearance, or may hereafter make its appearance, will spring from sources, blameless at least if not respectable—the honest errors of minds led astray by preconceived jealousies and fears. (1, p. 34)

One such honest error is an "over-scrupulous jealousy of danger to the rights of the people, which is more commonly the fault of the head than of the heart" (1, p. 35). Men who commit this error have sound hearts which feel a "violent love" for the rights of the people, a "noble enthusiasm of liberty." This noble enthusiasm is blameless and even "respectable" because it is patriotic rather than selfish. It is "noble" in the same way that the people's united efforts in the Revolutionary War were noble (2, p. 38). Such behavior is moved by a passionate enthusiasm rather than the cool calculation by which selfish men seek personal objects. That at least some men are moved by such noble motives might surprise readers who expect to find a "Hobbesian" view of man in The Federalist.[17]

But good motives do not ensure a good choice. Good-hearted opponents of the Constitution feel a patriotic attachment to existing local institutions, and are prejudiced against innovations. This kind of conservatism is not a problem in accounts of the "state of nature," where there are no existing institutions; but America's actual institution of government must choose to displace arrangements which respectably patriotic men are familiar with and attached to. Later in the book, The Federalist admits the value of "that veneration which time bestows on everything" (49, p. 314); men's "untractableness" protects them from easy persuasion by those who might make things worse (31, p. 194). But such stubbornness is not so useful in 1787.

Furthermore, precisely men with *good* motives will be angry with their opponents, and a "torrent of angry and malignant passions will be let loose" (1, p. 35). Men's own good motives will lead them to think their opponents' public professions are a hypocritical cover for private motives. While Anti-Federalists "stigmatiz[e]" the Federalists' "enlightened zeal for the energy and efficiency of government" as "the offspring of a temper fond of despotic power and hostile to the principles of liberty," the Federalists will think the Anti-Federalists' "over-scrupulous jealousy" a "mere pretense and artifice, the stale bait for popularity at the expense of public good." Good-hearted Federalists will interpret the Anti-Federalists' bad heads as bad hearts, while good-hearted Anti-Federalists will interpret the Federalists' good heads as bad hearts. Thus do righteously indignant patriots misinterpret their patriotic opponents. An additional complication is that some on each side do act from private motives—which means that the righteously indignant are unfair to some but warranted by others of their opponents, and will no doubt be seconded by the pretended indignation of their own nonrighteous allies.

Precisely this prospect of a divisive and angry struggle among a people which attempts to choose its own government was, according to *Federalist* 38, the reason why in ancient history one man rather than an assembly drafted the laws. While Madison calls those examples cases "in which government has been established with deliberation and consent," the deliberation was apparently by a single founder and the consent was given sometimes before and sometimes after he devised the laws, and sometimes not in a "strictly regular" fashion at all (38, pp. 231–32). That "a people, jealous as the Greeks were of their liberty," would "place their destiny in the hands of a single citizen" can only be explained by

> supposing that the fears of discord and disunion among a number of counselors exceeded the apprehension of treachery or incapacity in a single individual. (38, p. 233)

Besides this reliance on a single lawgiver,

> History informs us, likewise, of the difficulties with which these celebrated reformers had to contend, as well as of the expedients which they were obliged to employ in order to carry their reforms into effect. Solon, who seems to have indulged a more temporizing policy, confessed that he had not given to his countrymen the government best suited to their happiness, but most tolerable to their prejudices. And Lycurgus, more true to his object, was under the necessity of mixing a portion of violence

with the authority of superstition, and of securing his final success by a voluntary renunciation, first of his country and then of his life. (38, p. 233)

The "difficulties" of reform are not all spelled out but are summed up as the "prejudices" of the people, a problem also evident in *Federalist* 1's account of America. Lycurgus was "true to his object" in redistributing lands, requiring common meals, and instituting iron coins,[18] but he could not do so without violence, superstition, and suicide. Lycurgus's "portion of violence" was more like an implied threat of violence. Solon, who was "more temporizing," was a bit less temporizing than is suggested by the statement Madison cites. According to Plutarch, Madison's source (38, p. 232), Solon

> only altred that, which he thought by reason he would persuade his citizens unto, or else by force he ought to compel them to accept, mingling as he said, sour with sweet, and force with justice.[19]

Plutarch then cites to confirm this the statement by Solon which Madison reports, which only refers to the "sweet."

All of this, Madison says, teaches us "to admire the improvement made by America on the ancient mode of preparing and establishing regular plans of government" (38, p. 233).

The American Mode

But what is the American improvement? And how does it overcome the difficulties which gave birth to the ancient mode, difficulties which *Federalist* 1 suggests America faces as well? The problem is how to unite the choice of variously selfish and self-righteously unselfish men on a "good government." *The Federalist*'s solution is visible partly in the content of its argument, which reveals a Solon-like policy of "temporizing" with the mix of motives to which it must appeal; and partly in the important but informal role which *The Federalist*'s authors (among other "Founding Fathers") play in the process of "preparing and establishing" the Constitution.

The arguments of *The Federalist*'s first section are intended to demonstrate the *"utility of the UNION to your political prosperity"* (1, p. 36). In *Federalist* 1 Hamilton speaks to his "fellow citizens" and says he finds it "in your interest" to adopt the Constitution; it is safest for "your liberty, your dignity, and your happiness" (1, pp. 35–36; see also 2, p. 37). These statements preserve an ambiguity about what motives they address; they could refer to the nation taken as a whole, or to each individual, and thus appeal to patriotic or to selfish motives.[20]

Union is useful first of all because it provides "safety" against hostilities from abroad or at home. In adopting this starting point, *The Federalist* manifests agreement with the arguments of Hobbes and Locke, according to which a number of men voluntarily unite and institute a government out of a concern for the preservation of their lives and property. Not "wisdom and virtue" but only a modicum of prudence and a selfish concern for one's own life and comforts make this choice possible. The selfishness of this choice need not be insisted upon too starkly, since each man's interest in peace is in harmony with the interests of others; but a concern for the others is not a prerequisite.[21]

Foreign nations would be tempted by their interest and invited by our disunity to attack us. Safety depends on union, even if foreign nations will not "regard our advancement in union, in power and consequence by land and by sea, with an eye of indifference and composure" (4, p. 47). Neither the unthreatening weakness of disunion nor the formidable strength of union will make foreign powers complacent, but the latter will at least make them less sanguine about the prospect of gaining by war. Probably more shocking to *The Federalist*'s readers is its insistence that only union can prevent war between the states. Hamilton cites "innumerable" causes of hostilities and rebukes "idle theories" which hope that commerce or republican government prevent war (6, pp. 54, 59). *Federalist* 7 follows with a "more particular" explanation of the existing competitions between American states which could lead to war (pp. 60–66). Hamilton thus admits that the private interests of men in different states do indeed conflict, a consideration which might lead private-spirited men or men whose patriotic sentiments are confined to their own state to oppose a union in which their own state's interest would, at best, be compromised with other interests. For this reason, Hamilton's argument is that these conflicts of interest will not merely result in a competition from which different states emerge more or less prosperous; competition will rather lead to *war*. Those whose interests suffer will fight back if they can, and without union the separate states will think they can fight back. Just as Hobbes insists on the insecurity of all men in the state of nature—even the strongest—Hamilton insists that war, not a distribution of benefits which some enjoy and others lament, is the result of intrastate rivalries. Because one or both sides would seek help from foreign allies who could then act for their own advantage, not even the stronger American side would gain by war.[22]

If the "more powerful sentiment of self-preservation" can overcome the "zeal for . . . opinions and supposed interests" (38, p. 234)—if "sacrificing private opinions and partial interests to the public good" is seen not as a virtue but as a "necessity" (37, p. 231)—then the choice of union can be rooted in each man's selfish interest. But because it is America's "good fortune" to live in a time of "profound peace," that necessity is still disputable. The danger to Americans is still somewhat distant, and the "too feeble impulses of duty and sympathy" which make men concerned with the troubles of neighboring states are supplemented by the sharper "incitements of self-preservation" only when the danger has made a "near approach" to the self in question (29, p. 187). But if danger's approach is too near, it will be too late to choose to fight it. Thus while Americans have "hitherto been suffered to sleep quietly in their beds" (41, p. 261), they must anticipate the insecurity which will inevitably come. Men must "anticipate . . . the gathering storm," as Hamilton says in another context (25, p. 165). We note that Madison selectively paraphrases the Declaration of Independence when he says that men can "abolish or alter their governments as to them shall seem most likely to effect their safety and happiness" (40, p. 253). He thus deemphasizes the Declaration's suggestion that such action is taken when it "becomes necessary" by the old government's destructiveness. If men must anticipate, and act before the necessity is unequivocal (and perhaps overwhelming), the motive of "safety" will not eliminate the difficulties of uniting a society's choice. The temporary safety which makes choice possible also makes disagreement possible. In *Federalist* 15, Hamilton distinguishes between "the intelligent friends of the Union" who have long understood America's vulnerability, and others from whom "facts" have only recently "extorted . . . a reluctant confession" (p. 106).

In alerting men to the necessity of uniting for safety, *The Federalist* relies partly on predictions of future dangers, but also on descriptions of present "humiliation."

> We may indeed with propriety be said to have reached almost the last stage of national humiliation. There is scarcely anything that can wound the pride or degrade the character of an independent nation which we do not experience. (15, p. 106)

Hamilton offers a list of particulars, and concludes by urging a firm stand for "our safety, our tranquillity, our dignity, our reputation" (15, p. 107). Men's concern for their dignity and reputation might serve their safety and tranquillity, if the "last stage of national humiliation" precedes the last stage of national destruction. Can pride cause men to "make a firm stand" where a concern for safety regardless of dishonor might, by its cautious slowness to take offense, be unable to secure even safety? If so, pride would still need to be guided and perhaps moderated by those ("intelligent friends") who foresee dangers and understand possibilities. After all, it is an "inordinate pride of State importance" which resists the subordination of states to the Union which is necessary for safety (21, p. 140), and it is the "pride of states" which makes them unjustly provoke and refuse to conciliate foreign powers (2, p. 45).

However men's pride might contribute to their safety, *The Federalist* does not offer only safety to lure those of its readers whose selfishness cannot be cured. For selfish men moved by "ambition"—the love of power—*The Federalist* offers some prospect of satisfaction under the new Constitution. America will be an "empire" (1, p. 33) which can become the "arbiter of Europe in America" (11, p. 87), and its offices, notably the presidency, should be attractive. The new government will be able to deal with commerce, finance, negotiation, and war, which "seem to comprehend all the objects which have charms for minds governed by that passion" of ambition (17, p. 118). Those men who look to state offices to satisfy their ambitions may be reassured that those offices will be preserved; but those offices will decline in importance, and *The Federalist* often treats these men not as potential allies to be won with promises but as vulnerable targets in an appeal to the rest of the people (see 59, p. 366).

Men moved by economic interests may be more easily satisfied, and one can find in *The Federalist*'s defense of the new Constitution various campaign promises for men with particular interests: increased commerce, more prosperous agriculture and manufacturing, lower taxes on land, less oppression of the commercial interest, preserved fishing rights, etc. (see especially nos. 12 and 13). More generally, Madison says that "the great body of [the people of this country]"—i.e., most but not all— are "interested . . . in the effects of good government" (37, p. 227). They might out of prejudice resist the causes of good government, but as members of the public they may be individually interested in good government's service of the public good, even if they are not patriotically concerned with the public good as a whole. While such an argument underemphasizes the competitions among the public, *The Federalist* claims that the prosperity of *all* will be enhanced by the commercial benefits which union can secure (see no. 12, and chapter 7 below).

The Federalist also attempts to convince those unselfish, patriotic men who are justifiably suspicious of the private motives of others. In *Federalist* 2 Jay suggests that the people have reason to "respect the judgment and advice" of the "distinguished" men of the 1787 Convention (p. 41), meaning such men as Washington and Franklin. But *The Federalist*'s more fundamental argument is not a plea for trust, since the book freely admits that suspicion of men's motives is justified. In *Federalist* 6, Hamilton goes out of his way (that is, further than his subject there requires) to insist on the "agency of personal considerations"—"private passions"—"in the production of great national events, either foreign or domestic" (6, pp. 54–56). From Plutarch's *Life of Pericles* Hamilton derives some accusations that Pericles' personal motives led to calamitous policies. Plutarch reported those accusations but did not entirely endorse them; and Plutarch's own text gives as much or more emphasis to the difficulty posed by the people's *suspicions* that Pericles acted out of personal motives.[23] *The Federalist* appeals to suspicious people by arguing that they are not suspicious enough. They are too trustful of their existing "local institutions," and should notice the "obvious" motives of their state officers, and the less obvious "dangerous ambition" of seductive demagogues (1, pp. 33, 35). The people are not wary enough of the foreign ambitions which will lead to wars, and the domestic ambitions which will lead both to disunity in defense and to intra-American wars. Above all, *The Federalist* argues that under the new Constitution men's selfish ambitions can be controlled and put to the people's use without great danger. Thus the division of powers and the promise that "ambition" can be "made to counteract ambition" (51, p. 322) are offered not in opposition to but in agreement with the suspicions of those asked to choose this government. The jealous lovers of liberty are more likely to be reconciled to the necessary energy of government by arguments that acknowledge and promise a remedy for the known selfish ambitions of men, than by unconvincing denials of the power of those ambitions.

The Federalist's arguments thus seem intended to temporize with rather than to cure both human selfishness and the human suspicion of others' human selfishness. The great variety of *The Federalist's* arguments for the new Constitution corresponds to the diversity in motive and thought of the people being addressed. But if we liken *The Federalist's* strategy to the temporizing policy of the ancient lawgiver Solon—as the *Federalist* indeed invites us to do by adopting the pseudonym "Publius"[24]—our attention is drawn to the role of *The Federalist* itself and the proposal it recommends in the American "mode" of "preparing and establishing" a plan of government. *The Federalist* offers arguments which "may be judged of by all" (1, p. 36); the people need not begin their reflections on good government from scratch. The people do not spontaneously deliberate or devise their own plan of government, but are "called upon to deliberate" (1, p. 33) by a Convention which prepared a plan for them to accept or reject.[25] In *Federalist* 2 Jay exaggerates in asserting that the people "as with one voice, convened the late convention at Philadelphia" to correct the perceived and regretted defects of the Articles of Confederation (p. 39). In fact, the existing state legislatures appointed delegates for the convention. In *Federalist* 40, Madison speaks more frankly:

> in all great changes of established governments . . . it is impossible for the people spontaneously and universally to move in concert towards their object; and it is therefore essential that such changes be instituted by some *informal and unauthorized propositions,* made by some patriotic and respectable citizen or number of citizens. (40, pp. 252–53)

The "approbation" of the "supreme authority," *"the people themselves,"* would "blot out all antecedent errors and irregularities" (40, p. 253). The people can still reflect and choose, but they do so in a context formed by the reflections and choices of one or a few men. The people rely on some informal assistance in order to be "really capable" of moving in concert.

Even in giving their "approbation," the people act in the manner devised by the "informal" proposers, which is to elect delegates to ratifying conventions. Because those delegates are selected to consider this issue only, their decision more nearly manifests the people's "supreme authority" than would action by the state legislators already elected for other purposes;[26] but the elected delegates are still not quite *"the people themselves."* One might say that the people, or their representatives in state legislatures, delegated the Philadelphia convention to draft amendments; but since the mode of ratification was devised by the convention, it could also be said that the convention delegated the people to elect representatives to ratify amendments.

Still, this ultimate deference to the "supreme authority" of *"the people themselves"* differs from the irregular methods of ancient foundings, where a single lawgiver like Lycurgus used force, superstition, and suicide to institute his laws. While Lycurgus's irregular measures founded a "nation of soldiers," America's regular mode, obtaining the people's voluntary consent, preserves a people "absorbed in the pursuits of gain and devoted to the improvements of agriculture and commerce" (8, p. 69).[27] This reflects the difference between a founder who, in Rousseau's description, changes human nature,[28] and founders who temporize with the prejudices and selfish interests which antedate their own innovation.

Although America does not receive its government from a single man, it receives a single proposal from a single convention which deliberated in secret. That convention could privately compromise among interests which must be attracted, but can only be partly satisfied, by the new government (see 37, pp. 229–30). Different conventions of other men, Madison predicts, would be unable to agree on a better alternative (38,

p. 237). The Convention resembles Lycurgus in renouncing its official life, in that it will have no authority under the new Constitution. Still, it is open to the people's suspicions. It deflects this suspicion by the fact that it framed only a proposal; the people retain the "supreme authority." The American founders play an "informal" role in drafting a constitution and in writing arguments in its defense, and the people may accept or reject this informal assistance. However, because the people cannot in fact speak with "one voice" (2, p. 39), their rejection of this assistance would need to be followed by new offers of assistance from other men equally suspect. The people need "some patriotic and respectable citizen or number of citizens" to help them be "really capable" of choosing their own government; but they cannot help being suspicious of these respectable men.

Conclusion

It would be "most honorable to human nature" if societies of men were "really capable . . . of establishing good government from reflection and choice," rather than dependent for their governments on accident and force. Even without a society of perfect wisdom and virtue which might best reflect on and choose good government, there might be a sufficient common motive for a united choice in the "necessity" of "safety." After all, the "safety of the whole is the interest of the whole" (4, p. 47). According to Hobbes, this motive is universal and sufficiently self-evident to indicate to each man the necessity of choosing a good government. Locke modified this view by allowing man to choose government from a desire to preserve not only his life but his liberty and estate. These desires, while experienced separately by men, are not divisive because, as Locke says, everyone entering civil society has these things (including property);[29] so everyone will choose a government which protects them. But in practice this unity is undermined by men's particular interests and ambitions and prejudices and jealousies. Perhaps none of these things is as important as "safety," and perhaps they all presuppose safety; but it does not appear that men can easily be persuaded that this is so. In fact, precisely because *The Federalist* is recommending a choice which will secure safety before the necessities of force are so pressing as to prevent any choice, the necessity of that course can still be controversial. The real human beings choosing in 1787 insist on more than a natural or rational human being might; "good government" must not only provide safety but promise prospects for interests and ambitions, and allay prejudices.

The American example also shows that a society's choice of good government may depend on good luck. The vulnerability of societies to force, and their composition of men whose opinions and interests are not naturally unanimous, are difficulties whose solution in America depends on geographical good fortune and on those respectable citizens later called America's "founders." Referring to the institution of the state constitutions, and applying their example to the Federal Constitution, Madison says:

> Notwithstanding the success which has attended the revisions of our established forms of government and which does so much honor to the virtue and intelligence of the people of America, it must be confessed that the experiments are of too ticklish a nature to be unnecessarily multiplied. (49, p. 315; see 38, p. 233)

The dampening of partisan divisions because of the Revolutionary War cannot be expected in future times. If the choice of government is "ticklish" and risky, if it requires conditions or individuals which the people cannot necessarily provide for themselves, it should be attempted only sparingly. The respectable citizen George Washington conveniently illustrates the main difficulties I have mentioned. If the people can reject the proposal of 1787, employ a new convention with other citizens as respectable as Washington which can offer a better plan, and if, in the event of further wars, they can employ other Washingtons who can defeat enemies in more difficult circumstances, and who can be employed without danger of usurpation—then the honorable claim that the people are capable of choosing their own government gains credit. But if time is short, if future wars will be disastrous, if further conventions would be unable to agree, if new Washingtons, Hamiltons, and Madisons will not regularly reappear, then the people would seem to owe much to these particular circumstances and these particular men, or to the good luck or "finger of that Almighty hand" (37, p. 230) which brought them forth. If the people's ability to choose for themselves is grounds for pride, their dependence on a few, or on accident, is grounds for gratitude and reverence.

But the American "mode" of "preparing and establishing regular plans of government" avoids forcing this alternative. The assistance of the respectable citizens is "informal" and, correspondingly, later reverence for the Founding Fathers is informal.[30] The respectable citizens who took the lead improvised a mode by which their own contribution would not formally detract from the "supreme authority" of *the people themselves.* The honorable claim that the people can institute their own government is vindicated by use of a particular "mode" through which they give their decision. We shall see a similar approach in *The Federalist*'s account of the plan of government it recommends. The claim that the people are capable of self-government is perhaps even more honorable than the claim that they are capable of instituting a government. Hoping to vindicate that claim, *The Federalist* recommends a mode of government that allows respectable citizens to make their contribution without offending the people's honorable intention to rule themselves.

·[Two]·

The Necessity of Energy

The *ends* which attract and unite a people's choice of government (summarized as *"your political prosperity"*) are indicated in *The Federalist*'s first section (nos. 1–14). The *means* which the people must choose to secure those ends are described there only in general terms, often simply as "union."[1] A fuller statement of the necessary means occurs in the second and third sections of the book: The Articles of Confederation are insufficient (nos. 15–22), and an "energetic" government is necessary to preserve the Union (nos. 23–36).

Specifically, America needs a government more energetic than the Articles of Confederation, and "at least equally energetic"[2] as the proposed Constitution (1, p. 36). While the use of the word "energy" in this way is almost an invention of *The Federalist* and its contemporaries,[3] previous theorists of the social contract described the necessary qualities of government in parallel terms. Energetic government, according to *The Federalist*, requires that the most impressive powers of government— the purse and the sword—be possessed in a most impressive degree: "without limitation." The necessity of unlimited powers was argued by both Hobbes and Locke. For Hobbes, it is necessary for men to authorize a sovereign who can "do whatsoever he shall think necessary to be done ... for the preserving of Peace and Security, by prevention of Discord at home and Hostility from abroad. . . ."[4] Locke insisted that the "Supream power" is not "absolutely *Arbitrary,*" primarily because it may exert its power only for the proper ends; but it is nonetheless *"absolute"* in service of those proper ends.[5]

For America, the necessity of powers "without limitation" immediately conflicts with the opinion that national powers must be limited if state powers are to survive. In addition, men jealously attached to liberty (see 1, p. 35) are anxious to restrain the dangerous powers of purse and sword. In this chapter I will consider how the necessity of energy can be reconciled with a federal system and indeed with any limits on government.

Hamilton says the discussion of the "necessity of energy" in government "will naturally divide itself into three branches": "the objects to be provided for by a federal government"; "the quantity of power necessary to the accomplishment of those objects"; and "the persons upon whom that power ought to operate." Hamilton lists the "principal purposes" of union as if he were going to discuss each in turn, but in fact his discussion pursues only the first two: "the common defense of the members; the preservation of the public peace, as well against internal convulsions as external attacks." While union is also intended to regulate commerce and "superinten[d] . . . intercourse . . . with foreign countries" (23, p. 153), the objects of defense and peace are those which especially require energy. The claim that government can be "energetic" calls attention to the fact that a government consists of bodies in motion rather than simply of minds thinking or willing or writing laws on parchment. The necessity of such energy for peace and safety stems from the fact that both citizens and foreigners may put their own bodies in motion to resist the decisions of government.

"Upon Whom That Power Ought to Operate"

If energy is a matter of defeating men's resistance to rule, government is most energetic if it can exert its powers upon men least able or likely to resist. The existing Confederation lacks energy (15, p. 108) above all because of "upon whom" its powers operate.

> The great and radical vice in the construction of the existing Confederation is in the principle of LEGISLATION for STATES or GOVERNMENTS, in their CORPORATE or COLLECTIVE CAPACITIES, and as contradistinguished from the INDIVIDUALS of whom they consist. (15, p. 108)

In exercising its crucial powers—raising revenue and obtaining soldiers—the existing federal government must address states rather than individuals, which means that while its decisions are "in theory" "constitutionally binding," "yet in practice they are mere recommendations which the States observe or disregard at their option" (15, p. 108). Some have argued that this option would not be abused, since

> a sense of common interest would preside over the conduct of the respective members, and would beget a full compliance with all the constitutional requisitions of the Union. (15, p. 110)

But this view

> at all times betrayed an ignorance of the true springs by which human conduct is actuated, and belied the original inducements to the establishment of civil power. Why has government been instituted at all? Because the passions of men will not conform to the dictates of reason and justice without constraint. Has it been found that bodies of men act with more rectitude or greater disinterestedness than individuals? The contrary of this has been inferred by all accurate observers of the conduct of mankind. . . . (15, p. 110)

The necessity of energy arises from the fact that the "passions of men" cannot be restrained by "recommendations." A government must be instituted which suits "the original inducements to the establishment of civil power." One might object that the union being formed is not one of men leaving a "state of nature" but one of men already under the "civil power" of state governments. But this fact only heightens the necessity of energy, because it means that the men to be controlled are found not in their separate, natural bodies but in "bodies of men," meaning united groups of men acting in their "CORPORATE or COLLECTIVE CAPACITIES." Men in "collective bodies"—i.e., states—are less restrained in their passions than individual men are, for several reasons. First, collective bodies are less concerned with reputation because they divide up the infamy of bad deeds. Second, a "spirit of faction" hurries men in a way which overcomes the scruples which would ordinarily make them "blush." Third, collective bodies contain within them a "sovereign power" which looks with an "evil eye" on external restraints and which makes them fly apart from a common center.

> This tendency . . . has its origin in the love of power. Power controlled or abridged is almost always the rival and enemy of that power by which it is controlled or abridged. (15, p. 111)

Hamilton says this "proposition" is based on the "constitution of man"— even though it seems to refer to the "sovereign power" of a collective body rather than to other individual men.

The "constitution of man" is visible in collective bodies of men; or perhaps one should say that a certain part of man's constitution is visible in collective bodies. Individual men are concerned with their reputation among their fellows, and "blush" when violating standards they think they should respect. Men tend to be "timid and cautious" when they think or act alone (49, p. 315). In a collective body, men feel more invincible; they overcome the vulnerability of their individual bodies and the sense of limits which is connected with and enforced by their weakness. And the "love of power" is a passion whose satisfaction may seem more within reach for a "sovereign" of a collective body than for an individual body. Collective bodies manifest the qualities of men which make them least fit to be governed.

The view that a sense of common interest will lead states to obey mere "recommendations" is equivalent to the view that government is unnecessary. Compliance with recommendations would be at best and only at first unequal, and then be abandoned altogether as those most compliant decided to stop playing the fool (15, p. 112). Compliance can be expected only if the government's laws are not mere "advice" but rather contain a "penalty or punishment for disobedience."

> This penalty, whatever it may be, can only be inflicted in two ways: by the agency of the courts and ministers of justice, or by military force; by the COERCION of the magistracy, or by the COERCION of arms. The first kind can evidently apply only to men; the last kind must of necessity be employed against bodies politic, or communities, or states. (15, p. 110)

These two forms of coercion are previously described as "the mild influence of the magistracy" as distinguished from "the violent and sanguinary agency of the sword," and again described as "the mild and salutary *coercion* of the *magistracy*" as distinguished from *"violence"* (15, p. 108; 20, p. 138). The magistrate's "mild influence" is more precisely a "mild . . . *coercion*," that is, undeniably a "COERCION" which may involve force and violence. Hamilton refers to the "arm of the ordinary magistrate" as the proper executor of laws (16, p. 116). The coercion of an "arm" is different from the coercion of "arms," because the latter supposes that there will actually be a fight. A "sword" would be used against someone who also has a sword. The magistrate can coerce with locks, and even a gallows, but does not use a sword because he does not expect a real struggle from individual men; it will usually be enough for the authority to "manifes[t]" its "majesty" (16, p. 116).

The sword is needed for coercion against "bodies politic" because these collective bodies are strong enough to resist, and thus not so impressed by the majesty of the magistrate's arm. States not only show man's will-fulness rather than his shame and concern for reputation, they show his strength and courage rather than his weakness and fear.

> In an association where the general authority is confined to the collective bodies of the communities that compose it, every breach of the laws must involve a state of war; and military execution must become the only instrument of civil obedience. Such a state of things can certainly not deserve the name of government, nor would any prudent man choose to commit his happiness to it. (15, p. 110)

For this reason, the fact that the present confederation has no coercive power at all is not its most "radical vice" (15, p. 108); for to give it coercive power while it remains confined to governing "collective bodies" would not make it a "government" but would only institute a continually re-curring "state of war." Hamilton likens such a system based on military coercion of collective bodies to the "romantic" "monster-taming spirit, attributed to the fabulous heroes and demigods of antiquity" (16, p. 115). Indeed it resembles the real confederacies of antiquity too, in which the individual cities retained the proud independence of separate col-lective bodies, and were tamed—when they were tamed—by the sword (see no. 18). Reliance on the sword would destroy the American Union:

> When the sword is once drawn, the passions of men observe no bounds of moderation. The suggestions of wounded pride, the instigation of irritated resentment, would be apt to carry the States against which the arms of the Union were exerted to any extremes necessary to avenge the affront or to avoid the disgrace of submission. (16, p. 114)

America must therefore give its central government authority over *in-dividuals,* and enable it to use the coercion of magistrates.

> The government of the Union, like that of each State, must be able to address itself immediately to the hopes and fears of indi-viduals; and to attract to its support those passions which have the strongest influence on the human heart. (16, p. 116)

Government must address the hopes and fears of individual men, rather than offend "the passions of men" such as "pride" and "resentment" which are stirred by an appeal to the sword. Those hostile passions are more likely in a collective body which feels able to avenge affronts and avoid disgrace than in an individual man who must stand alone before the magistrate. Collective bodies are a kind of "monster" which it would be "romantic" to expect to tame by the sword; the sword kills or antagonizes, but it does not tame. The monster must instead be deconstructed into the parts which compose it: individual, natural men with their natural hopes and fears.

Unlimited Powers and Limited Government

Even in order to impress individual passionate men enough to rule them without a fight, government needs some "powers." In addition, it cannot guarantee against, and must expect, men's uniting themselves into collective bodies to oppose it. The danger is obvious in the case of foreign men united into the collective body of a nation's army. The less evident danger, which Hamilton does not discreetly neglect to discuss, is the violence of a domestic insurrection. "[S]editions and insurrections are, unhappily, maladies as inseparable from the body politic as tumors and eruptions from the natural body" (28, p. 178). The threat that these energetic assaults pose both to the government itself and to the people's "tranquillity" and "safety" requires that the government possess the powers which will give it the energy to defeat them. The powers in question are raising and maintaining an army; and taxation, discussed here for its contribution to defense. Because these powers are "necessary," in these respects Americans cannot choose a novel form of government but must respect the "usual maxims of prudence and policy," and imitate the "customary and ordinary modes practiced in other governments" (24, p. 162; 23, p. 155). But the harsh necessity is not merely that the government must have these powers; it is that it must have these powers *without limit.*

> The authorities essential to the common defense are these: to raise armies; to build and equip fleets; to prescribe rules for the government of both; to direct their operations; to provide for their support. These powers ought to exist without limitation, *because it is impossible to foresee or to define the extent and variety of national exigencies, and the correspondent extent and variety of the means which may be necessary to satisfy them.* (23, p. 153)

Hamilton says this principle is self-evident, and rests upon simple, universal axioms which he later likens to the maxims of geometry. These "maxims in ethics and politics" are

> [1] that there cannot be an effect without a cause; [2] that the means ought to be proportioned to the end; [3] that every power ought to be commensurate with its object; [4] that there ought to be no limitation of a power destined to effect a purpose which is itself incapable of limitation. (31, p. 193)

The three "ought" statements—more a reiteration than a list—seem to derive from the first "is" statement. Ethics and politics presuppose the principle of causation,[6] and they require that men be guided by an "end" or "object" or "purpose." According to *Federalist* 3's assertion that *"safety* seems to be the first" object for a wise and free people (p. 42), the necessity of the "means" to this appears undeniable.

Hamilton's explanation of this necessity focuses on two powers granted by the new Constitution which the Anti-Federalists would like to limit: the power to raise and maintain a "standing army," and the power to tax. Some advocate writing an explicit ban on standing armies in peacetime into the Constitution because of the danger which they pose to liberty—a danger Hamilton admits (8, pp. 67–68). Without a standing army, America would rely on militia for defense. But, as we have seen, a militia is insufficient in "modern times" (8, p. 69). Even a "simple view" of America's need for frontier garrisons against the Indians shows the importance of a small permanent corps. To rotate ordinary citizens in the task would result in a substantial "loss of labor and disconcertion of the industrious pursuits of individuals"—if indeed men will submit to being "dragged" from their "occupations and families" in a time of "profound peace" (24, pp. 161–62). Even if in wartime men are ready to pick up their rifles, normally they are "private citizens," as Hamilton calls them in this context, concerned with occupation and family. And as to real war, the bravest of America's militiamen from the War of Independence will admit that they could not have won that war alone. When other nations fight with disciplined armies, America must oppose them with disciplined armies.[7]

Regarding the nation's power to tax, Hamilton again insists that no limits can reasonably be imposed in the Constitution.

> Money is, with propriety, considered as the vital principle of the body politic; as that which sustains its life and motion and enables it to perform its most essential functions. A complete power, therefore, to procure a regular and adequate supply of revenue, as far as the resources of the community will permit, may be regarded as an indispensable ingredient in every constitution. (30, p. 188)

The view that taxation must be able to reach "as far as the resources of the community will permit" is another statement of the principle that *"in the usual progress of things, the necessities of a nation, in every stage of its existence, will be found at least equal to its resources"* (30, p. 190). Presumably those nations whose necessities exceed their resources will fail; but no nation ever enjoys the luxury of a real surplus. Even if it does not always need to use all of its resources, it must be able to call on all those resources when the necessity arises; "all the sources of revenue" must be "open to its demands" (12, p. 96). Other nations would always look on a rich nation which is unable to tax its riches as a target for conquest which is both attractive (because rich) and easy (because its riches cannot be applied to defense). Modern wars require borrowing (30, p. 192); and creditors look not merely at a nation's resources but at a government's ability to draw on those resources in the future (12, p. 96). To think that the power of taxation should be restricted is to assume that

> there was some known point in the economy of national affairs at which it would be safe to stop and to say: Thus far the ends of public happiness will be promoted by supplying the wants of government, and all beyond this is unworthy of our care or anxiety. (30, p. 191)

In reply to those who say that the states, too, need money, Hamilton explains that for both governments to have full taxing powers[8] is the only alternative to federal superiority in taxation. Hamilton hints that he might even prefer the latter (34, p. 211); but certainly no plausible division of taxation (e.g., "internal" vs. "external") would correspond with the proportion of resources which each government is likely to need (34, pp. 206–11).

The "necessity" of these unlimited powers for the sake of defense is not that they are always necessary but that they may sometimes be necessary. Even though "safety" is certainly a limited object—and is explicitly contrasted with the more ambitious aim of acquiring power and dominion (see 6, p. 54)—this limited object is threatened with unlimited dangers and thus seems to require unlimited powers in its service.[9] But the logic of this argument suggests the imprudence not only of the restrictions the Anti-Federalists propose, but also of the Constitution's own project: a government of enumerated powers. If the *"extent and variety of the means which may be necessary"* (23, p. 153) for national safety are unforeseeable, any attempt to limit government by defining certain "means" or "powers" which it is granted would seem ill-advised. Even a list of means which it may *not* employ—a "Bill of Rights"—would pose the same problem. It is possible that there are some ends other than safety for which the necessary means can be foreseen and defined. And perhaps we can know in advance that only certain categories of means will be needed for safety—even if the quantity cannot be known in advance. Hamilton seems to limit the category for which there can be no limit on quantity when he says that there should be in the Constitution

no limitation of that authority which is to provide for the defense
and protection of the community in any matter essential to its efficacy—that is, in any matter essential to the *formation, direction,* or
support of the NATIONAL FORCES. (23, p. 154)

Perhaps certain powers could come in handy—including, say, *ex post facto*
laws and bills of attainder—which would nonetheless not be "essential."
But if the possible exigencies are really infinite, might not some usually
nonessential but useful means be called for in the most extreme exigency? Hamilton later admits his

> aversion to every project that is calculated to disarm the govern-
> ment of a single weapon, which in any possible contingency might
> be *usefully employed* for the general defense and security. (36, p.
> 223; emphasis added)[10]

Thus the useful as well as essential powers should be available.

Not only is "fettering the government" in ways which "run counter to
the necessities of society" ill-advised, it is likely to be to no avail. In case
of necessity, the fetters will be broken. Hamilton cites historical examples
which teach "how unequal parchment provisions are to a struggle with
public necessity." Necessary breaches of a Constitution which attempts
to restrict too much will undermine reverence for the Constitution and
set a precedent for unnecessary breaches (25, p. 167, and 41, p. 257).

How can a government of enumerated powers avoid this "fettering"?
Even if the Constitution's enumeration includes the essential powers of
taxing and raising armies in an unlimited degree, might it not exclude
some useful powers, or even some necessary powers whose necessity is
not now foreseen? Part of the answer to this question is indicated by *The
Federalist*'s repeated description of the Constitution's enumeration of
powers as an enumeration of "objects" (see 14, p. 102; 27, p. 177; 39,
p. 245; 41, p. 263).[11] Not the allowable means but the allowable *ends* are
"foreseen and defined." The means are implicitly authorized:

> No axiom is more clearly established in law, or in reason, than
> that wherever the end is required, the means are authorized;
> wherever a general power to do a thing is given, every particular
> power necessary for doing it is included. (44, p. 285)

Each enumerated power is a "general power to do a thing," that is, a
statement of the "end"; and while "the means" could not practically be
enumerated, they are "authorized." The Constitution's famous "necessary and proper" clause is only an unnecessarily explicit statement of
Madison's "axiom . . . in law, or in reason." Congress would in any case

be authorized to "make all Laws which shall be necessary and proper for carrying into Execution" the powers granted by the Constitution.

But the Constitution's grant of the "necessary and proper" means might seem more restrictive than *The Federalist*'s argument for all "useful" means. If the clause is taken literally, some useful means would be excluded because they were not strictly "necessary." And useful or even strictly necessary means would be excluded if they were not "proper."

Madison quietly but unmistakably construes the necessary and proper clause in a much more permissive direction. He treats "necessary and proper" as if it meant necessary *or* proper, i.e., as if Congress may make all laws which shall be necessary *and* all laws which shall be proper— rather than only those laws which are both. Three times in one paragraph Madison writes as if the opposite of "necessary and proper" laws were laws which are *"not necessary or proper,"* i.e., which are "unnecessary and improper" (44, p. 285).[12] That is, the permitted category includes all necessary and all proper laws, and excludes only those which are neither. According to this formulation, not only the proper means to the authorized ends, but even those improper means which are necessary, are granted. Borrowing the terms from Hamilton quoted earlier, *Federalist* 44's language implies that government may use all means which are "usefu[l]" if they are proper, and all means which are "essential" even if they are improper.[13]

By enumerating "objects" or ends, the Constitution does not sharply restrict the *"extent and variety of the means."* The restriction imposed by enumeration is further denigrated in Hamilton's account in *Federalist* 78 of the judiciary's role in enforcing America's "limited Constitution":

> By a limited Constitution, I understand one which contains certain specified exceptions to the legislative authority; such, for instance, as that it shall pass no bills of attainder, no *ex post facto* laws, and the like. Limitations of this kind can be preserved in practice no other way than through the medium of courts of justice, whose duty it must be to declare all acts contrary to the manifest tenor of the Constitution void. (78, p. 466)

Thus Hamilton understands a limited Constitution to be one with "certain specified exceptions to the legislative authority"—rather than as one limited to a certain specified enumeration of the legislative authority. And in explaining his position, he says that to deny the court's authority is to put the legislative servants above their master, the people, which is to say that "men acting by virtue of powers may do not only what their powers do not authorize, but what they forbid" (78, p. 467). Thus Hamilton unnecessarily suggests the possibility of men doing "what their powers do not authorize," and distinguishes it from doing what their powers "forbid"—reiterating that "limited" government means specified exceptions, not enumerated powers.[14] Perhaps this is because a commission of powers is not precise but has a "tenor," and men do not exactly exercise a certain power, they act "by virtue of" certain powers. Hamilton's defense of judicial review leaves room for a loose construction of national powers.

These explanations interpret the proposed "parchment" as not attempting the impossible task of forbidding what is "necessary." The Court is not urged to enforce an "enumeration" when it enforces the limited Constitution, and the enumeration is presented as a list of ends. Such a loose construction of the parchment restrictions is not surprising in light of *The Federalist*'s insistence that parchment restrictions are frail in any case. But what, then, is the security for the people against abuses by a government which can raise armies and taxes in amounts unlimited by parchment? Does the necessity of energy require abandonment of the wish not to be ruled with unnecessary energy? If we cannot foresee and define in advance the real *"national exigencies,"* we cannot define in advance, let alone forbid, those tyrannical exercises of power which are not necessary or even intended to meet exigencies. Even if one could safely rule out a few powers—*ex post facto* laws, bills of attainder (a possibility to be discussed further below)—one cannot safely limit those powers which are most dangerous. They are necessary precisely because they are dangerous, because an energetic government must be able to endanger those who oppose it.

The Federalist insists that the real protection against abuse is to be found not in any limitation of the government's powers but in the government's *structure*, in how it is "modeled."

> It will indeed deserve the most vigilant and careful attention of the people to see that it be modeled in such a manner as to admit of its being safely vested with the requisite powers. . . . A government, the constitution of which renders it unfit to be trusted with all the powers which a free people *ought to delegate to any government*, would be an unsafe and improper depositary of the NATIONAL INTERESTS. (23, p. 156)

The debate on the proposed Constitution should therefore focus on its "internal structure," not on "inflammatory declamations and unmeaning cavils about the extent of the powers" (23, p. 156; see 31, p. 196). While Hamilton allows that perhaps certain powers ought not be delegated to any government, he insists that the powers now given to the state governments could safely be given to the federal government—or to any federal government worth trusting. The modeling of the federal government is the key. But since the necessary federal powers—taxation and war—are the decisive ones, a government trusted with these could surely be trusted with any lesser powers the states may have. Whether or not the federal government would use these lesser powers as well (or better), its possession of them would not be "unsafe."

How to model a government so that it can be trusted is more fully discussed in the second half of *The Federalist*, which describes and defends the proposed government's "structure" (see chapters 5 through 7, below). For example, a trustworthy "separation of powers" depends on the modeling of institutions so that "ambition" will "counteract ambition" (51, p. 322), rather than on "a mere demarcation" of powers on "parchment" (48, p. 313). This contrast between "modeling" or "structure" and "parchment" or "rules" is developed in the present context in Hamilton's discussion of the constitutional provisions for taxation. Both assuring sufficient revenue, and discouraging excessive taxation, are best accomplished when inflexible fixed rules are avoided.

The Constitution permits the Federal government to impose indirect (excise) taxes, as well as direct taxes, although the latter must be proportioned to population. Excise taxes are preferable, because they "contain in their own nature a security against excess." If they are raised too high, men will reduce consumption or smuggle, which means that government will find them self-defeating. This fact that " 'in political arithmetic, two and two do not always make four' " is a "natural limitation of the power of imposing" excise taxes (21, pp. 142–43). There is no such natural limitation on direct taxes (for example, a property tax), since men have no real "option" by which to avoid paying. The Constitution introduces an artificial limitation on direct taxes by its requirement that they be proportional to population.

> In a branch of taxation where no limits to the discretion of the government are to be found in the nature of the thing, the establishment of a fixed rule, not incompatible with the end, may be attended with fewer inconveniences than to leave that discretion altogether at large. (21, p. 143)

This fixed rule "may" have fewer inconveniences than an unlimited discretion, but it certainly does have inconveniences. Making taxation proportional to population does not take into account the "infinite variety of causes" of the "wealth of nations" (21, p. 141). A fixed rule for direct taxes will err because it—like fixed rules which would limit the extent of powers which are designed for unforeseeable exigencies—cannot be suited to the variety of human affairs. The preferable "natural limitation" found in excise taxes stems from natural human passions which make men averse to paying high taxes. More generally, *The Federalist* defends a "structure" of government which limits government by the interaction of men's natural passions. While passionate men may overestimate or underestimate the requirements posed by the exigencies they face, they provide a more flexible limit on government than fixed rules do.

But because excise taxes do have natural limits which might fall short of the government's need for revenue, the Constitution must permit other forms of taxation as well. A government which could impose only excises would have to try to overcome their natural limits:

> if the avenues to [other resources] were closed, HOPE, stimulated by necessity, might beget experiments, fortified by rigorous precautions and additional penalties [against smuggling], which, for a time, might have the intended effect, till there had been leisure to contrive expedients to elude these new precautions. The first success would be apt to inspire false opinions, which it might require a long course of subsequent experience to correct. Necessity, especially in politics, often occasions false hopes, false reasonings, and a system of measures correspondingly erroneous. (35, p. 213)

This observation applies "especially in politics" because in politics men must make choices rather than resign themselves to the necessity of failure. If men cannot choose wisely from a range of options, they must choose what necessity allows them and hope for the best. A fixed rule forbidding direct taxation would be "incompatible with the end," because there will sometimes be a necessity to tax to the natural limits of taxation altogether. Hamilton admits that the Union might have some difficulty collecting nonexcise taxes, if it is given the power. But this, he says, will "impose a disposition to greater care in the choice and arrangement of the means" (36, p. 222). Thus while necessity leads to hopes and erroneous measures, difficulty leads to care in choosing. The new Constitution avoids fixed rules which create necessities, hopes, and errors, but is modeled so that the natural passions of men make governing difficult enough to encourage careful choice.

Standing armies, too, must be controlled not by fixed rules but by a well-modeled structure. The importance of that control is clear from the question raised in chapter 1: Can a people, in modern times and when exposed to dangers accidentally absent in 1787, avoid surrendering their choice to the force which can defend them? The proposed Constitution limits military appropriations by Congress to two years, so the executive cannot maintain an army by himself. This should allay those fears which in the past led men to oppose a standing army as an instrument of oppression in the executive's (e.g., the English king's) hands. Under the proposed Constitution, a dangerous standing army could be created only by a "conspiracy," a "combination between the executive and legislative in some scheme of usurpation" (26, p. 172; 25, p. 165). The "separation of powers" is therefore a useful element in a safe "structure" (see chapter 5 below). But even more important is the fact

> that the whole power of the proposed government is to be in the hands of the representatives of the people. This is the essential, and, after all, the only efficacious security for the rights and privileges of the people which is attainable in civil society. (28, p. 180)

Not parchment definitions of powers but *representation* is the safeguard. While Hamilton here speaks of "civil society," he had just previously contrasted "civil society upon an enlarged scale" with the agitations and revolutions of "petty republics" (28, p. 179). Perhaps seeking an efficacious security for the people's rights in a direct democracy on a small scale leads to such agitations and revolutions that only civil society upon an enlarged scale deserves the name of civil society; and hence representation is the necessary safeguard. Outside "civil society" strictly speaking is, of course, the protection the people may find in their "original right of self-defense" (28, p. 180), the right of revolution which Hamilton mentions here and to which I will return.

Hamilton's elaborations of how the people may be safe from abuse of the power to raise armies are revealing about the importance of representation. For one thing, giving the power to the national rather than the state governments has (besides the advantages for defense) an additional advantage. The power

> had better be in those hands of which the people are most likely to be jealous than in those of which they are least likely to be jealous. For it is a truth, which the experience of all ages has attested, that the people are commonly most in danger when the means of injuring their rights are in the possession of those of whom they entertain the least suspicion. (25, p. 164)

Since the people cannot keep their own power in their own hands, they must go against their instincts. They must trust those they are jealous of so that their natural jealousy will be useful, and be jealous of those they trust so that their natural trust will not be duped. The people may be too trustful of *themselves* to suspect the possibility of being duped. The Constitution should go against men's grain so that their grain will be a check on it; this of course implies that the choice of such a constitution in the first place will not come easily. The people must confide in men they are jealous of.

The people's suspicion of representatives will in practice be most effective when it is led or even fomented by—paradoxically, perhaps—representatives. The "spirit of party" both in the national legislature and in state legislatures will cause some representatives to be poised to "arraign the measures and criminate the views" of other representatives (26, p. 171). Appropriations for a standing army will surely attract such "declamation." The partisan motives of representatives can supplement or even take the place of suspicions by the people.

A similar reliance on representation is visible in Hamilton's proposal for the organization of the militia as a supplement to whatever standing army is necessary. Rather than have the entire population distracted from "productive labor" by a rigorous discipline for a universal militia, emphasis should be placed on organizing a "select corps" within the militia.

> This will not only lessen the call for military establishments, but if circumstances should at any time oblige the government to form an army of any magnitude that army can never be formidable to the liberties of the people while there is a large body of citizens, little if at all inferior to them in discipline and the use of arms, who stand ready to defend their own rights and those of their fellow-citizens. (29, p. 185)

Despite the fact that war is a "science" and requires specialization (see 25, p. 166), "discipline and the use of arms" can be mastered easily enough by these nonprofessionals—perhaps because they are selected for ability; and perhaps they remain inferior in more sophisticated aspects of war. This "select corps" guards the people's liberty by a kind of representation. They are men who are "daily mingling with the rest of their countrymen" and "participate with them in the same feelings, sentiments, habits, and interests" (29, p. 186). This "select corps" is to the citizen militia what representation is to direct democracy. A portion of the people trusted by the people undertakes the task of defending their liberties, because modern, industrious private citizens cannot really do this for themselves. We will see below that even in exercising their "original right of self-defense" (revolution)—when civil society's security of representation fails—the people again benefit from and rely on a process of representation.

It is in such structural elements of a well-modeled government and not in the parchment's careful listing of powers that the people must find safety. The structure is intended to preserve the necessary energy while discouraging its unnecessary use or abuse. I have already noted the difficulty posed by those "specified exceptions to the legislative authority" which Hamilton admits "limit" the government; such elements of a "bill of rights" as were written into the proposed Constitution (see 84, p. 511) seem to be "parchment" limits, fixed rules of the kind said to be dangerous or inefficacious rather than the recommended structural limits. A more radical difficulty is the fact that the structure is itself a kind of "fixed rule." Hamilton argued that the necessarily unlimited powers must be under the direction of the "same councils which are appointed to preside over the common defense," since "the persons from whose agency the attainment of any *end* is expected ought to possess the *means* by which it is to be attained" (23, p. 153). He rejects the idea of dividing the power between the federal and state governments; but it is clear that the "councils" or "persons" to whom the new Constitution gives the "means" are themselves divided into different branches of government. While this presumably makes concurrence easier than it would be if the states had to agree also, there remain certain obstacles to the action which "exigencies" may demand. Perhaps this is why Hamilton says not that "wise politicians" will simply avoid "fettering the government with restrictions that cannot be observed" when necessity prevails, but only that they will "be cautious about" fettering the government in this way (25, p. 167). There may be an unavoidable element of what others call "prerogative"[15] in all government. A provision as fundamental and innocuous as that laws shall be passed by Congress could at some time be a fetter in the face of necessity; even if an infinite exigency would require its abridgement, one could hardly have a constitution without such provisions. *The Federalist* takes a tolerant view of certain apparently necessary usurpations by the Congress under the Articles of Confederation, and notes that such "assumptions" of powers had been "warranted, in the public estimation" (40, p. 252). And the 1787 convention itself may have exceeded its powers (notably by its provision that nine states would suffice to adopt the proposed Constitution, rather than the thirteen which the Articles of Confederation themselves required for amendment)—but even so, the members "were not only warranted, but required as the confidential servants of their country, by the circumstances in which they were placed to exercise the liberty which they assumed" (40, p. 254). A well-modeled government will largely avoid, but may not altogether escape, the necessity to act outside of its constitutional limits.

The States

If the central government must as a matter of necessity possess the most important powers without limit and be able to exert those powers on individual citizens, the Anti-Federalists' fears that the states will be submerged in a "consolidated" national government seem well founded. *The Federalist*'s authors speak as "federalists" (10, p. 84), by which they mean supporters of union as distinguished from those who support the states at the expense of union. Those latter are called "Anti-Federalists" on the grounds that their attachment to states in effect opposes union. However, *The Federalist* defends not a "federal" Constitution strictly speaking, but a "partly federal and partly national" Constitution (39, p. 246). A "federal" union, also known as a "confederacy," was understood traditionally and by the so-called Anti-Federalists to be a "society of societies"—Montesquieu's phrase—meaning a union whose parts are states rather than individuals.[16] This was thought to imply that member states would retain full control over their "internal administration," that they would unite as equals in the federation, and that the federation would instruct its members in their "collective capacities" only. In *Federalist* 9, Hamilton attempts to denigrate this account of what distinguishes a *"confederacy"* from a *"consolidation"* of the states;[17] but his main point is that "as far as the principle contended for has prevailed, it has been the cause of incurable disorder and imbecility in the government" (p. 76).[18] The traditional federal principle is untenable in light of the necessity of energy described above. In *Federalist* 39 Madison uses the word "federal" the way the Anti-Federalists use it, and meticulously demonstrates that the proposed Constitution is a "compound" of federal and national features. Its federal features recognize the states as states—e.g., ratification of the Constitution by state conventions, election of senators by states, ratification of amendments by states, and limiting the central government to "certain enumerated objects" and thereby leaving "supremacy" with respect to other objects in the state governments. Its national features treat America as if it were one state—e.g., the election of representatives by districts of equal population, and the "operation" of the government on individual citizens.

Of Madison's five points of analysis, this matter of the government's "operation" on individuals (his third point) is the only one unqualifiedly said to be simply "national." The importance of this feature has already been discussed earlier in this chapter; its consequence is that the central and state governments both give their commands to individual citizens. All men have two masters, although each is only a master with respect to its own "objects." This of course will lead to questions about the "proper line of partition" between the authority of the two governments (37, p. 227). As is evident in the case of the power to tax, certain means to their objects are held by both governments. The "partition" is a division of ends; each government's "sphere" is to pursue its own "objects." The problem is similar to the problem of *one* government, if that one government is understood to have full authority to pursue limited objects.[19] According to Locke, the government may do whatever is necessary as long as it is directed toward the correct objects. The people are the final judge of whether that government, or either government in America, is in fact serving its legitimate objects.

The Federalist suggests that the "partition" between nation and state will be determined by the degree to which the people are or become attached to one or the other. Since they elect both governments, they can elect more assertive officers to one and more restrained officers to the other, depending on which government seems to deserve a larger role. *The Federalist* tries to soothe fears that the states will be extinguished by pointing to the much greater attachment of the people to their state governments. This attachment is based on the natural affection men feel for what is closest to them, the importance of local interests, and particularly the "transcendent advantage" the states have from "the ordinary administration of criminal and civil justice," which

> is the most powerful, most universal, and most attractive source
> of popular obedience and attachment. It is this which, being the
> immediate and visible guardian of life and property, having its
> benefits and its terrors in constant activity before the public eye,
> regulating all those personal interests and familiar concerns to
> which the sensibility of individuals is more immediately awake,
> contributes more than any other circumstance to impressing upon
> the minds of the people affection, esteem, and reverence towards
> the government. (17, p. 120)

The federal government is able to address men's "hopes and fears" by ruling individuals rather than collective bodies. But the states continue to address those most powerful hopes and fears moved by the visible "benefits" and "terrors" which criminal and civil justice display. Crime, and the punishment which more visibly replicates its terror and promises the benefit of halting the criminal's terror, makes clearest to men the advantage of being governed rather than living in a "state of nature." If men's first object is safety (3, p. 42), the drama of crime and punishment attaches men to the states which visibly serve that object.

The national government's contributions will be more remote and less visible (17, p. 120). Still, in time of war its contribution to safety will become visible, and may win it some affection, esteem, and reverence (45, p. 293). And Hamilton qualifies his statement of men's natural affection for what is near. That affection will attach men to state governments "unless the force of that principle should be destroyed by a much better administration of the [government of the Union]" (17, p. 119). Ten papers later, Hamilton completes this thought:

> Various reasons have been suggested in the course of these papers to induce a probability that the general government will be better administered than the particular governments. . . . (27, p. 174)

I will discuss the "various reasons" below (chapter 3); Hamilton here is rather emphatic in suggesting that the central government can, if it does its job well, win the popular attachment away from its natural object, the states.

> I believe it may be laid down as a general rule that [the people's] confidence in and obedience to a government will commonly be proportioned to the goodness or badness of its administration. (27, p. 174)

Hamilton says the "exceptions" to this rule rest on "accidental causes." The impressiveness of good administration can overcome the ties of natural affection. And over time, the people's experience with the central government's "ordinary" operations will give it the support of men's "habit" (27, p. 176). *The Federalist* gently advises the new government on what policies would best win confidence and obedience (see 27, pp. 176–77, and 29, p. 187).[20]

Thus the relative spheres of the central and state governments will depend on the relative attachment of the people, which may be expected to change in the future. The central government will have to prove itself by good administration. The natural trust which supports the states is less powerful than the acquired taste for the benefits of sound policies. While the Constitution does enumerate the objects of the central government, the partition between states and nation will not be as much a legal issue as a political one. "[T]he people ought not surely to be precluded from giving most of their confidence where they may discover it to be most due . . ." (46, p. 295). Parchment can neither limit the nation's powers, nor assure them against state encroachment. Two governments competing for the people's support form a structure more useful than fixed rules.

The Federalist's own position is on the whole unsympathetic to the importance of the states. Because not all matters can be "advantageously administered" by the central government (46, p. 295), the states are useful for "local" objects; but Hamilton does not conceal his disdain for those objects in arguing that even an ambitious national government would be uninterested in them (17, p. 118). The danger in 1787 is that the states will be too powerful. Not only the necessity of a union with "energy," but also the internal defects of state governments (see below, chapter 3) argue for the nation's preeminence. *The Federalist*'s main contribution to what we call "federalism" was to "compound" traditional federalism with a "national" government so that it would avoid "imbecility" and come to appear respectable and tenable; but this mixing was less for the sake of preserving the federal principle than for the sake of introducing the national principle in a way which could win the voluntary choice of a people whose "local institutions" had attracted men's "prejudices" (see 1, p. 33).[21]

But *The Federalist* does make one important argument about the usefulness of states. The division of powers between two distinct governments guards the "rights of the people" in the same way that separation of the branches of a single government guards those rights.

> Hence a double security arises to the rights of the people. The different governments will control each other, at the same time that each will be controlled by itself. (51, p. 323)

This "control" is a bit more subtle than the control of bicameralism or a president's veto, because it seems that the two governments will be acting by themselves in their independent spheres. Because the national laws are supreme, and the national courts will judge the partition between the two spheres, the nation can control the states in some matters (39, pp. 245–46). One might think that this control is not an advantage of federalism, since a purely national government would avoid the possibility of state government abuses by abolishing state governments. But perhaps the powers are safer when controlled than when exercised directly.

But how do the states control the nation? Because of the necessity of national supremacy, this control is not an institutionalized feature of government (as the later doctrine of "nullification" would have it) but appears especially in informal agitation and, most dramatically, when the people resort to their right of revolution. I noted earlier *The Federalist*'s prediction that state officers would stand poised to "criminate" even the good and certainly the bad measures of the national government. They are in a position of prominence, and have their own selfish motives for sounding alarms; they can display their "frowns" and invent "devices" in opposition (46, p. 297). State legislators themselves elect senators, and can influence the people's election of the members of the House (45, p. 291).

In a more extreme situation, the national government can be controlled by being overturned by a people exerting their "original right of self-defense which is paramount to all positive forms of government" (28, p. 180). A united America will have several notable advantages in asserting this right if the occasion arises. First, the size of the country means that the people's "natural strength" is greater in proportion to the government's "artificial strength" than it is in a small country; and there would be more territory in which to resist the troops of the central government. Second, the existence of state governments would give the people a valuable means both of detecting and exposing usurpations, and of organizing resistance. Even though the states have no legal authority to resist the national government's legal acts, they will be very useful in this extralegal situation. By contrast, in a country without such local institutions

> The citizens must rush tumultuously to arms, without concert, without system, without resource; except in their courage and despair. (28, p. 180)

The people's "natural strength" needs an artificial organization which can alert it and coordinate its actions. Confederation institutionalizes a place for those informal leaders who could be expected to lead the people's revolutions;[22] this is such an improvement that in this circumstance "the people, without exaggeration, may be said to be entirely the masters of their own fate" (28, pp. 180–81). While the creation of two governments with distinct objects does not, I have suggested, differ much in principle from the Lockean proposal of one government with limited objects, the second government does make more practical the Lockean enforcement of limits by revolution.[23] The people master their own fate by "throwing themselves into either scale"; they "make use of" one government to defend themselves against the other (28, p. 181). Their mastery in vindicating their right is like their choice in instituting government; they have power, but they depend on others to enable them to use it successfully.

While *The Federalist*'s account of the role of the states in protecting men against oppression by a central government has been cited as a groundwork for later doctrines of "nullification" and even "secession,"[24] there are some important differences. First, such state actions are not officially allowed by the form of government; they are revolutionary acts. The national government, quite properly, will resist such actions and forcibly attempt to suppress them. A revolutionary struggle would be a last resort for an oppressed people, and its success would depend upon the inability of a tyrannical national government to retain loyalty among the people. Second, Hamilton does not refer to particular states acting in behalf of the people of those states. The states altogether would lead a people who as a whole find their government oppressive. Indeed such a united front would be crucial to the success of an uprising; otherwise the national government could use the forces of the loyal parts against the disloyal parts (9, p. 75). Revolution is a recourse in practice for the people as a whole, when there is a "general alarm" which forms a "common cause" (46, p. 298).

Thus the secession of 1776, not that of 1861, is the kind of resistance intended. Madison cites that successful resistance as proof that Americans need not fear a new, oppressive central authority, because they could (as a last resort) repeat their experience of 1776, and with an even more favorable prospect of success:

> Plans of resistance would be concerted. One spirit would animate and conduct the whole. The same combinations, in short, would result from an apprehension of the federal, as was produced by the dread of a foreign, yoke; and unless the projected innovations should be voluntarily renounced, the same appeal to a trial of force would be made in the one case as was made in the other. But what degree of madness could ever drive the federal government to such an extremity? In the contest with Great Britain, one part of the empire was employed against the other. The more numerous part invaded the rights of the less numerous part. The attempt was unjust and unwise; but it was not in speculation absolutely chimerical. But what would be the contest in the case we are supposing? Who would be the parties? A few representatives of the people would be opposed to the people themselves; or rather one set of representatives would be contending against thirteen sets of representatives, with the whole body of their common constituents on the side of the latter. (46, p. 298)

The last sentence quoted suggests the importance of representatives in making the "whole body" of the people an effectual force.

Madison then analyzes the worst case: a federal government with an enormous standing army to enforce its usurpations. I have already discussed *The Federalist*'s various assurances regarding structural controls on the necessary power to raise armies, which suggest that the people can choose a forceful government which will not forcibly deprive them of their choice. Hamilton admitted that, while these arrangements could prevent unnecessarily large standing armies, they could not alter the possibility that a large standing army could be necessary:

> if the defense of the community under such circumstances should make it necessary to have an army so numerous as to hazard its liberty, this is one of those calamities for which there is neither preventative nor cure. (26, p. 173)

This circumstance is necessity incarnate. There is, admittedly, no way men can guarantee their liberty by any choice they could make. Fortunately, this danger is "altogether unlikely." Later, *The Federalist* goes further, and Hamilton implies by a rhetorical question (28, p. 182), and Madison says "it may be affirmed with the greatest assurance" (46, p. 300), that the American people's advantages in exerting their right of revolution can indeed save them even from the largest possible standing army. The "hazard" cannot be prevented, but it can eventually be defeated by the military superiority of

> near half a million of citizens with arms in their hands, officered by men chosen from among themselves, fighting for their common liberties and united and conducted by governments possessing their affections and confidence. (46, p. 299)

A well-modeled government can only make the extinction of the people's choice by military force improbable. The final security of the people's choice rests in their own force, as exerted in revolution—although even in this most striking display of popular sovereignty, the people need to be "united and conducted" by some few among them whom the well-modeled American system keeps available. America is not like the ancient republics which were "nation[s] of soldiers," but the American private citizens are nevertheless armed. The people's latent force is sufficient to vindicate its choice eventually, or—what is probably more useful—to pose an impressive threat to do so.

Thus the states could help the people in a revolution if the national government had the "madness" to push things to that extreme. The states remain potentially the kind of "collective bodies" of men which can resist being ruled, even if in ordinary times the central government can successfully rule by issuing commands to men's individual bodies. *The Federalist*'s invocation of 1776 reminds us that some Anti-Federalists feared that the proposed Constitution would result in the same kind of distant, centralized, and eventually tyrannical authority which the Revolutionary War had thrown off. *The Federalist* answers that fear partly by this assertion that Americans can, if necessary, successfully repeat the Revolution. But this assurance surely implies that a repetition of 1776 would lead to a repetition of the unsatisfactory situation of 1776 to 1787. The states can help the people reclaim their rights, but the people would then face again the necessity of instituting a new "energetic" government for the Union. The states can help overthrow government, but they cannot themselves replace it, for the same reasons which in 1787 require a national government. The states resemble what Locke called "society." Society can resist a tyrannical government, but must institute some other government, because *some* government is necessary to preserve society as distinguished from the state of nature.[25]

The states' role in revolution or the threat of revolution is clearly a last-ditch check on central tyranny; the primary safeguard is the general form and particular structure of the central government itself, which I will examine in chapters 4 through 7. Madison also claims that the new government provides a remedy for a problem which revolution cannot really remedy even in the last resort; that is, the problem of the "unjust and unwise" but "not . . . absolutely chimerical" attempts by the "more numerous part" to invade the "rights of the less numerous part." That is one subject of the famous *Federalist* 10, and of the next chapter.

·[Three]·

A Study of *Federalist* 10

Federalist 10 is today the most famous and highly regarded essay of the book—perhaps even of all American political writings.[1] External evidence indicates that the analysis had been worked out over a long period of time and in relation to a wide variety of particular political issues, and that its presentation in *The Federalist* had the benefit of considerable care.[2] But the very clarity of argument which supports *Federalist* 10's reputation as a classic of political writing has made the essay seem readily available for quotation and summary, rather than in need of interpretation. *Federalist* 10's conclusion is familiar: Contrary to the conventional wisdom that popular governments suit only small and homogeneous cities, only an extended republic with a wide variety of groups and a "scheme of representation" can cure the effects of popular government's mortal defect, "faction." But the carefully composed argument in support of that conclusion has not received the scrutiny which it both rewards and deserves—not only for the importance and fame of the conclusion itself, but for the importance of the principles underlying it to the political theory of *The Federalist* as a whole.

Readers who confidently summarize the essay do not stop to wonder about the very important distinctions contained even in Madison's definition of faction:

> By a faction I understand a number of citizens, whether amounting to a majority or minority of the whole, who are united and actuated by some common impulse of passion, or of interest, ad-

·[59]·

verse to the rights of other citizens, or to the permanent and aggregate interests of the community.[3]

Why does Madison say "of passion, or of interest"? How are these two impulses related or different? How are the factions they engender related or different? Even less noted is Madison's distinction between "the rights of other citizens" and "the permanent and aggregate interests of the community" as the two objects which faction threatens. What is the relation between those two objects?

Most interpreters have focused on factions moved by economic interest. While these are indeed the "most common and durable" factions in a modern, liberal regime, Madison describes a separate category of factions moved by passionate attachment to fallible opinions; he thus recalls the prevalence of political conflict based on religious opinions and appears to anticipate the rise of ideological politics. Madison's distinction shows the incompleteness of a psychology of human "self-interest." It also sheds light on *The Federalist*'s relation to a liberal tradition in which men's economic interests play a prominent part, and to a republican tradition of self-government in which citizens are free to passionately promote their own opinions.

Throughout *Federalist* 10, Madison also preserves a distinction between "the rights of other citizens" (also called "justice," "private rights," etc.), and "the permanent and aggregate interests of the community" (also called "the public good," "the good of the whole," "the public weal," etc.). The importance of these terms is suggested by the fact that each is, in other parts of *The Federalist,* described as the fundamental object of government (see p. 162 below). While the republican tradition stressed a patriotic concern for the "public good," liberalism insists that government protect the "private rights" of individuals. I will consider in this chapter the meaning of each of these two terms, and their relation to each other.

While these are the two fundamental objects of government, *Federalist* 10's "inquiries" have an additional "great object":

> To secure the public good and private rights against the danger
> of such a [majority] faction, and at the same time to preserve the
> spirit and the form of popular government, is then the great object to which our inquiries are directed.

Federalist 10's immediate context is a series of papers showing the contributions of *"the UNION"* to *"political prosperity."* It appears that not only does political prosperity require that the public good and private rights be secured, but that they be secured by a "republican remedy," one which will "preserve the spirit and the form of popular government," so that "this form of government can be rescued from the opprobrium under which it has so long labored and be recommended to the esteem and adoption of mankind." Madison's diagnosis of popular government's mortal vice does not lead him to abandon popular government to the opprobrium it has earned. Popular government itself is, it seems, part of political prosperity. *Federalist* 10 thus links the theme of volume 1 (political prosperity) with the announced theme of volume 2 (*"the true principles of republican government"*).

Federalist 10 "unfold[s] the true principles of Republican Government"[4] by its treatment of the three themes I have mentioned: the "interest" and "passion" which generate men's political activities; the "justice" and "public good" which are the proper objects of government; and the basis for thinking republican government is part of political prosperity despite its depressing history and poor reputation. In elaborating those themes, I will pay close attention to the details of the text, and conclude with a restatement of major findings.

The Problem of Faction

Before defining faction and systematically dissecting its causes, effects, and possible remedies, Madison begins with a report of how the problem of faction appears to two different types of people: the "friend of popular governments," and "our most considerate and virtuous citizens."

The friend of popular governments is "alarmed" at the effect of faction on the "character and fate" of such governments. Faction has introduced "instability, injustice, and confusion" in the public councils, and these have "in truth, been the mortal diseases under which popular governments have everywhere perished. . . ." Besides this effect on popular government's "fate," there is an effect on popular government's "character" (i.e., reputation)[5] in that these diseases are the "favorite and fruitful topics from which the adversaries to liberty derive their most specious declamations."

Our "most considerate and virtuous citizens" are concerned with the vices which faction introduces into "our" (American) governments. They have three complaints:

> [1] that our governments are too unstable, [2] that the public good is disregarded in the conflicts of rival parties, and [3] that measures are too often decided, not according to the rules of justice and the rights of the minor party, but by the superior force of an interested and overbearing majority.

·[61]·

Two of these problems—instability and injustice—distress both the friends of popular governments and the considerate and virtuous citizens, although for somewhat different reasons. Good citizens complain about the quality of "our governments"; good democrats are alarmed that these vices injure the prospects for "popular governments."

But one additional problem named by the considerate and virtuous citizens was not said to threaten popular government's reputation or fate: "the public good is disregarded." Disregard of the public good, which is appropriately enough a particular concern of good *citizens,* appears (for reasons which will become clear) not to be as much of a mortal disease to popular governments as injustice and instability are, or as injurious to its reputation. Although one might be tempted, on the basis of looser or different usage in other times or by other writers, to consider justice and the public good as equivalent expressions, Madison preserves this distinction throughout the essay.[6]

Madison describes our most considerate and virtuous citizens as "equally the friends of public and private faith and of public and personal liberty." Public liberty, one of their concerns, means "popular government" *or* the popular element of a mixed government like England's.[7] The friendship for public liberty is similar to, but not quite so discriminating as, the attachment to certain "principles" shown by the "friend of popular governments." England's mixed government is not a popular government, but it does preserve "public . . . liberty" in that it has "one republican branch" (the House of Commons) (39, p. 240; see 9, p. 72). Public liberty exists where government is at least partly popular; popular government is wholly popular.

Although considerate and virtuous citizens are friends of, among other things, public liberty, they are not necessarily friends of popular government. They complain about "an interested and overbearing majority." Perhaps when they contemplate popular government's propensities and history they are tempted to prefer England's mixed government, which combines the public liberty of an elected House of Commons with the steadiness of a hereditary monarchy. But, unlike the friend of popular governments, these virtuous citizens are not dogmatic about the *form* of government; their concern is that it serve its proper *ends*—the ends which faction threatens. To anticipate: In seeking to protect those ends, Madison's argument is the work of a good citizen;[8] in insisting on a "republican remedy" for faction, Madison writes as a friend of popular governments.

But *Federalist* 10's first paragraph makes one wonder why the friend of popular governments is so attached to their "principles" if he "contemplates their propensity to this dangerous vice." If popular governments have "in truth" everywhere perished from the instability, injustice, and confusion induced by faction, the "declamations" against them might seem justified.[9] The existing American popular governments may or may not have made "valuable improvements" on ancient and modern constitutions[10] (the improvements "cannot certainly be too much admired," Madison ambiguously says). But it would be an "unwarrantable partiality" to say that they have solved the problem of faction. Is it then an unwarrantable partiality to be a friend of popular governments? Or could there be such a thing as a warrantable partiality—a bias which could be justified but not necessarily by all of its holders and perhaps never completely in any case?

Having outlined the concerns of the friends of popular governments and of considerate and virtuous citizens, Madison turns to "known facts" which show that faction is a problem for America. Some distresses may have other causes,[11] but "many of our heaviest misfortunes" must be blamed on "the operation of our governments," particularly

> that prevailing and increasing distrust of public engagements and alarm for private rights which are echoed from one end of the continent to the other. These must be chiefly, if not wholly, effects of the unsteadiness and injustice with which a factious spirit has tainted our public administration.

Thus the only known facts to which Madison appeals to support the complaints of the considerate and virtuous citizens are a "prevailing and increasing distrust . . . and alarm." Distrust and alarm—rather than particular actual violations of private rights or public engagements—are the most politically relevant facts. Government should be such as to give men what Montesquieu called an "opinion . . . of . . . safety."[12]

The distrust and alarm concern "public engagements" and "private rights." Madison had called the most considerate and virtuous citizens "equally the friends of public and private faith and of public and personal liberty." It would appear that there is no widespread alarm about private faith or public liberty. The public liberty of America's popular governments must seem fairly well entrenched—except perhaps to their close friends who see their dangerous propensities. Private faith may be more secure than public faith because of the need of individual men to preserve their credit for future use; public faith is more problematical because the government can redefine "faith" for itself, command obedience, and prevent revenge. Private faith is more secure and personal liberty less secure because individual men are weak. Public faith is less secure and public liberty more secure because the whole people seems to be strong.

The chief if not the only cause of the alarm and distrust is "the un-steadiness and injustice with which a factious spirit has tainted our public administration." These problems were mentioned before ("instability," "too unstable"; "injustice," "not according to the rules of justice"). Conspicuously absent is an additional complaint made by the most considerate and virtuous: "that the public good is disregarded."

Disregard for the public good has no effects which arouse a widespread alarm or distrust; it is a kind of neglect which is itself easy to neglect. Alarm about private rights and public engagements can grow out of or even remain confined to each man's alarm for his own rights and his own investments in government bonds. The public good is less immediate. The people disregard the public good because of the distraction of party conflicts in which they themselves participate. The absence of any prevailing alarm for the public good is itself a manifestation of the disregard for the public good. The fact that disregard for the public good concerns only the most considerate and virtuous citizens, and raises no general alarm, is certainly consistent with its not being a cause of popular government's mortality. Injustice is a mortal disease because, according to *Federalist* 51 (p. 324), those who suffer under it eventually fight back, making their oppressors insecure and fearful enough to overturn the regime. Disregard for the public good may not afflict anyone so directly or harshly or immediately. It may result in the failure to gain advantages which are possible or even vital for the country as a whole. But the most considerate and virtuous citizens who realize that, will probably not overturn the regime.[13]

Madison then gives his precise explanation of what a faction is:

> By a faction I understand a number of citizens, whether amounting to a majority or minority of the whole, who are united and actuated by some common impulse of passion, or of interest, adverse to the rights of other citizens, or to the permanent and aggregate interests of the community.

Any number can be a faction. Whether or not any particular set of united citizens is a faction depends upon whether or not they are united and actuated by the kind of common impulse specified. Factions are evidently mischievous and dangerous, and one should not assume in advance that all organized or unorganized groups are factions. A faction's impulse is either passionate or interested (a distinction which will be developed below), and is adverse either to the "rights of other citizens" or to the "permanent and aggregate interests of the community." This latter distinction is another statement of two ends we have already encountered: justice ("rules of justice and the rights of the minor party," "private rights"), and "the public good." "Instability" drops out as a separate theme, perhaps because it is an indirect outcome of the clash of factions rather than inherent in the "impulse" of any one faction.

What groups does Madison include in his "understand[ing]" of faction? For example, are what we call lobbies or "interest groups" necessarily "adverse" to the "permanent and aggregate interests of the community"? Madison's repetition of the word "interest" might suggest that many interests could be *part* of the aggregate interests and therefore not really "adverse." An interest group may watch out for the prosperity of the part it is concerned with and thereby even contribute to the "aggregate" prosperity. In that case, interest groups would be factions only when they go too far, and try to profit at the expense of the whole. Similarly, an interest group adverse to the "interests" of other groups is not a faction as long as it is not adverse to the "rights" of others. However, Madison defines faction not by the harmful content of its plans or program but by the *impulse* which both joins its members together and sets them in motion. He does not say that a faction does something adverse to the rights of others or the public good, but only that its passionate or interested impulse is adverse to the rights of others or the public good. Even if wheat growers or dockworkers do not actively oppose the public good or propose programs to enrich themselves at everyone's expense, is it not still true that the impulse which moves them, taken in itself, is adverse to the permanent and aggregate interests of the community? Even if a particular interest is part of the aggregate of interests, that interest as an impulse uniting and actuating a group is indifferent to the aggregate and would, if not restrained by some other impulse, further its interest even against the aggregate. And the possible restraining impulses would not seem to be those which unite and actuate the group, since they are not intrinsic to its reasons for being a group. Madison's definition seems to detect a factious impulse at the heart of even a respectable lobby.

Madison's phrase "the permanent and aggregate interests of the community" provides some further information about the content of the "public good." This formulation bears some resemblance to the definition by Francis Hutcheson (an author well known to Madison)[14] of "the *greatest* or *most perfect Good*" (for each man) as

> that whole Series, or Scheme of Events, which contains a greater Aggregate of Happiness in the whole, or more absolute universal Good, than any other possible Scheme, after subtracting all the Evils connected with each of them.[15]

The necessary additions and subtractions would yield a calculation of the highest possible total of interests—taking into account the indefinite future ("permanent"). The interests of the community are an "aggregate" because the community is a nonhierarchical whole; none of the parts has a higher dignity than the others. But the whole is more than the sum of its parts because the whole has or is intended to have a permanence which the parts (individual men) lack. The present parts have no higher dignity than the future parts. An individual or group interest may conflict with the aggregate by gaining less for itself than it loses for others, or by neglecting the fact that the public good must be "permanent." The distribution of gains and losses among different men would seem to be irrelevant to the total as long as the balance of gain is maximized.

Although a resourceful utilitarian theorist might devise arguments to show that tradeoffs which yield a net gain but seem rather hard on the losers are in fact not beneficial to the whole, Madison appears not to rely on such computations. The "rights of other citizens" (i.e., justice) is an end which Madison specifies separately from this "aggregate" good. While these ends may overlap, Madison's "or" suggests that factions which violate rights may not always diminish the aggregate interests; and that factions may sometimes diminish the aggregate interests without harming rights.[16] This can be explained by the fact that the profitable oppression of one or a few might not diminish an aggregate good; and the fact that men have interests which are more inclusive than their rights.[17]

In the next two paragraphs Madison establishes the outline for the rest of the essay. Either by removing faction's causes or by controlling its effects, one can cure "the mischiefs of faction"—that is, cure the effects of faction. Madison first discusses and dismisses removing the causes; this discussion is important because in considering removing the causes Madison shows what the causes are. He thus gives a more systematic account of the problem he had previously presented only as a current problem for America and a typical problem for popular government. Even though Madison concludes that a proper cure will not attack the causes, a proper understanding of why the disease is so persistent and fundamental does require us to understand the causes.

The causes of faction which Madison considers "removing" are (1) "the liberty which is essential to [faction's] existence," and (2) the diverse "opinions," "passions," and "interests" of citizens.

Liberty

Removing liberty to cure faction would be a remedy worse than the disease. "Liberty is to faction what air is to fire, an aliment without which it instantly expires." Liberty is thus not a sufficient cause of faction, but a necessary condition; it is a medium in which some friction or kindling will be destructive.

> But it could not be a less folly to abolish liberty, which is essential to political life, because it nourishes faction than it would be to wish the annihilation of air, which is essential to animal life, because it imparts to fire its destructive agency.

Liberty should not be abolished because it is "essential to political life." Evidently the liberty meant is what the first paragraph called "public . . . liberty," the liberty of participation in politics. We will see in Madison's next paragraph that a more private liberty—the liberty of exercising one's fallible reason—also contributes to faction. One might object that some forms of "political life" can exist without the liberty of popular participation. But even if political participation were confined to a few, their liberty would permit factions among them.[18]

But why would it be so foolish to abolish liberty? Is political life so important? Madison does not claim that this (political) liberty is necessary to social life or to life itself. Indeed we learn later in the essay that faction can cause the "sacrifice" of an "obnoxious individual"; faction can ruin or destroy some men's lives. Might we not be better off without political life—or, if that is impossible, with this "liberty" and the consequent sacrifices and destructive fires confined to a few? A similar question may be asked about the analogue. Animal life, as *Federalist* 37 indicates, is not the whole; nature also includes "vegetable" and "unorganized" matter (p. 228). Might not some nonanimal forms be better off without air, which they do not need, and without fire, which can destroy them? Madison's argument seems both political-centric and animal-centric.

The statement of the analogy is instructive: It would be as foolish to abolish liberty as it would be to wish the annihilation of air. Liberty apparently can be abolished, but air's annihilation can only be a wish— or so it seemed in 1787. And regardless of the improvements in their condition which might result, vegetables and minerals are in no position to wish for the elimination of air or for anything else. To "wish" would seem to be an activity of "animal life"; to "abolish" would seem to be an activity of "political life." For animals, or humans acting in their capacity of animals, to wish to eliminate air would be to wish their own destruction as wishing beings, for the benefit of nonwishing matter. For men with political life to abolish liberty would be to politically choose not to have a political choice, for the sake of nonpolitical life. While there might be something to be said for that, perhaps choosing men are unlikely to say it.

The Federalist's insistence on popular government has sometimes been interpreted as a prudent concession to its readers' prejudices or as (for Madison) an unexamined premise.[19] Alternatively, popular government could be understood as merely a necessary but not a sufficient condition for the real end, the protection of men's rights.[20] That view is not refuted by the fact that Madison points to severe conflicts between popular government and private rights, since he clearly intends his plan to mitigate those conflicts and since he also points to severe conflicts between non-popular governments and private rights. But I find in this passage and elsewhere a stubbornness about political liberty and popular government[21] apart from or in spite of its effects. Men choose to live a "political life" and not only an "animal life."

Passions and Interests

The other methods of removing the causes of faction—"giving to every citizen the same opinions, the same passions, and the same interests"— is as "impracticable" as the abolition of liberty would be unwise. Thus Madison does not say that these diversities should be preserved for their own sake or for their fruits; it is only impractical to make men uniform in these respects. Perhaps Madison refrains from a more direct defense of diversity because of the possibility of true opinions, well-ordered passions, and enlightened and permanent interests which would be desirable for all men if they could be discovered. In any case, human diversity appears intractable; and this diversity leads to the friction which sets off the "fire" of faction when the "air" of liberty is available.

Although factions were said to be moved by certain impulses of passion or interest, Madison now discusses men's diversity in opinion, passion, and interest. Diverse opinions are a cause of faction even though opinion is not the "impulse" which unites and actuates a faction. Opinions will differ "[a]s long as the reason of man continues fallible, and he is at liberty to exercise it." The liberty to exercise one's reason seems to be a different liberty from the public liberty which permits faction. Men could be free to form opinions without being free to act politically; this follows the distinction between personal liberty and public liberty suggested in Federalist 10's first paragraph. The fact that the free exercise of fallible reason leads to different opinions, rather than to a shared error or a shared uncertainty, suggests that the "reason of man" is fallible in different degrees or different ways in different men.

Madison then turns to the impracticality of giving men the same passions. But, contrary to what we might expect, he does not directly assert that different men have different passions or that different men's passions have different objects. Instead he blends his discussion of opinion with his discussion of passion, and suggests a threefold "connection" between "reason" and "self-love."

> As long as the connection subsists between his reason and his self-love, his opinions and his passions will have a reciprocal influence on each other; and the former will be objects to which the latter will attach themselves.

The reason of man is fallible because man is a fallible creature; but apart from the distortions suffered by pure reason due to our species' imperfections, an additional distortion is introduced by the fact that the reason of man occurs in individual men and is connected in them with their self-love. The "influence" of men's passions on their opinions is perhaps clearest. Men's reasoning is biased by the attractions they feel; they may believe to be good what they are attracted to by passion. In particular, self-love may incline them toward opinions which flatter or favor themselves. The apparently anthropocentric defenses of liberty and air in the previous paragraph may manifest this influence of passion on opinion.

The "reciprocal" influence Madison asserts, that of opinion on passion, may seem almost contradictory. It implies that our opinions do not merely report in words our passionate reactions of attraction or aversion; our opinions are instead the foundation of those reactions. We love what we think good, rather than thinking good what we love. (Madison, observing a "reciprocal influence," indicates that we do both.) The influence of opinion on passion was noted by Francis Hutcheson:

> [O]ur Affections must very much depend upon the *Opinions* we form, concerning any thing which occurs to our Mind, its *Qualities, Tendencies,* or *Effects.*[22]

This position would seem to make our passions educable and less imperious than might be expected.

The paradox of a "reciprocal influence" is clarified by the fact that an influence is not a cause. Each can influence the other if each is only partly the result of the other; thus there is apparently an element of opinion which cannot be reduced to passion, and some passion which does not depend on opinion. This implies that men are not infinitely persuadable, because the attempt would run into the resistance of some core of passion; nor are they utterly obstinate, since not all of their opinions are products of passion.

Madison's concise formulation leaves an unresolved ambiguity regarding what kind of reasoning is independent of, and influences, men's passions. One might say that the influential opinions are opinions about one's own prospective pleasures and pains; thus men's fallible reason would calculate the intensity of various pleasures, the pains to which they might be annexed, the best means of attaining them, etc. Madison's view would then agree with Locke's *Essay Concerning Human Understanding,* according to which men may "raise" their desire for "any good proposed" by "a due consideration" of its value; and may "in most cases" suspend the execution and satisfaction of any desire so as to weigh, examine, and compare objects.[23] Alternatively, Madison could mean that men form opinions about the intrinsic goodness or badness of objects quite apart from any "self-love," and that those opinions can then influence men to desire objects which they do not desire for themselves. This latter alternative would provide a good explanation of how the "virtuous," patriotic, justice-loving men to whom Madison refers later in the essay are possible. They could form opinions about the good of the whole or the rights of others even if their self-love moved them in contrary directions. But there is an ambiguity precisely because those men can also be explained by the former hypothesis. Virtue could be grounded on the passion for salvation and eternal life (one of Locke's arguments); or on passions which attach us to the happiness of others which were variously described by David Hume ("humanity"), Adam Smith ("sympathy"), and Francis Hutcheson and Madison's Hutchesonian professor at Princeton, John Witherspoon[24] ("moral sense");[25] or on the passion for reputation and glory. In any of these cases, reason would merely compare the pleasures of and calculate the means to the objects of desire.

Although we may regret our inability to specify the precise influence which opinions can have on passions, this theoretical ambiguity supports Madison's practical point. Even to the extent that men's opinions do affect their passions, the fallibility of reason means that the result will not be unanimity. There is no agreement on exactly what instructions reason gives to the passions even when it is in a position to instruct. And (reciprocally) different passions of different strengths can be expected to interfere in different ways and degrees with the reasoning which would instruct them.

There is a third connection between passion and opinion; opinions are "objects" to which passions "attach themselves." While the "reciprocal influence" already discussed explains the inevitable diversity of passions and opinions, this additional relation shows how the "impulse" of a faction is constituted. Men become passionate about their opinions. In the next paragraph, when Madison gives examples of opinionated factions, he speaks of a "zeal" for those opinions. While the notion of a passionately held opinion may seem unexceptional and entirely consistent with common experience, it does warrant examination. Certainly the passionate attachment to an opinion is not quite an appetite or desire for something, or even an aversion. It is more like a love (since the object is not absent) but it is a love for something intangible, and the passion is not satisfied by merely holding the opinion one is attached to. To be passionate about an opinion is to struggle on its behalf and to insist that the opinion be respected by others who would deny its worth. Without passion, one might hope that the opinion will persuade by its own reasonableness, or regret that others are not wise enough to be persuaded, or even consider that one's opinion could be in error. But a passionate opiner feels a stake in his opinion because it is his; his desire that his opinion prevail resembles the desire to rule other men. This passion explains why men ask questions "with an air of seeming triumph" (7, p. 60), or find in facts which support their viewpoint a cause for "malicious exultation" (9, p. 72). This is not a passion which (in Hobbes's words) desires commodious living and "encline[s] men to Peace"; it is more like "that exultation of the mind which is called GLORYING"[26]—a passionate self-assertion manifested in an insistence on whatever opinions are one's own.

As Madison's definition of faction indicates, a mere opinion is not a sufficient impulse to unite and actuate a faction. An opinion needs the assistance of passion to become politically forceful. At the same time, passions may equally depend on opinions for a political object to which to attach themselves. Passion is a strong impulse, but it is not necessarily a "common impulse." Apart from any diversity in passions from one man to the next, each man's self-love, his concern with the passions he feels separately in himself, sufficiently divides him from other men. But faction implies both division and unity; a faction is a "number of citizens" with a common impulse. For several men's separately felt passions to become a common impulse may require the assistance of opinion. Contrary to this suggestion, Madison's next paragraph gives as examples of passionate factions groups based on an "attachment" to leaders or other interesting persons. Thus a kind of shared love seems to be a uniting impulse; one can imagine a similar effect from shared hatred. But in other cases (and perhaps in these), passion becomes political by influencing opinion, and by making opinions an object of attachment. This politicized passion may be amenable to change insofar as the opinion on which it relies is vulnerable to persuasion—although, in practice, the heat of zeal may keep the opinion relatively immune from examination. Madison then explains why diversity of *interests* is unavoidable.

> The diversity in the faculties of men, from which the rights of property originate, is not less an insuperable obstacle to a uniformity of interests. The protection of these faculties is the first object of government. From the protection of different and unequal faculties of acquiring property, the possession of different degrees and kinds of property immediately results; and from the influence of these on the sentiments and views of the respective proprietors ensues a division of the society into different interests and parties.

Diverse interests stem from diverse property which in turn is the result of men's diverse faculties. The first sentence quoted above uses the phrase "not less" without clearly indicating what is being compared; it permits but does not require us to think that the previously discussed obstacles to uniformity of passion and opinion were *also* examples of the diversity in the faculties of men;[27] and hence that men's fallible reason and passions are included among men's "faculties." In any case, men's faculties, as well as—or (by the interpretation suggested) including—his fallible reason and passions, are inherent qualities of his species; thus these "latent causes of faction" are not the result of transient conditions but are "sown in the nature of man."

But Madison's summary assertion obscures part of his analysis. Diverse interests result from men's (natural) faculties, but only insofar as those faculties are "protect[ed]" by government. Similarly, diverse opinions result from men's naturally fallible reason, but only so long as men are "at liberty to exercise" their reason. And diversity altogether only leads to faction if there is the public liberty which allows "political life." Thus the causes of faction seem to be sown not simply in the nature of man but in a political arrangement, i.e., a government which attends to its "first object," the protection of men's faculties, and which leaves men free to opine and to participate in politics. Madison may imply that such a political arrangement is itself "sown in" the nature of man in that it is the arrangement justified by or suited to man's nature; I will consider this below. But we should not overlook this premature intrusion of politics into the argument's structure. Faction is partly the result of the benign government which it endangers.

Madison's assertion that the "rights of property" "originate" from men's "faculties" appears to align him with those theorists who argue that men have a right to property which antedates government and is secured by

government. Madison elaborates his position only by apparently iden-
tifying the "faculties . . . from which the rights of property originate"
with the "faculties of acquiring property." Man's ability to acquire property is the basis of his right to it, although Madison does not here discuss
various questions which might be raised concerning the manner or extent
of rightful acquisition. He seems to echo John Locke's famous argument
for the naturalness of property. Locke found a right to property in men's
labor. Since each man is *"Proprietor of his own Person,"* his labor is his
own.[28] Even the trivial labor of picking up an acorn is a kind of mixing
of oneself with a natural resource sufficient to give one a better claim
to it than anyone else; and some such claim is necessary, since many
essential resources can only be put to use (e.g., eaten) separately.[29] More
fundamentally, labor gives a right to property in land because a cultivator
takes only "almost worthless" materials from nature and contributes 9
or 99 or 999 times as much value by his own "pains."[30] He even adds to
the common stock by reducing his reliance on the almost worthless natural resources. If acquisition of goods by labor is essentially the *creation*
of those goods, there can be "no doubt of Right, no room for quarrel."[31]
Madison in a later essay referred to "Heaven" "decreeing man to earn
his bread by the sweat of his brow."[32]

But a right to property originating in men's "faculties" seems broader
than a right to property based on labor. Madison emphasizes the "diversity" of these faculties, and speaks of the "rights" of property, as if
to underline the variety of legitimate modes of acquisition. Locke discusses the fairly primitive acquisition in the "State of Nature," where
physical labor may be applied to different tasks of picking up, gathering,
digging, felling, framing, tilling, etc., but always seems to involve an
expenditure of "pains" (or "toil" or "sweat"). Madison says men's faculties
of acquisition are "different and unequal," meaning that different men
may have different faculties and may have the same faculties in different
degrees, by which they acquire, respectively, different "kinds" and "degrees" of property. Locke explains different degrees of acquisition by
the fact that "different degrees of Industry were apt to give Men Possessions in different Proportions."[33] To this apparently natural difference
in men's industry, i.e., effort, Madison seems to add other natural differences in men's "faculties" which make one man's efforts more fruitful
than another's. Locke also suggests the differences in *kind* of men's modes
of acquiring by an example showing that some men hire servants,[34] and
perhaps more generally by the distinction between "the *Labour* of [a
man's] Body" and "the *Work* of his Hands."[35] To the extent that "Hands"
are not merely part of "Body," they reflect the element of skill as distinguished from strength.

While Madison's formulation is Lockean in spirit, his emphasis on men's "faculties" rather than on the labor which men perform using those faculties draws attention to the natural differences among men. Locke, in arguing for the natural equality of men, said that men are "Creatures of the same species and rank promiscuously born to all the same advantages of Nature, and the use of the *same faculties.*"[36] As a result, no man has a natural right to dominion, which leaves every man "*Proprietor of his own Person,* and the actions or *Labour* of it."[37] But according to Madison, to be proprietor of one's own person is to be proprietor of one's *unequal* faculties of acquisition. Madison's elaboration might seem to embarrass Locke's original premise (equality). But apparently the faculties by virtue of which each man can claim his own acquisitions for himself are more equal than men's faculties of acquisition are.[38]

Madison does not say that government is instituted to protect the rights of property, but rather that the "first object of government" is the "protection" of the "faculties of men." Madison elsewhere indicates that he agrees with a social-contract theory of government.[39] Men's faculties are theirs by nature but are not sufficiently protected by nature. As in Locke's account, men enter society for the purpose of protecting something which they enjoy precariously prior to society. But Madison's specification of that something is an apparently original formulation. Men do not seek to protect any particular property but rather their faculties of acquiring property altogether. Government secures men's ability to acquire more property in the future.[40]

The "faculties of men" which it is government's first object to protect are not precisely the "faculties of acquiring property." They are the "faculties of men, from which the rights of property originate." The comma could imply that the "faculties of men" altogether are meant, even if some of those faculties are not the basis of property rights.[41] Or, in any case, acquisition would be only one activity of the faculties which are useful for that purpose. The meaning of the "faculties of men" may be illuminated by other texts. Jefferson expressed concern in his *Notes on the State of Virginia* that Americans after the Revolutionary War would "forget themselves, but in the sole faculty of making money"—implying that there are other faculties.[42] In *Federalist* 37, Madison speaks of the various "faculties of the mind" (p. 227). And Madison's Professor Witherspoon spoke in his Princeton lectures on moral philosophy of a range of "faculties"—including the understanding, will, affections, and perhaps the body—which are the "parts" of "human nature."[43] I will return to the possible broader implications of the "faculties of men" below.[44]

Madison says that the protection of men's different and unequal acquisitive faculties leads "immediately" to "the possession of different degrees and kinds of property." Thus the protection of faculties means protecting the exercise of those faculties and especially protecting each man's possession of the fruits of his exercise of his faculties. This protects men's faculties by giving sufficient incentive for the possibly arduous exercise of those faculties. In order to secure to men the fruits of their labor, government would surely need to define and punish theft. One might object that the thief, too, exercises an acquisitive faculty.[45] Madison's rather broad usage seems intended to include various gainful occupations besides physical labor, and the distinction between those and outright theft, if not an unmistakably sharp one, would turn on whether the occupation is somehow productive. An "unmerited" profit[46] would be one not gained by a man's own faculties but "harvest[ed]" by him from the "toils and cares" of others (62, p. 381).

The possibility of "unmerited" gains means that not all unequal property is the result of unequal faculties of acquisition. Actual inequality does not perfectly correspond with natural inequality. But Madison's point is that one cannot expect to eliminate inequality if one protects men's natural faculties.

Although protecting men's faculties implies protecting the resulting unequal possessions, Madison in a later essay defended the mitigation of inequality. Government should make use of "the silent operation of laws, which, without violating the rights of property, reduce extreme wealth towards a state of mediocrity, and raise extreme indigence towards a state of comfort."[47] The "rights of property" forbid direct expropriation but permit indirect devices such as the abolition of primogeniture. Perhaps "extreme indigence" is in itself destructive of men's faculties. Or one man's huge acquisitions (of land, for example) might deprive others of the opportunity to exercise their faculties.[48] According to Hutcheson, since "property is constituted to encourage and reward industry, it can never be so extended as to prevent or frustrate the diligence of mankind."[49]

Diverse faculties lead to diverse property; diverse property leads to diverse "interests and parties" because of the "influence" which property has on its proprietors' "sentiments and views." Men must, so to speak, take an interest in their own property in order to form an "interest." This would appear to be an extension of the human self-love that Madison already said influences men's opinions. While "sentiments and views" resemble "passions" and "opinions," the difference is noteworthy. Sentiments are calmer than passions;[50] unlike opinions, which seem to need the assistance of passion to be a sufficient "impulse," interests may move men more cold-bloodedly. And perhaps the "views" of men interested in their property do not quite deserve the honor of being called "opinions," i.e., fallible and biased attempts to express the truth. In short, unequal faculties give men different opinions and property; self-love heatedly attaches them to the former and coolly interests them in the latter.

Madison then turns to the activation of these "latent causes of faction" in different "circumstances of civil society." The degree of faction and the particular factions will differ from time to time and place to place, but the latent causes make some kind of faction predictable. Madison again discusses opinion, passion, and interest, and again more closely links the first two.

> A zeal for different opinions concerning religion, concerning government, and many other points, as well of speculation as of practice; an attachment to different leaders ambitiously contending for pre-eminence and power; or to persons of other descriptions whose fortunes have been interesting to the human passions, have, in turn, divided mankind into parties, inflamed them with mutual animosity, and rendered them much more disposed to vex and oppress each other than to co-operate for their common good. . . . But the most common and durable source of factions has been the various and unequal distribution of property.

The parties of opinion, as previously noted, show a "zeal" for their opinions. Madison's description appears to follow Hume's essay "Of Parties in General," which found parties based on political or other practical opinions ("Where different principles beget a contrariety of conduct") easily explained, but which found parties on speculative questions, including religion, quite extraordinary, and explained them by the "nature of the human mind" which "as it is wonderfully fortified by an unanimity of sentiments, so it is shocked and disturbed by any contrariety."[51] It is clear from Madison's previous versions of *Federalist* 10's argument that religious factions were his primary concern among opinionated parties.[52]

What might be called more purely passionate parties are based on attachments which men feel for ambitious leaders or for others cryptically described as "persons of other descriptions whose fortunes have been interesting to the human passions."[53] This may refer to notable religious figures or afflicted private men (Shays?) who do not appear to be politically ambitious; or perhaps even to enslaved blacks, whose situation was noted by Madison in the speech at the Constitutional Convention which outlines *Federalist* 10's argument.[54] The "circumstances" which activate factions of opinion and/or passion are the presence of some charismatic persons and the availability of certain opinions which men fasten on. Madison says these things have "in turn" divided men, implying that people are at any one time capable of being moved by a limited number of such attachments—perhaps only one. Zeals and attachments come and go and one may overshadow another; this is in contrast with the "durable" factions based on property.

Madison's assertion that these zealous opinions and attachments have "divided mankind into parties, inflamed them with mutual animosity, and rendered them much more disposed to vex and oppress each other than to co-operate for their common good" is crucial. Before this assertion, Madison's explanation of the causes of faction had shown only an intractable basis for human *diversity*. He had not established that different opinions, passions, or interests necessarily bring about an impulse which is "adverse to the rights of other citizens, or to the permanent and aggregate interests of the community." But now Madison indicates that men with contrary zealous opinions and attachments are not content to agree to disagree or to attempt to persuade each other. They are angry at each other and even wish to "oppress" each other. Diversity, although natural among men, irritates men. Madison carries the argument a striking step further:

> So strong is this propensity of mankind to fall into mutual animosities that where no substantial occasion presents itself the most frivolous and fanciful distinctions have been sufficient to kindle their unfriendly passions and excite their most violent conflicts.

Thus not only does disagreeing make men angry, as argued above; now Madison almost says that anger makes men disagree. Men's fighting spirit is always looking for a pretext. This sentence uses the word "passions" in a new way. Heretofore, passions had been a cause of diversity; now Madison speaks of unfriendly passions which are kindled even by a frivolous diversity. Passions have shifted from being the spark to being the fuel. Madison had already indicated a stubbornness in human nature by the fact that men's passions "attach themselves" to their opinions. Self-love makes men defend the opinions which their fallible reason adopts. But now self-love seems to prompt men to stubbornly assert themselves, and to adopt whatever grounds of division can serve as a vehicle for their belligerence.[55]

This discussion of men's hostile dispositions to "vex and oppress" their opponents precedes, and does not seem to apply to, the analysis of factions of interest. The "various and unequal distribution of property" is the "most common and durable source of factions"; those interested factions are not as extraordinary, intermittent, or heated as the passionate factions discussed above.

> Those who hold and those who are without property have ever formed distinct interests in society. Those who are creditors, and those who are debtors, fall under a like discrimination. A landed interest, a manufacturing interest, a mercantile interest, a moneyed interest, with many lesser interests, grow up of necessity in civilized nations, and divide them into different classes, actuated by different sentiments and views.

That there have "ever" been some men "without property" suggests that the unequal faculties of acquiring property are so unequally distributed that some men acquire only enough to consume and have nothing left to "hold." Or perhaps those with greater faculties acquire so much that some who could acquire find nothing left.[56] The division between property-holders and the propertyless and the division between creditors and debtors are permanent circumstances of human society. By contrast, the divisions according to *kinds* of property "grow up of necessity in civilized nations." Societies smaller or more primitive than civilized nations have more uniformity but are not homogeneous in interest; and a civilized nation is necessarily further divided. In contrast to the hotly contentious conflicts of passionate factions, these factions of interest are mildly described as "interfering"; thus

> The regulation of these various and interfering interests forms the principal task of modern legislation and involves the spirit of party and faction in the necessary and ordinary operations of government.

While they have a permanent root in human nature and are troublesome when they arise, passionate factions are not necessarily ordinarily involved in government. But interested factions will be there all the time.

Madison's statement of the "principal task of modern legislation" invites comparison with his previous statement of the "first object of government":

> The protection of these faculties [the faculties of men] is the first object of government.

> The regulation of these various and interfering interests forms the principal task of modern legislation. . . .

(1) The relation between "object" and "task" is the relation between end and means. Interfering interests should be regulated in such a way as to protect men's faculties; this would imply allowing those acquisitions which do not foreclose other men's use of their faculties of acquisition.

(2) "Legislation" is less inclusive than "government." Men's faculties may also be protected by the execution and adjudication of well-established laws, for example those against murder and robbery; and by defense against conquest by governments less likely to protect men's faculties. The regulation of interfering interests seems to be what requires the continued attention of lawmakers; it is their "task." (3) Madison refers only to "modern legislation." Do premodern legislatures not have this task? Although the wide variety of interests is only a necessity of (modern?) civilized nations, all society features the conflict of propertied and propertyless, and of creditors and debtors, and even a premodern legislature would have to regulate those conflicts. But they may have had a different principal task. Madison's statement of government's "first object" is unqualified; thus we may infer that while the (proper) purpose of government is always the protection of the faculties of men, nonmodern governments deduced a different task from this object. In *Federalist* 8, Hamilton had described a difference between "the ancient republics of Greece" and "modern" times to explain why standing armies result from frequent conflict in the latter but not in the former:

> The industrious habits of the people of the present day, absorbed in the pursuits of gain and devoted to the improvements of agriculture and commerce, are incompatible with the condition of a nation of soldiers, which was the true condition of the people of those republics. (8, p. 69)[57]

For ancient republics, the "faculties of men" were not so much their ability to pursue gain and improve the sources of gain as the faculties brought out in a "nation of soldiers," presumably including physical strength, courage, and prudence. More generally, according to Montesquieu, ancient republics encouraged "virtue" in their citizens.[58]

Modern legislation is apparently based on a disputable interpretation of the faculties of men. Madison's general statement that "[t]he protection of these faculties is the first object of government" is not as far as one might expect from Aristotle's statement that "the good life" is the end of political association. The good life is activity in accordance with virtue, i.e., that excellence of which a human being is capable, which is appropriate to his "proper function."[59] There is some resemblance to this in Madison's presentation of man as a being with certain faculties to be exercised rather than simply a being with certain needs or desires to be satisfied. However, Madison does not say that government should cultivate or perfect human faculties.[60] His emphasis on *protecting* the faculties which constitute man's (individual) nature draws Madison much closer to the Lockean contract.

Modern legislation regulates interfering interests so as to protect men's acquisitive faculties. This "involves the spirit of party and faction in the necessary and ordinary operations of government" by making politics an everyday concern of the durable factions of interest. Madison thus clearly associates these three elements: acquisitive faculties, factions of interest, and modern politics. Also associated are their three opposites: nonacquisitive faculties, factions of passion (/opinion), and nonmodern politics. Nonmodern governments protected human faculties in such a way as to make the more tempestuous passionate factions concerned with the ordinary operations of government. In particular, governments which took an active interest in men's faculties from the point of view of religious salvation aroused the passion of men attached to different religious opinions.[61] Modern legislation, by concerning itself with the acquisitive faculties, is open to the interference of durable interests, but stays away from the more destructive rage of factions moved by passions. Or at least it does not of necessity involve the latter. But even if, according to the principles of modern legislation, religion is not a *necessary* political issue, passionate men may try to make it one. As long as there is the "liberty" of "political life," these natural but unnecessary factions[62] will still be a problem.

This consideration led the notable modern Thomas Hobbes to disparage the liberty of political life. In *Federalist* 14 Madison notes that "some celebrated authors, whose writings have had a great share in forming the *modern* standard of political opinions" defended the monarchical governments they lived under (p. 100; emphasis added). And indeed, while the premodern governments of Greece were republics, most pre-American modern governments were not. Republics allowed men to exercise their faculties in forming opinions and in passionately defending their opinions. These activities give scope to a form of the same belligerent spirit which is manifested in a "nation of soldiers." By his advocacy of popular government, Madison seems to support these political faculties as well as the acquisitive faculties emphasized in modern times. While Hobbes thought that men's faculty of passionately opining was too volatile to be indulged, Madison seeks to show that this faculty may, in the right circumstances, be safely protected.

To sum up: Modern politics attempts to protect man's acquisitive faculties and to make his more inflammatory faculty of passionately opining politically irrelevant. But even if this understanding of which human faculties should be protected were accepted, modern politics would face difficulties: (1) it cannot guarantee that passionate men will confine themselves to what is politically relevant, and (2) it is faced with less spectacular but very important and durable conflicts caused by men's acquisitive faculties.[63] In both of these respects, modern politics needs the improvements which Madison will offer.

Legislative Judging

The principal task of modern legislation—regulating interfering interests—requires the legislature to act in effect as a judge. According to Locke, the great virtue of a legislative authority is its ability to enact "settled standing Rules, indifferent, and the same to all Parties."[64] Criminal laws are a good example of such settled, impartial rules. But no regulation of diverse and interfering interests will be the same to all parties. Law cannot be impartial by being general when the men it equally applies to have unequal interests; a law taxing imports can apply to all citizens, but those in the importing business will find their plans unequally discouraged. Legislation is thus deprived of its implicit impartiality and is better understood as the more delicate function of judging:

> what are many of the most important acts of legislation but so many judicial determinations, not indeed concerning the rights of single persons, but concerning the rights of large bodies of citizens?

Contrary to Montesquieu's suggestion that judicial determinations could be made less offensive by parceling out each individual's case to one of many relatively invisible judges,[65] the legislative judgment will visibly affect the case of "large bodies of citizens."

Madison's phrase "judicial determinations" also emphasizes that judgment must be according to some principle. Legislating, even if it should respect and attempt to enforce the laws of nature, involves a greater scope for variety based on the opinion or will of the legislator. Indeed Professor Witherspoon had suggested that precisely in the case of regulatory laws directing "in what way arts and commerce may be carried on," the legislature may be guided by "common utility" in handling these matters which are "arbitrary and mutable" in themselves.[66] In contrast, Madison insists that regulating interests involves judging men's *rights*. If men consent to government so as to protect their faculties, in particular their acquisitive faculties, then rules which affect the exercise of those faculties become issues not merely of individuals' interests or wishes or even of "common utility," but of individuals' rights. At the same time, because the exercise of men's faculties leads to "interfering," there is clearly no absolute right to exercise one's faculties without limitation. Thus these rights require a judicial determination, which means not a deliberate enactment of positive rights but a thoughtful discovery of the rights men already have.

The problem is that legislators are not fit to judge men's rights impartially; they are "advocates and parties to the causes which they determine." No man is fit to "be a judge in his own cause," because "his interest would certainly bias his judgment, and, not improbably, corrupt his integrity." According to Locke this unfitness makes a legislative authority's "settled Standing rules" preferable to the individual judgment men make about their own cases in the state of nature.[67] According to Madison, the problem visible in the state of nature remains visible in the legislature, where "large bodies" of men (rather than individuals) can badly judge their own case.

Interested men do not have the angry inclination to "vex and oppress" others which characterized passionately opinionated men; they are biased and perhaps corrupt, but not belligerent. Thus one might wonder whether their "impulse" is really factious in Madison's strict sense (adverse to the rights of others or to the permanent and aggregate interests of the community). Madison shows that it is by giving three examples. (1) A proposal concerning private debts will divide creditors and debtors. Although "justice" should "hold the balance," in fact "the most numerous party, or in other words, the most powerful faction must be expected to prevail."[68] Here and in the third example Madison anticipates the theme of the second half of the essay: the majority. He bluntly restates "most numerous" as "most powerful," depriving it of the luster it might derive from the principle of majority rule. An unjust majority relies on its power and asserts "force as the measure of right."[69] (2) Whether or how much to encourage domestic manufactures by restricting foreign manufacturers would be decided differently "by the landed and the manufacturing classes, and probably by neither with a sole regard to justice and the public good." (3) Apportioning taxes on "the various descriptions of property" requires "the most exact impartiality";

> yet there is, perhaps, no legislative act in which greater opportunity and temptation are given to a predominant party to trample on the rules of justice. Every shilling with which they overburden the inferior number is a shilling saved to their own pockets.

The third example is the most emphatic; the winners do not merely "prevail" or show some "regard" for self-interested considerations—they "trample on the rules of justice." This is because the opposed parties have in this case seemingly no common interest; what one gains, the other loses. While other executive or judicial acts might give more occasion for grossly self-serving favoritism, taxation is the leading opportunity for the legislature. The other branches constantly deal with particular cases, while the legislature is often constrained to make laws which apply equally to everyone. Madison's example derives from the American Revolution,[70] and echoes American complaints of the 1770s that if Parliament could tax America it would be constantly tempted to save the shillings of its own constituents. Even if America had representatives in Parliament (some said), they would be the "inferior number."[71] The root of the problem was the natural division of the empire, so that Americans were a distinguishable target for abuse. Unfortunately, according to *Federalist* 10, all civil societies are naturally divided and offer comparable targets.[72] For this reason "representation" in the legislature is by itself an insufficient solution to the problem of taxation.

In adducing the examples of factions impelled by interest, Madison preserves the distinction between "justice" and "the public good" which had been suggested in the essay's opening paragraph and in the definition of faction. In all three examples, Madison refers to the faction's likely disregard for justice. This emphasis on justice is consistent with the statement that the legislature makes "judicial determinations" of men's "rights." Justice requires that each man's rights be respected. But in the second example, and not in the others, Madison also refers to the public good. Neither the landed nor the manufacturing class will have "a sole regard to justice and the public good." Madison thus implies that, at least in this case, a good legislator would have regard for both justice and the public good—not a sole regard for either.

The justice at stake in the first and third examples is relatively clear. Justice means, or at least includes, the protection of each man's right to exercise his faculties. The paper-money schemes of debtors are a not very well disguised form of theft from creditors, thus depriving the latter of the fruits of their acquisitive faculties. Taxation is impartial if it assesses men in proportion to their ability to pay, or perhaps according to the benefit they will receive.[73] Here again, government protects men's faculties by protecting their acquisitions; and perhaps in taxation of luxuries there is some of the "silent" moderating of wealth which also protects faculties (see p. 75 above). There could be different interpretations of what Madison's principle of protecting men's faculties requires in each of these cases. However, Madison's claim is not that only one mode of regulation would be just, but only that some regulations would be unjust.

The meaning of justice in the second example seems more problematic. Neither the landed nor the manufacturing interest proposes to rob the other of the fruits already gained by its enterprise. Regulation would be more a matter of encouraging or discouraging the future exercise of men's acquisitive faculties in a certain way, by affecting the possibility of gaining by that activity. To justly protect men's acquisitive faculties would seem to mean to protect all of those faculties, or at least to protect all of them equally. But precisely because the faculties are diverse it is difficult to specify what would constitute an impartial protection of all. The faculty of acquisition by agriculture and the faculty of acquisition by manufacturing are both entitled to protection; but the principle of protecting all of men's faculties does not provide a standard by which to choose between or even to compromise between two incommensurable faculties.

A standard of judgment would be available if Madison interpreted the "protection of [men's] faculties" more radically. In a later essay on the "distribution" of citizens, i.e., their distribution into different occupations, Madison concluded that

> Whatever [occupation] is least favorable to vigor of body, to the *faculties* of the mind, or to the virtues or the utilities of life, instead of being forced or fostered by public authority, ought to be seen with regret as long as occupations more friendly to human happiness, lie vacant.[74]

Different occupations are more or less favorable to men's faculties. Echoing and enlarging upon Jefferson's famous remarks in *Notes on the State of Virginia*,[75] Madison ranks highest the "life of the husbandman" and ranks lowest that of the sailor, for their respective effects on men's health, virtue, intelligence, and competency. Manufacturing and mechanical industry vary in their effects on men, and "their merits" must be "graduated accordingly."[76] One might say that if government is to protect human faculties, it must exert itself against those activities by which men degrade themselves and act, as animals or machines, without human faculties. But Madison does not say this. Indeed he says the reason he proposes his "theory" of "distribution" is

> not because it could be reduced to practice by any plan of legislation, or ought to be attempted by violence on the will or property of individuals: but because it would be a monition against empirical experiments by power, and a model to which the free choice of occupations by the people, might gradually approximate the order of society.[77]

Legislation should not attempt to protect men's faculties in a way which offends men's "free choice." The "will" which makes men insist on free choice in exercising their faculties might itself be considered a faculty which government should protect; it resembles what I have previously described as men's political faculties. Nonetheless, while Madison says that bad occupations should not be "forced or fostered," he says that good occupations should not be "reduced to practice" by a "plan" or "attempted by violence"—implying that government may not be able to avoid "foster[ing]" one kind of life or another. Perhaps in this case, as in mitigating inequalities, the laws may have a "silent operation" fostering healthy occupations while not offending men's wish to have a "free choice."

Madison's view of justice subordinates a concern for the effect of various ways of life on the faculties of men to a respect for men's faculty of free choice. Given this emphasis, justice does not depend on a "plan of legislation" imposing conditions favorable to men's faculties. While just legislators might quietly consider the merits of the life of manufacturing and the life of farming, their principal problem would be to regulate those interests in a way which respects the free choice of those men engaging in each.

As noted above, Madison refers in this example to the likely disregard for justice and also for "the public good." It is possible that justice permits a broad range of regulations and forbids only such extreme policies as might impoverish or destroy one of the competing interests; the public good would then be a more precise guide to policy. Thus whichever just regulations would most add to the permanent and aggregate prosperity should be adopted.

Madison's insistence on a regard for both justice and the public good raises the question of whether those ends are ever in conflict. Madison gives no explicit examples of such conflict but finds it worthy of note when the ends coincide. Thus protection for copyrights and patents both serves "the public good" and respects "the claims of individuals" (43, p. 272); paper-money schemes offend "justice" and injure the "public prosperity" (44, p. 281).[78] But there could be cases where the community's aggregate interests are in conflict with the rights of individuals.[79] Considerations such as the nation's need to develop domestic industry in order to build a navy for defense, or the need to placate powerful nations who wish to export a particular product, might favor a policy which would "[bear] hard on"[80] the landed or manufacturing men's right to exercise their faculties. The more indirect and subtle policies by which government protects men's faculties may also be in tension with the public good. A wish to discourage degrading occupations may oppose the aggregate interests which rely on them. The fact that sailors were worst-off in health, intelligence, and virtue led Madison to the following reflection:

> How unfortunate, that in the intercourse, by which nations are enlightened and refined, and their means of safety extended, the

immediate agents should be distinguished by the hardest condition of humanity.[81]

Government may face a similar difficulty when it attempts to preserve an open field for men's acquisitive faculties. Madison advocated policies

> withholding *unnecessary* opportunities from a few, to increase the inequality of property, by an immoderate, and especially unmerited, accumulation of riches.[82]

"Unmerited" accumulations would be those which are not the product of one's own faculties, but draw too heavily on the exertions of others. A concern for justice would "especially" try to prevent this. "Immoderate" accumulation could deprive others of opportunities to exert themselves; this would be a second concern of justice. But Madison says only that "*unnecessary* opportunities" should be withheld, implying there will be some necessary opportunities for immoderate, and even for unmerited, accumulation. They might be necessary because they cannot be withheld without too much intrusion on men's free choice; because they cannot be successfully withheld at all; or because they cannot be withheld without injury to the aggregate prosperity of society. The public good may require policies which permit some men to be undeservedly rich, or encourage some men to live the life of sailors.

In Madison's previous versions of the argument of *Federalist* 10, his subject was the danger posed by majorities to the rights of others, i.e., to justice. In *Federalist* 10 itself the public good is introduced as another endangered object; but as the three examples suggest, justice is given most emphasis. In the first and third examples Madison does not mention the public good but he does mention the majority. The majority may tend to identify its own interest as the public good—a mistake not discouraged by the fact that the public good is an "aggregate." *Federalist* 10 appeals to justice against the overbearing majority; the majority has no right to sacrifice other men's rights to its own interests. But Madison does not quite say that men's rights may never be sacrificed to anything. The protection of each man's faculties is the first object of government because the right to exercise their faculties is what men seek when they create "civil society" in the first place.[83] But precisely because men can protect their faculties only by instituting a civil society ("community," "public"), the permanent and aggregate interests of that community cannot be ignored. While one might think that only the community's safety, rather than its broader "permanent and aggregate interests," is the necessary condition for "private rights," this narrower view is undermined by the dependence of safety on revenue and the dependence of revenue on economic prosperity (see p. 41 above). Men who wish their individual faculties protected should not deny the claims of the public good even if they rightfully deny the claims of the majority's good.

The legislators who should be judging are in fact "advocates and parties"; this may be simply because they are themselves men with interests of their own, or because they speak for interested constituents. The analysis would apply even to nonpopular legislative bodies; the "predominant party" will still have the "opportunity and temptation" to be unjust. Madison considers a possible objection to his unhappy conclusion, but dismisses it:

> It is in vain to say that enlightened statesmen will be able to adjust these clashing interests and render them all subservient to the public good.

This suggestion, although "in vain," is not as optimistic as might be expected. Despite the fact that Madison's examples emphasized the problem of a disregard for *justice,* the suggestion is only that enlightened statesmen could serve the "public good." We recall from *Federalist* 10's first paragraph that, although injustice was a subject of widespread alarm, only an elite of the "most considerate and virtuous citizens" were concerned with the public good as well as with justice. "Enlightened statesmen" are apparently included in the elite who concern themselves with the public good; in *Federalist* 12 Hamilton says the "political cares" of "enlightened statesmen" center on "national wealth" (p. 91). If statesmen adjust interests to serve the public good, do they pay less attention to justice? Do they resolve the possible conflicts with private rights in favor of the public? While that might seem consonant with an enlarged statesmanship which must consider the whole nation and be unsentimental about whatever partial sacrifices that requires, Madison deflects that suggestion in his explanation of why "it is in vain" to rely on enlightened statesmen to adjust interests for the public good.

> [1] Enlightened statesmen will not always be at the helm. [2] Nor, in many cases, can such an adjustment be made at all without taking into view indirect and remote considerations, which will rarely prevail over the immediate interest which one party may find in disregarding the rights of another or the good of the whole.

By mentioning "rights" which a party might disregard, Madison implies that the adjustment which would serve the public good would have to show a regard for the rights of all parties as well as for the good of the whole. Although I have just suggested that the public good is a necessary condition for private rights, private rights appear here as a necessary means to the public good—a relation which will become clearer below.

The reasons Madison gives for thinking it in vain to rely on enlightened statesmen do not altogether rule out the suggestion, since enlightened statesmen may *sometimes* be at the helm, a more direct adjustment might in some cases be possible, and distant considerations can prevail, although "rarely." Since there will, according to the second reason, be interested parties in a position of authority even when an enlightened statesman is at the helm, I infer that the helm is some position of leadership in the legislature or the executive; that is, the man at the helm cannot simply impose an enlightened adjustment. His difficulty is that the authority remains with the partisans whom he must persuade. But respect for the rights of others is an "indirect" consideration, since it relies on a reciprocal respect which the stronger party may never need and might not receive anyway; and regard to the "good of the whole" is "remote" because the whole may be expected to persist for a while even if partisans damage it. Thus the partisans, although shortsighted, are not simply mistaken. There is not a solution which will satisfy the impulses of both sides; in practice, an "adjustment" will thwart one or both. The meaning of "enlightened statesmen" shares the ambiguity found earlier concerning the influence of opinion on passion. Enlightened statesmen might be men whose reason sees that the community's permanent, aggregate interests are a greater good than their own interest; or they might simply understand the "indirect and remote" effects which their policies will have—on their own good. In the latter case, they may see that a prosperous state would give future glory to an enlightened statesman—an incentive probably not as available to the other men, not at the "helm," who control the legislature.

Controlling the Effects of Faction

Madison then makes a fresh start in accordance with the outline he has given. Since faction's *"causes"* cannot be removed, "relief is only to be sought in the means of controlling its *effects*." One might think that in the two paragraphs preceding he had been discussing faction's effects—i.e., its involvement in the legislature and the improbability of enlightened statesmen curbing its tendencies. But Madison instead considers the political opportunities for factions to be part of their cause. If there were no legislature regulating interests, there would be no temptation for men to unite to serve their own interest at some other interest's expense. Indeed in a situation without a legislature, men might be most tempted to turn against those whose interests most resembled their own.

If a cloth manufacturer cannot join with other cloth manufacturers to legislatively "[bear] hard on" merchants who import cloth, his selfish impulses might incline him to individual violent attacks on competing clothmakers. What Madison calls faction's "effects"—and what the rest of the essay discusses—is the *success* which faction attains in its political endeavors.

The effects of faction depend decisively on whether it is a majority or a minority. The "republican principle" of majority rule serves to "defeat" a minority's "sinister views," but enables a majority "to sacrifice to its ruling passion or interest both the public good and the rights of other citizens." A solution to the problem of majority faction—the "great object to which our inquiries are directed"—"is the great desideratum by which alone this form of government [popular government] can be rescued from the opprobrium under which it has so long labored and be recommended to the esteem and adoption of mankind." Majority faction is a special case of the problem of faction Madison has been discussing, but it is the important case for popular governments. The word "form" or "forms" occurs four times in this paragraph, drawing attention to the fact that popular government is one among several possible forms, and it is not one with a very good reputation. This form needs to be vindicated by an assurance that its substantive results will be justice and the general good, rather than their opposites. Thus the popular form is apparently not a sufficient end in itself. In addition, the fact that majority faction relies on the form of popular government for its success should be sobering to those who believe that rule by the greater number is simply inevitable. A nasty majority is not an unstoppable force but rather depends for success on a form whose existence cannot be taken for granted.[84] Madison also suggests that formal injustice is worse than informal injustice. Minority faction can "clog the administration" and "convulse the society," but not "execute and mask its violence under the forms of the Constitution." As is admitted in the next paragraph, individuals too commit acts of injustice and violence. Formal government imperfectly controls a sometimes unruly human material, but for the form to be the instrument of injustice removes the last refuge for justice.

Thus "controlling the effects" of faction means keeping a faction from being a majority. In discussing faction's causes Madison had shown that the "impulse" and "opportunity" were inherent in human nature[85] and in political life; now he will try to show how the impulse and opportunity for *majority* faction may be avoidable:

> Either [referring to the impulse] the existence of the same passion or interest in a majority at the same time must be prevented,

or [referring to the opportunity] the majority, having such coexistent passion or interest, must be rendered, by their number and local situation, unable to concert and carry into effect schemes of oppression.

Madison rules out another possible suggestion:

If the impulse and the opportunity be suffered to coincide, we well know that neither moral nor religious motives can be relied on as an adequate control. They are not found to be such on the injustice and violence of individuals, and lose their efficacy in proportion to the number combined together, that is, in proportion as their efficacy becomes needful.

An "adequate control" on a larger number is more needful because individuals can be punished and minorities outvoted, while majorities in popular governments have apparent impunity. Madison does not completely rule out the suggestion of moral and religious motives but says that they cannot be "relied on"—just as Hobbes dismissed motives for promise-keeping other than fear as not to be "presumed on" or "reckoned upon."[86] A form of government which men can esteem and adopt must be reliable. What Madison here calls "moral . . . motives" appears to be or at least include the concern for "character" or reputation to which he referred in earlier versions of his argument. A well-known passage in Hume's *Essays* argued that men in groups are less moved by such concern than they are individually.[87] Regarding "religious motives," Madison is understandably more reticent than at the Constitutional Convention where he said that "Religion itself may become a motive to persecution & oppression," and considerably more reticent than in his letter to Jefferson in which he said that religion "has been much oftener a motive to oppression than a restraint from it."[88] Some trace of this view is visible in *Federalist* 10's discussion of religious opinions as a source of faction.

Moral and religious motives appear here as a possible but insufficient control on *action* once the impulse and opportunity for faction have coincided. Apparently these motives would not change the impulse which they oppose; they would merely keep it from succeeding. They could be considered a separate impulse. This may explain Madison's rather rapid deduction from the existence of different interests to the existence of opposed factions. An interest group's impulse adverse to others' rights or to the common good could sometimes be overshadowed by other impulses (or be thwarted by external restraints), but it would not cease to exist.

A "pure democracy," where the people assemble and rule in person, cannot prevent the impulse or the opportunity for majority faction. "A common passion or interest [i.e., impulse] will, in almost every case, be felt by a majority of the whole"—presumably because of the small number of citizens. There is always an opportunity for "communication and concert" because of the "form of government itself"; the people assembled in person can easily concert. Thus "there is nothing to check the inducements to sacrifice the weaker party or an obnoxious individual." Madison makes a slight change from the preceding paragraph where he had said majority factions "must be rendered . . . unable to concert and carry into effect schemes of oppression." In a democracy, majority factions find "communication and concert" automatic; but Madison does not say that they are easily able to "carry into effect" their schemes. This omission is consistent with Montesquieu's judgment that democracies are relatively incompetent in executing their plans:

> the people . . . is not fitted to administer by itself. . . . [T]he people always acts too much or too little. Sometimes with a hundred thousand arms it overturns everything; sometimes with a hundred thousand feet it moves only like insects.[89]

> Monarchical government has a great advantage over republican: affairs being conducted by one alone, there is more promptness in execution.[90]

Thus while nothing checks "the inducements to sacrifice" a minority or individual, sinister plans may not always be fully successful.

> Hence it is that such democracies have ever been spectacles of turbulence and contention; have ever been found incompatible with personal security or the rights of property; and have in general been as short in their lives as they have been violent in their deaths.

Democracies' turbulence and mortality can be attributed to the combination of majority faction and the deficient execution which prevents the majority from being simply and successfully despotic. The predominant party encounters resistance and the result is contention and violence rather than a majority which rules the minority with the iron hand which it would need to match its oppressive intentions.

While Madison had defined faction as "adverse to the rights of other citizens, or to the permanent and aggregate interests of the community," the majority faction in a pure democracy is described only as adverse to men's "rights." It wishes to "sacrifice the weaker party or an obnoxious

individual"; it threatens "personal security" and the "rights of property."
Madison does not say that these factions oppose the public good. Injustice
may have the indirect result of harming the public good, as in this
example it does by leading to turbulence and the violent death of the
regime. But Madison consistently distinguishes justice from the public
good, and here he speaks only of justice. Although Madison is often said
to have overturned the "small republic" theory of Montesquieu, he does
not deny Montesquieu's argument that

> In a great republic, the common good is sacrificed to a thousand
> considerations; it is subordinated to exceptions; it depends on ac-
> cidents. In a small [republic], the public good is better sensed,
> better known, closer to each citizen; abuses there are less ex-
> tended, and consequently less protected.[91]

A direct democracy may well have merit in its attention to the good of
the community as a whole. But this will not satisfy the individuals or
minorities being sacrificed. Direct democracy does not provide a sufficient guarantee of justice for its individual citizens. This defect may be
related to, although it is clearly more extreme than, the "principle" of
"virtue" which Montesquieu ascribes to democracy.[92] Since democracy
requires citizens to repress their private desires and even sacrifice themselves out of love of country, individuals cannot really insist on "private
rights." Partisan repression is certainly a perversion of the impartial
repression which democracy imposes, but according to Madison the demands of the whole may in practice be the demands of the majority.
However, injustice carries its own punishment. The oppressed fight back
and the oppressors lose the security they seek from civil society (see 51,
pp. 324–25). Direct democracies overlook the extent to which justice is
ultimately necessary to the public good even as they do not overlook the
importance of the public good.

Unnamed "theoretic politicians"[93] have "erroneously supposed"

> that by reducing mankind to a perfect equality in their political
> rights, they would at the same time be perfectly equalized and as-
> similated in their possessions, their opinions, and their passions.

That this is an error has been established by Madison in his explanation
of faction's "latent causes." Possessions which are "equalized and assimilated" would be not only equal in amount but the same in kind, so that
men with different kinds of property could not find legislative methods
of favoring their kind. For passions to be assimilated would require each
man's passions not to conflict with other men's passions; thus for men
to have equal amounts of assertive self-love would not solve the problem.

In the letter to Jefferson containing *Federalist* 10's argument, Madison developed his account of this "theoretic" democracy. If all men did have "precisely the same interests, and the same feelings in every respect,"

> The interest of the majority would be that of the minority also;
> the decision could only turn on mere opinion concerning the
> good of the whole, of which the major voice would be the safest
> criterion; and within a small sphere, this voice could be most eas-
> ily collected, and the public affairs most accurately managed.[94]

By "mere opinion" Madison seems to suggest that there would not be passionate opinion. If there is no diversity among men, the only political question is the "good of the whole." Diversity raises the question of the good of each part, i.e., the question of justice. Madison here even endorses a Montesquieuan "small sphere" for easy and accurate management of the public good. But "civilized Societies" cannot avoid diversity and therefore must consider arrangements which will also serve justice.

"A republic," meaning a government with "the scheme of representation," "promises the cure for which we are seeking." Madison acknowledges that his usage of the words "republic" and "democracy" is not well established,[95] by saying "I mean" when he defines each of them; he had said "I understand" when he gave his definition of faction. Madison outlines the rest of the argument: "Let us examine [1] the points in which [a republic] varies from pure democracy, and we shall comprehend both [2] the nature of the cure and [3] the efficacy which it must derive from the Union."

Representation

A republic differs from a pure democracy both in delegating "the government . . . to a small number of citizens elected by the rest," and in the "greater sphere of country" a republic can embrace. Madison considers the effect of each of these differences. Delegating representatives to govern can apparently be either better or worse than direct democracy. "[O]n the one hand," the "public views," meaning the prevailing or majority views, can be refined and enlarged by

> a chosen body of citizens, whose wisdom may best discern the
> true interest of their country and whose patriotism and love of
> justice will be least likely to sacrifice it to temporary or partial
> considerations. Under such a regulation it may well happen that
> the public voice, pronounced by the representatives of the people,
> will be more consonant to the public good than if pronounced by
> the people themselves, convened for the purpose.

While Madison's criticism of democracies was for their oppression of private rights, his praise of representation centers on the public good. A chosen body of citizens can discern and pursue "the *true interest of their country*," and act for "the *public good*," as "proper guardians of the *public weal*" (emphasis added). These representatives may remind us of the suggested solution of "enlightened statesmen" which Madison had dismissed. The difference is that while enlightened statesmen were expected to adjust the clashes of the partisans in the legislature, it is now suggested that the legislative body's entire membership can be improved, replacing partisans with men of patriotism and wisdom. But Madison again suggests that the public good is the concern of a kind of elite: wise representatives share this concern with enlightened statesmen and with the most considerate and virtuous citizens. Private rights, by contrast, appear to be a subject of wider interest, because they concern both just men who care about the rights of others,[96] and other men who care about their *own* rights. Although one might think that everyone should be concerned with the public interest insofar as they are part of the public and will be affected by what affects the public, this is too "remote" a consideration, as Madison says. And this may well be due to the fact that American republics are not the small cities in which Montesquieu had said the public good was "closer" and "better known." The considerate and virtuous notice how in America the public good is disregarded, apparently by those less considerate and virtuous. The American republic needs a substitute for the direct concern with the public good which Montesquieu claimed for small republics. Madison finds this substitute in the possibility of selected men being wise enough to see what is necessarily remote in a large republic.

These fit characters are characterized not only by wisdom and patriotism but also by "love of justice." Madison's reference to the love of justice in this passage on the public good is surprising but revealing. In the discussion of enlightened statesmen and in the discussion of pure democracies, justice appeared as a necessary means to the public good. In this passage, justice appears as a means in Madison's analysis, but as an end in itself to the chosen citizens who "love" it. Perhaps a statesman who considered justice only as a necessary means to the public good would be too easily tempted to cut corners and inadvertently injure the public good. Madison says these representatives will discern the public good by their wisdom, and be unlikely to "sacrifice it to temporary or partial considerations" because of their patriotism and love of justice. Patriotism, i.e., love of country or, we might say, love of the public good, is by itself insufficient to serve the public good; patriotism might be "partial" and interpret the public good as being especially the good of the majority, with the bad effects on the public good observed in pure democracies. The "love of justice" prevents "partial considerations." At the same time, the love of justice is insufficient; it is perhaps a "temporary" consideration in its wish to respect each mortal man's rights in each transitory controversy. A patriotic statesman would not wish the country to lose a war justly, or to sacrifice its strength to an attempt to be strictly impartial at home—as in the example of tariff policy mentioned above. "Patriotism" prevents temporary considerations by its love of a country intended to be permanent.

Madison quickly throws cold water on this elevating prospect of "fit characters" being elected:

> On the other hand, the effect may be inverted. Men of factious tempers, of local prejudices, or of sinister designs, may, by intrigue, by corruption, or by other means, first obtain the suffrages, and then betray the interests of the people.

The "interests of the people" indicates Madison's theme here is still the public good rather than the rights of any part of the public. The people is considered as a whole and is vulnerable to bad men. A "chosen body" is no guarantee of a good choice; the "other means" besides intrigue and corruption presumably include relying on the gullibility of a people already admitted to have a defective understanding of the public good. Madison's description of the bad men preserves his triad of passion, opinion, and interest, but makes passionate faction a matter of men's "tempers" rather than making passion the uniting principle of the faction. Thus he reiterates his description of men's "unfriendly passions" which are looking for an issue to fight about (see p. 77 above).

The fact that representation can either improve or worsen government's service of the public good means that the advantage of a republic over a democracy in this respect has not been established. Except for the violence and political mortality which result from injustice (not a minor exception), pure democracies may be successful in keeping men's attention on a "closer" public good. Dropping the comparison between democracies and republics, Madison instead compares small republics with large republics and finds two "obvious considerations" showing that the latter are more "favorable to the election of proper guardians of the public weal." This procedure is justified by the fact that "pure democracy" is not an available choice in the debate of 1787.

Both obvious considerations are elegantly mathematical and rest on the fact that in a large republic each representative will necessarily represent a larger number of people, since the number of representatives cannot be expanded or contracted in full proportion to the size of the population without danger of confusion or cabal. As a result, each representative is (1) chosen *from* a greater number, and (2) chosen *by* a greater number. Regarding the first,

> it follows that if the proportion of fit characters be not less in the large than in the small republic, the former will present a greater option, and consequently a greater probability of a fit choice.

One might object to this that the proportion of "fit characters" (men of wisdom, patriotism, and love of justice) would differ according to size, insofar as a small republic more closely approximates a pure democracy's patriotism and insofar as less wisdom would be sufficient to understand its less complex public good, even if love of justice might not increase in a smaller sphere. In any case, why should "a greater *probability* of a fit choice" result from a "greater option"? Would not the existence of a single fit character be sufficient to allow the voters to choose him? Unless Madison implies that the number of fit characters is so small that a small district might have *none,* he implies an element of randomness in the voters' selections; the goodness of the draw depends on the goodness of the field. Perhaps it seems to men more like a "choice" when they have more options; if there were, say, only one plausible candidate, to choose him would be more like acceptance or deference than choice. The importance of options may be related to Madison's remarks about men's eagerness to divide themselves up even without a reason. If men insist on disagreeing, it is useful if they have several "fit" options to divide themselves around rather than one best candidate against unfit others to whom divisive men might stubbornly give their vote. Men's wish to be choosey is not sufficiently respected in a small district where one man seems to be, so to speak, the natural choice.

The fact that in a large republic representatives are chosen by a greater number means that

> it will be more difficult for unworthy candidates to practise with success the vicious arts by which elections are too often carried; and the suffrages of the people being more free, will be more likely to center on men who possess the most attractive merit and the most diffusive and established characters.

"Vicious arts" seems to refer primarily to bribery, which is presumably more expensive and less easily concealed in a large district. It is an art because it relies on certain predictable qualities in the material it uses, i.e., human beings. Without this art, the people's suffrages are "more free." But the suffrages are at once more free and more likely to be exercised in a certain way. Even relatively free men are somewhat predictable insofar as they will choose intelligently—although this must be qualified by the suggestion above that men are somewhat stubborn in their choosing and unwilling simply to accept the one best. Choosing is both irrational, in insisting on options, and rational, in choosing the meritorious. However, even the rational element is imperfectly rational; men will vote not for the wise, patriotic, and justice-loving, but for those with "the most attractive merit and the most diffusive and established characters." The most attractive merit is not the most merit.

Both paragraphs on elections raise the following problem: If the political liberty men have in popular government is important to them for its own sake, i.e., apart from the protections it may or may not afford to private rights, then there must be something about the exercise of political authority which men find satisfying. Yet the type of popular government recommended by *The Federalist* is one in which the people do not themselves exercise political authority but merely elect particular men to exercise authority (see 63, p. 387). How, then, can men express their freedom merely in electing others? If men wish to live a "political life," can they be satisfied with a "scheme of representation" rather than participation in a "pure democracy"?

A partial answer is available in *Federalist* 10's suggestions about the nature of elections. For one thing, candidates must be men who have made their merits attractive to the people, men who have established and diffused their reputations among the people. This reflects the people's wish to assert *themselves* in voting rather than merely accepting those most intrinsically fit. But if candidates can master the art of making themselves attractive to a populace whose likely feelings of attraction are predictable, the people's free choice seems compromised.[97] Still, men's divisive insistence on options may prevent their freedom from being fully submerged by artful candidates. Men may be attracted, but they stubbornly divide among attractive options rather than agreeing on the most attractive. Elections are therefore not usually unanimous or nearly unanimous, a result which reminds candidates and voters alike of the voters' free choice.

Madison qualifies his assertion of the superiority of large districts by "confess[ing]" that, as in "most other cases," the best solution is "a mean." He had just illustrated this principle in his argument that the size of a legislative body should avoid smallness ("cabals of a few") and largeness ("confusion of a multitude"). In the present case,

> By enlarging too much the number of electors, you render the representative too little acquainted with all their local circumstances and lesser interests; as by reducing it too much, you ren-

der him unduly attached to these, and too little fit to comprehend and pursue great and national objects.

Madison's diction distinguishes local from national in a manner consistent with Montesquieu's defense of small republics. Men must be "acquainted" with the local good, but must "comprehend" the national; they can be "attached to" the local, but "pursue" the national. A smaller sphere yields a more simple, accessible, immediate public good.

Madison had judged large districts more likely to select men who have "fit" qualities in general: wisdom, patriotism, and love of justice. Now it appears that the subjects of the representative's knowledge and the object of his patriotism will be more local or more national depending on the size of the district. But while "too much" local attachment is called an inconvenience, too little local attachment is not. The sole drawback of very large districts is too little local *acquaintance;* and the force of that objection becomes less clear when Madison explains that

> The federal Constitution forms a happy combination in this respect; the great and aggregate interests being referred to the national, the local and particular to the State legislatures.

The existence of state governments may make less local acquaintance necessary to a Congressman, and thus make larger districts possible (see 56, p. 346). This "happy combination" of nation and states does not observe "a mean"; it combines relative extremes. Local governments[98] remove an "inconvenienc[e]" from Madison's proposal; but Madison's obvious considerations in support of large districts suggest that those local governments will be manned by less fit characters.

Here, as throughout the section on representation, Madison is speaking of the public good (compare "the great and aggregate interests" with "the permanent and aggregate interests of the community") rather than of the private rights which are the subject of the preceding section (critical of "pure democracy") and the succeeding section (on the extended sphere). Even though justice, i.e., a respect for private rights, appears to be a necessary means to the public good, and even though fit representatives have a "love of justice" and are (we learn later) "superior to . . . schemes of injustice," Madison insists on their utility to the public good, rather than to private rights. Two explanations for this seem plausible.

First, Madison may mean to emphasize that the proper practical task of the legislature is to promote the good of the public as a whole. Justice requires that men's rights be respected, but when the legislature taxes and regulates, it shows only what Hamilton later calls a "negative merit of doing no harm" by refraining from engaging in "schemes of injustice." Justice, as Madison understands it, does not generally require an overt legislative "plan," although it can be "fostered" by certain quiet policies.[99]

Second, Madison may simply think that even excellent representatives will find it more feasible to "refine and enlarge the public views" in pursuit of the public good than in the service of private rights. A faction in the electorate which carelessly disregards the public good in pursuit of its own aims might be convinced by its attractively meritorious representatives that its own good ultimately depends on the prosperity of the community as a whole. But an "overbearing" faction which sets out to profit or bully at the expense of a minority's rights may be less persuaded by a justice-loving representative's appeal to justice, or even by his very "indirect" argument that justice is necessary to the public good, which is in turn necessary to the faction's good. A majority's disdain for the rights of others may be harder to refine and enlarge (by moral or prudential arguments) than is a majority's shortsighted disregard for its own dependence on the permanent and aggregate interests of the community. The better remedy in the former case is therefore to prevent such factions from becoming a majority in the first place—by extending the sphere.

The Extended Sphere

Besides representation, the other difference between republican and democratic government is size, i.e., "number of citizens" and "extent of territory." Madison makes clear that this—rather than representation— is the "circumstance principally which renders factious combinations less to be dreaded in the former than in the latter." Representation in itself is not as important because its effects may be good or be "inverted." Madison's explanation of the crucial "circumstance" has become famous:

> The smaller the society, the fewer probably will be the distinct parties and interests composing it; the fewer the distinct parties and interests, the more frequently will a majority be found of the same party; and the smaller the number of individuals composing a majority, and the smaller the compass within which they are placed, the more easily will they concert and execute their plans of oppression. Extend the sphere and you take in a greater variety of parties and interests; you make it less probable that a majority of the whole will have a common motive to invade the rights of other citizens; or if such a common motive exists, it will be more difficult for all who feel it to discover their own strength and to act in unison with each other. Besides other impediments,

it may be remarked that, where there is a consciousness of unjust or dishonorable purposes, communication is always checked by distrust in proportion to the number whose concurrence is necessary.

This argument is structured by Madison's earlier distinction between the impulse and the opportunity for majority faction. In an extended sphere there will be more different impulses at work, and each will "probabl[y]" be felt by less than a majority. This depends on the "variety" of a large country, since groups in different localities with the same impulse would feel an impulse to merge. The large nation's economic diversity leads to a wide variety of interests.[100] The fact that Madison speaks here of the variety of "parties and interests" indicates that a diversity of passionately opinionated groups (as well as interest groups) is expected in the extended sphere. This may be due to the diversity (noted by Hamilton) in "genius, manners, and habits" or "temper and sentiments" of men in different parts of the Union which is "nourish[ed]" by "causes, as well physical as moral" (60, pp. 367–68).[101] The men and opinions which arouse people's passions may differ from place to place. As to a majority faction's "opportunity" to carry out its plans, Madison suggests there will be various "impediments" imposed by the large sphere, but explains only one of them. Men will be more reluctant to communicate their unjust or dishonorable purposes to the larger number of people necessary for a majority in a large country. A conspiracy of very many men is inhibited by "distrust."[102] But this principle would seem to apply only where there is "consciousness" of bad motives, and not to cases where men's judgment is merely biased by interest. Other "impediments" would be the physical obstacles to any long-distance communication and the difficulty in knowing whether and how many men far away are really allies.

In presenting this "principa[l]" solution to the problem of majority faction, Madison refers to the problem in terms of justice ("plans of oppression," "invade the rights of other citizens"), rather than in terms of the public good, which was prominent throughout the discussion of representation. The public good is not guaranteed by an extended sphere, but rather requires the active attention of fit rulers. While the public good is endangered by a factious majority, the impotence of or bargaining between fragmented minority factions would not suffice to serve the public good either. The public good all along appeared as the concern of a sort of elite: the "most considerate and virtuous citizens"; the unavailable or inefficacious "enlightened statesmen"; and finally the "fit characters" who might become representatives. An enlightenment beyond that of most men is needed to understand the permanent, aggregate interests of society, especially when that interest has been complicated by society's being large. But an enlightened elite is not suggested as the essential solution to the problem of justice. Madison calls the extended sphere the principal solution to the dangers of faction partly because it is the solution to the principal danger of faction, injustice. The relative impotence of oppressive partisans, rather than the refinement of their views by a "chosen" elite, is the best available cure for oppressive partisanship. While the public good depends on the existence and election of proper guardians of the public weal, men's rights gain security from the extended sphere even if those proper guardians are unavailable.

Scholars looking for the source of Madison's argument for an extended sphere have found its "embryonic form" in David Hume's essay "Idea of a Perfect Commonwealth."[103] Hume insisted that the "common opinion" that a large country could not be a republic ("commonwealth") was a "falsehood."[104] In summary,

> In a large government, which is modelled with masterly skill, there is compass and room enough to refine the democracy, from the lower people who may be admitted into the first elections, or first concoction of the commonwealth, to the higher magistrates who direct all the movements. At the same time, the parts are so distant and remote, that it is very difficult, either by intrigue, prejudice, or passion, to hurry them into any measures against the public interest.[105]

Verbal similarities, as well as the basic point (defending a large republic), indicate Madison's debt. But there are some important differences between Madison and Hume. Hume's "Idea" proposes a division of a nation into 10,000 parishes, and a system of indirect elections. The people in each of the 10,000 parishes elect one representative for their parish; the 100 such representatives in each county in turn elect a "senator" and ten "county magistrates." In contrast: (1) Madison does not recommend in *Federalist* 10, and he opposed at the Constitutional Convention, a system of indirect elections. The people's views are to be "refined" by representatives they elect directly. (2) Madison's defense of large election districts is clearly at odds with Hume. Hume confines the people to local elections because they

> in their parochial meetings, will probably choose the best, or nearly the best representative: but they are wholly unfit for country meetings, and for electing into the higher offices of the republic. Their ignorance gives the grandees an opportunity of deceiving them.[106]

(3) Hume's plan recommends a kind of federalism, with local matters handled locally and each level of government electing the next. The apparent similarity between this system and the American one led Douglass Adair, in an excellent article on Madison and Hume, to characterize "Madison's analysis" as follows:

> Compound various economic interests of a large territory with a federal system of thirteen semisovereign political units, establish a scheme of indirect elections which will functionally bind the extensive area into a unit while "refining" the voice of the people, and you will have a stable republican state.[107]

But *Federalist* 10 not only does not suggest indirect elections, it does not exactly recommend a "federal system."[108] Neither the multiplicity of parties in an extended sphere nor the election of representatives from large districts depends fundamentally on the division of America into states (although the existence of state governments to handle "local" affairs makes very large districts less inconvenient).[109] Indeed *Federalist* 10 is an implicit indictment of the states. It begins by citing complaints against "our governments"—at least primarily our state governments—and concludes by showing the superiority of the "large . . . republic" constituted by a new government for the Union. Except insofar as the states will be controlled or replaced by the central government, they will remain defective, small republics. That is why Madison proposed to the Constitutional Convention that the national legislature be given a veto over state acts; and it was in support of that proposal that Madison presented the arguments of *Federalist* 10. While Madison feared that the constitutional prohibitions on states (e.g., regarding *ex post facto* laws, and paper money) and federal judicial review of state acts would be inadequate substitutes for his proposal, the case *Federalist* 10 makes for an extended republic applies to America only if the central government becomes the essential political arena—or if (as *Federalist* 56 suggests) future developments diversify the states themselves, making them more like large republics.[110]

(4) While Hume suggests that his plan will reduce the opportunity for the success of malign proposals, he does not argue as Madison does that national diversity will make a similar impulse less likely in the majority. This principle could have been suggested to Madison by various political experiences. In *Federalist* 51's recapitulation of *Federalist* 10's argument, Madison notes that a "multiplicity of sects" is a security for "religious rights" (51, p. 324). In his earlier career, Madison was a leader in a fight in Virginia against state-established religion; and he noted in a letter to Jefferson that the hatred between Presbyterians and Episcopalians had

prevented their acting as a coalition against religious liberty.[111] Madison also saw the effects of diversity in the American confederacy of the 1780s, which was often unable to agree. The seeds of the extended-sphere argument are visible in a letter Madison wrote to Lafayette in 1785. There he argued that it was in Spain's interest to encourage American expansion to the Mississippi, because this would further diversify American interests and make Spain safe.

> Her *permanent* security . . . lies in the Complexity of our foederal Govt. and the diversity of interests among the members of it which render offensive measures, improbable in Council, and difficult in execution.[112]

Here "offensive measures" are against foreign rivals rather than domestic minorities. Although the Constitution of 1787 would enable the Union to act more easily, "diversity of interests" would still be an impediment. But Madison denied even in 1785 that diversity would prevent all action and lead to stalemate or weakness. If Spain counted on "the pacific temper of republics, unjust irritations on her part will soon teach her that Republics have like passions with other Governts."[113] The "passions" which resent injustice and lead to self-defense are the ones which Madison assumes or hopes can overcome the obstacles posed by the extended sphere. In the 1787 letter to Jefferson expounding *Federalist* 10's argument, Madison admitted that while an extensive sphere would be helpful, "too extensive" a sphere would make a "defensive concert" "too difficult against the oppression of those entrusted with the administration."[114] Madison's concern parallels but is more limited than that of modern scholars who infer a difficulty of mobilizing any kind of majority in a large, diverse nation. The only necessary mobilization suggested is a "defensive" one, and Madison implies that men's defensive impulses are stronger than their offensive ones.

Students of American politics since Madison have been impressed by his analysis of the variety of interests found in the extended sphere. But that analysis seems vulnerable in an important practical respect. The diversity of interests which one might find in a united America was overshadowed, according to Madison's own view, by one primary division: the difference of states "having or not having slaves."[115] In this case the extended sphere created not a multiplicity of interests but a division into two. The South later argued that the nonslave majority made its own rights unsafe. How can the principles of *Federalist* 10 apply to this fundamental distinction between slave states and nonslave states?[116]

While *Federalist* 10 does not explicitly discuss slavery,[117] Madison's convention speech setting forth the principle of the extended sphere discusses it very prominently. Madison there gives seven examples of oppression resulting from conflicts of interests, "real or supposed"; the first two are from antiquity, the third is from America's colonial period; and the fourth is:

> We have seen the mere distinction of colour made in the most enlightened period of time, a ground of the most oppressive dominion ever exercised by man over man.[118]

Then Madison proceeds to consider "What has been the source of those unjust laws complained of among ourselves?" and gives three contemporary examples. Slavery may be an injustice "among ourselves" which is less "complained of," but it is the "most oppressive dominion ever exercised by man over man." It is the most extreme example of tyranny by the majority. While Madison served in the Virginia legislature he saw antislavery bills almost "throw[n] . . . under the table."[119] Perhaps, then, in the extended sphere, the slaveholders' factious rule would be broken by the introduction of diverse interests, i.e., nonslaveholders. But this cannot be quite what Madison had in mind, if only because he insisted that the federal government would have no right to abolish slavery.[120] He even explained how the federal government could protect the slaveholders. One of the "vices" of the Confederation was its failure to secure states against internal violence:

> According to Republican Theory, Right and power being both vested in the majority, are held to be synonymous. According to fact and experience a minority may in an appeal to force, be an overmatch for the majority.[121]

Madison gives two examples of the minority's strength in appealing to force, and then adds:

> 3. Where slavery exists the republican Theory becomes still more fallacious.[122]

"Still more fallacious" because in this case the official majority has neither power in an appeal to force nor "Right." But Madison explains that the federal government may intercede nonetheless to protect states against such insurrections (43, p. 277).

Later in his life, Madison insisted that a plan of emancipation must do justice both to the slaves and to the slaveholders; he proposed freeing the slaves and compensating the owners with money from sale of the western lands. The money would also finance a plan of colonization, which was necessary because prejudice against blacks was based on a physical distinction, and was "not likely soon if ever to be eradicated."[123]

The plan would require a constitutional amendment to implement. The North would not object to spending money from western lands to compensate slaveholders because Northerners understood slavery was a national problem; and they had shown a "meritorious alacrity" in promoting colonization.[124]

Extension of the sphere weakens both the political power of the slaveholders and the physical power of the slaves. Madison wanted the slaveholders to retain enough political power to be able to insist on compensation; for this reason he proposed both in the Federal Convention and in a Virginia constitutional convention giving slaveholders additional weight in the senate by counting slaves in the apportionment of that branch. Apparently Madison thought either a slave rebellion or an uncompensated emancipation imposed by a nonslaveholder majority would be inconsistent with the permanent and aggregate interests of the community. But a continuing exercise of the "most oppressive dominion ever exercised by man over man" would be unjust, and perhaps also opposed to the public good.[125] An extended sphere could take in interests not dependent on slavery which might show a "meritorious alacrity" in advocating emancipation. If the sides were balanced, as Madison wished, a settlement which did justice to both might be adopted. As it turned out, the issue was settled by force. While this is not what Madison intended, it is a striking and important outcome of the extended sphere: the power of other areas of the republic could defeat a local majority which had oppressed a local minority.

Madison sums up the ways in which faction is better controlled by republics, especially large republics, in particular "the Union": (1) representation, (2) variety of parties, (3) difficulty in concerting. He calls the third point the "most palpable advantage," presumably because the first two are only probabilities. Good representatives are only more likely and factious majorities only less likely in a large sphere, while the difficulties of distances and numbers are more palpable, i.e., visible and solid. Madison's recapitulation of the first advantage speaks of "representatives whose enlightened views and virtuous sentiments render them superior to local prejudices and to schemes of injustice." He is less clear here than he was earlier in making the public good, rather than justice, the end especially served by representation—although he is consistent with his earlier implication that statesmen must act justly and even love justice (along with being patriotic, i.e., loving the public good)[126] in order to serve the public good. Madison also refers in this summary to the "secret wishes of an unjust and interested majority." Factions are defined by their impulses, rather than by their deeds. Interested men have an impulse which produces secret unjust wishes even if those wishes are restrained by either virtuous motives or external obstacles.

Madison then gives examples of how the Union will be relatively immune to the dangers of faction, as compared to "particular States." He again follows exactly his triad of passion, opinion, and interest, making clear that not only economic diversity but also diversity in passionate attachments to leaders and religious opinions are the beneficial effects of the extended sphere. The view that these passionate factions will be diversified in the larger nation could be explained by the human fallibility and stubbornness which accounted for their existence in the first place, or by the distinctive "temper" of men in different regions (see p. 100 above). Whatever the reason, in a greater population religious sects fragment rather than simply expand.

> A religious sect may degenerate into a political faction in a part of the Confederacy; but the variety of sects dispersed over the entire face of it must secure the national councils against any danger from that source.

Although religious sects are not necessarily and ordinarily involved in modern politics, they may "degenerate" and act as political factions. Regarding factions of interest, Madison's examples of "improper or wicked" projects—"A rage for paper money, for an abolition of debts, [or] for an equal division of property"—cast some additional light on what justice and/or the public good require in the regulation of men's interests. Throughout this discussion Madison stresses that the Union *as a whole* will not be in danger; in the center of the discussion he makes this more specific: "the national councils" will not be in danger. Factions may pervade parts of society or perhaps even appear all over, but be unable to dominate the national councils. By contrast, everything in the society of a pure democracy is immediately reflected in its councils.[127]

Madison concludes that the "extent and proper structure of the Union" provide the remedy. He had previously referred to a "well-constructed Union" (p. 77) and simply "the Union" (p. 81) as crucial. The "proper structure" may refer to large districts, or to the "happy combination" which allows large districts for the central government, or to the "scheme of representation." But the Union's *extent,* that is, the mere existence of this union as a union with one government, is decisive. Finally:

> And according to the degree of pleasure and pride we feel in being republicans ought to be our zeal in cherishing the spirit and supporting the character of federalists.

"Federalists" here means Unionists as distinguished from men attached
to state governments. Union is a necessary ingredient in successful republicanism, and should be supported in proportion to "the degree of
pleasure and pride we feel in being republicans." Thus Madison again
alludes to the attractiveness of popular government. Is one's pleasure
in being a republican the result of the "pride" one feels? Men's desire
to act politically seems to be based not merely on the goods, selfish or
public, which the political process might produce. There is an element
of pride, which is called in *Federalist* 39 an "honorable determination"
(p. 240). By asserting oneself as a citizen one exercises the human faculty
of choice, a faculty not evident in "animal life." The passion with which
men defend their own opinions, and (even more) the passion with which
men seek out subjects of disagreement, manifest their determination to
assert their own will. By saving popular government from faction, *Federalist* 10 seeks to protect men's private exercise of their faculties from
factious oppression, and to make possible the continuing public exercise
of faculties which men's pride makes them insist on.

Conclusion

Federalist 10 attempts to rescue republican government from opprobrium by showing how the effects of faction can be controlled even
though its causes cannot or should not be. Even though the essay's
essential structure and practical conclusion are relatively self-explanatory,
my study suggests the importance of a series of distinctions which Madison makes and which scholars have not understood with sufficient
precision.

1. *The distinction between the causes of faction.* Factions are moved by an
"impulse of passion, or of interest." Passionate factions are often passionately attached to an opinion. Charles Beard and his successors have
emphasized *interested* factions, and have especially quoted Madison's remarks that economic divisions are the most "common and durable," and
that their regulation is the "principal task of modern legislation."[128] But
even though interested factions are durable and necessarily involved in
politics, passionate factions are more explosive. They show man at his
most contentious, angrily and intentionally vexing and oppressing his
fellow man. Interested factions oppress each other only as a means to
their own profit; for passionate factions oppression is almost an end in
itself. Madison's distinction is similar to that which Albert Hirschman
has developed with reference to earlier authors who hoped to tame men's
self-aggrandizing, "aristocratic" passions by developing in men a calmer
"bourgeois" appreciation of their (especially economic) interests.[129] But,

somewhat at odds with Hirschman's implied chronology,[130] Madison treats the belligerent, passionate side of man's nature as an enduring political problem. Modern legislation tries to make passionate conflicts unnecessary by taking economic regulation as its primary task; but man's passionate nature is precisely to fight unnecessary fights. The "popular government" Madison recommends opens a field for men to exercise their faculty of passionately opining, in contrast to previous nonpopular modern governments which sought to protect only the faculties of acquisition.

2. *The distinction between the effects of faction.* Factions oppose the rights of others or the permanent, aggregate interests of the whole, i.e., justice or the public good. These are the fundamental objects of government. Justice is an issue because society is composed of parts, of individual men with "rights"; the public good is an issue because society is a whole, and it prospers or perishes as a whole. We have seen the dependence of justice on the public good (rights presuppose national defense), and the dependence of the public good on justice (peace is disturbed by insurrections by the oppressed). This mutual dependence suggests a large degree of harmony between the two objects when they are properly understood, rather than understood in "temporary" or "partial" ways. But neither relation of dependence will apply in every case. More fundamental than the prudential arguments for respecting rights (so as to forestall rebellion, and also to stimulate the enterprise which creates society's wealth) is the fact that "civil society" is created in the first place by men who wish to secure their rights. A just government secures men's right to exercise their faculties freely; justice does not depend on an elaborate "plan" of legislation. The public good is the ordinary, practical object of government's concerns, and the good which can be attained goes beyond the preservation of rights to the promotion of interests.[131] However, a public which does not secure rights but is otherwise prosperous contradicts the purpose for which it was created.[132]

3. *The distinction between the methods of controlling faction.* Large republics have two distinct advantages in controlling faction: better representatives, and the variety of parties and obstacles to concert. The former is presented as serving the public good; the latter is presented as serving justice. Robert J. Morgan, in an attempt to show the importance of representation, says Madison concluded that "representatives chosen from large, heterogeneous districts are likely to be independent of any single interest."[133] But while this would have neatly linked the two parts of Madison's solution, Madison made no such claim in *Federalist* 10, presumably because no plausible district will be large enough to be heterogeneous in the way that the Union will be heterogeneous. A sufficient

diversity requires a sphere larger than the current states;[134] and the aim is therefore not that a faction will be incapable of winning an election in a district, but that it will be incapable of winning a majority of districts. This implies that factions may successfully elect representatives, but that each faction's representatives will be a minority. But if factions can elect representatives, how can that be consistent with the election of "fit characters"? The two parts of Madison's solution seem to conflict.

The relation of the two solutions must be understood in light of the two effects of faction. The diversity of parties is in Madison's view the more important solution; its effect is to make each faction too small to successfully commit injustices. Injustice is the crucial problem; it directly violates the ends of government, and it can lead to violence and the destruction of the regime. If factions are minorities, even if they can elect factious representatives who are also minorities, injustice will be less likely. A representative with a sinister impulse in his own case, but unable to prevail (because outvoted) in his own case, may still be a fit judge in cases which do not affect him directly. Unfit characters will be unable to cause injustice if they speak for diverse minorities; and even fit characters (who love justice) may be unable to prevent injustice if they must face the votes of a determinedly unjust majority.

The public good is an object which seems less urgent; it tends to be overlooked. The hope is that fit characters who are elected representatives will actively promote the public good. The extended sphere with a diversity of parties does not suffice to secure the public good. Madison does not reject Montesquieu's claim that the public good is "closer" to the citizens of a small republic; he insists on a large sphere for the sake of justice, and suggests that fit characters may be able to understand the less obvious good of a large, complicated public.

The importance of the public good, even if not immediate, is still great. To weaken the country or even to neglect to strengthen the country can make it vulnerable to destruction. This ought to concern even the cosmopolitan friends of popular government, since a form of government cannot persist in a conquered country or expect to be esteemed or adopted by other countries which see that tendency. Perhaps the public good as a "permanent" consideration does not at all times demand equal attention;[135] perhaps luck can sometimes be a substitute for fit characters. Concern for the public good would be characteristic of a Madisonian regime at its most successful; but even without the fit characters hoped for, there is some protection for private rights in the diversity of motives of the less fit characters.

4. *The distinction between government as a means and as an activity.* The first object of government is to protect the faculties of men. This means

especially in modern times to ensure that men's unequal faculties of acquisition can be exercised and the fruits of those faculties enjoyed. These are among the "private rights" which men institute government to protect. But Madison also refers to "public . . . liberty" or simply "liberty," which is "essential to political life." "Liberty" means popular government, or at least popular participation in a mixed government such as England's. Men take "pride" in being republicans because political life allows them to exercise faculties which separate them from "animal life." Men's pride is seen in their passionately attaching themselves to opinions and asserting themselves against other men. An election is therefore not a unanimous or nearly unanimous acquiescence in a natural leader but reflects the divisiveness of men who insist on being the choosers among options. A partiality to popular government is warrantable because popular government respects men's "honorable determination" to exercise their faculty of opining, even if their opinions reflect reason's fallibility and passion's influence. Madison thinks men's proud but dangerous self-assertion can be more safely indulged in an extended sphere. The fact that men are not merely interested in receiving benefits but are also determined to assert their own will complicates the construction of government and guides the analysis of *The Federalist*.

·[Four]·

Theoretical Uncertainty and Honorable Determination

After some introductory remarks in *Federalist* numbers 37–38, *Federalist* 39 begins the "candid survey of the plan of government reported by the convention" (p. 240) which occupies the remainder of the book. The survey begins by considering the "form" of that government: Is it "strictly republican"? Is it *"federal"*? As we saw in chapter 2, the answer to the question about federalism is *not* that the proposal is strictly federal, but that it is "partly" federal. But Madison claims the proposal is "republican" "in the most rigid sense" (39, p. 242). His compact account of this matter casts some light on a question raised above regarding *Federalist* 10: Why the insistence on popular government? Why not a "partly" popular government, like England's?

I will turn to that account after granting Madison's wish to be indulged some introductory "reflections" which will contribute to a "just and fair result" (37, p. 224). The principal burden of these remarks is that the "merits of this Constitution" do not include perfection, because a "faultless plan was not to be expected." Madison explains five "difficulties inherent in the very nature of the undertaking referred to the convention." The last two of those difficulties are the conflicting claims of different-sized states and of different interests which the convention had to reconcile; the first three are difficulties of devising a plan of "theoretical propriety" even apart from those conflicts (37, pp. 224–30). Madison thus returns to the question of the possibility of instituting good government by "reflection and choice." Not only the various motives and

·[111]·

prejudices among the people affect their reflection and choice; even the thoughtful few who composed the convention faced certain difficulties in reflecting on the nature of good government. These difficulties show the "necessity of moderating . . . our expectations and hopes from the efforts of human sagacity" (37, p. 228). I will suggest a connection between the limits of human sagacity explained in Madison's preface and the necessarily assertive rather than conclusive nature of the case for popular government. Madison's preface is also important for its summary statement of the ingredients of good government which the later essays elaborate.

Theory

The first difficulty faced by the convention was the "novelty of the undertaking." Since both the existing confederation and other historical confederations were founded on "principles which are fallacious," the convention could only "avoid the errors suggested by the past experience of other countries, as well as of our own" (37, p. 226). Although "experience" is "the oracle of truth" (20, p. 138) and "the guide that ought always to be followed whenever it can be found" (52, p. 327), in the construction of a federal government for America experience furnishes "no other light than that of beacons, which give warning of the course to be shunned, without pointing out that which ought to be pursued." One might add that the histories of "petty republics" (9, pp. 71–72) and of large monarchies (14, p. 104) suggest additional courses to be shunned. These experiences provide "beacons" only if unsatisfactory effects can be traced to "fallacious" "principles." But to replace fallacious principles with new ones is risky; novel principles are not solid until they have been tested by experience. Thus in *Federalist* 9 Hamilton could only "venture" a new improvement in the modern science of politics (p. 73); and in *Federalist* 1 the theory of the Declaration of Independence (which replaced fallacious principles) was presented as in need of a practical demonstration. The fact that *The Federalist*'s new theories are not fully tested makes its enterprise problematic, but also admirable. If the theories work out, future countries can imitate America more closely than America could imitate anyone else. They will escape the difficulty posed by novelty but will miss the "glory" of America's "new and more noble course" of raising "the fabrics of governments which have no model on the face of the globe" (14, p. 104). If there were past experiences of success, one might try to imitate them in a rough, approximate way without fully understanding the (true) principles which explained their success. But the experience of failure demands a more theoretical approach that detects fallacious principles and replaces them by novel ones which seem reasonable but are unproven because they are "still in the womb of time and experience" (23, p. 157).

A second difficulty ("a very important one") faced by the convention's attempt to reflect on and choose good government

> must have lain in combining the requisite stability and energy in government with the inviolable attention due to liberty and to the republican form. (37, p. 226)

That this combination "could not be easily accomplished will be denied by no one who is unwilling to betray his ignorance of the subject." While in stating the previous difficulty Madison had suggested the necessary tentativeness of theorizing, here he is quite emphatic about a theoretical point. Everyone who wishes to appear knowledgeable about "the subject" (politics?) will admit the difficulty of combining "stability and energy" with "liberty and . . . the republican form." Even though experience offers no examples of "the course . . . which ought to be pursued," men can learn from experience or otherwise (1) that certain elements or qualities are needed in government, and (2) that they are difficult to combine. Experience could show the effects of the presence or absence of these various qualities, as well as the lack of examples of their successful combination.

Madison does not here explain why liberty and the republican form are due "inviolable attention," but he does make a brief argument for stability and energy in government:

> Energy in government is essential to that security against external and internal danger and to that prompt and salutary execution of the laws which enter into the very definition of good government. Stability in government is essential to national character and to the advantages annexed to it, as well as to that repose and confidence in the minds of the people, which are among the chief blessings of civil society. (37, p. 226)

Madison explains that the people find unstable legislation "odious" and will not be satisfied until the state governments improve in this respect. Madison does not say that the people care about "energy;" stability is more attractive because it encourages "repose and confidence in the minds of the people, which are among the chief blessings of civil society." This statement of civil society's blessings recalls the formulations of Hobbes and Locke, according to which men wish to leave the state of nature so as to be free of fear and uncertainty.[1] And it resembles Montesquieu's statement that political liberty "in a citizen is that tranquillity of spirit which proceeds from the opinion which each has of his safety."[2] The energy which secures men against dangers and promptly executes the laws contributes to repose and confidence. But stability both contributes to repose and resembles repose; energy is not so popular because it does not resemble repose but defeats the enemies of repose in a way that may remind men that their repose is threatened. Men want the blessing of living under stable laws on which they can depend; and this blessing partly depends on the energy by which a good government can defeat dangers to stability.

Madison here suggests no difficulty in combining energy with stability; the difficulty is in "mingling" them both with "the vital principles of liberty."

> The genius of republican liberty seems to demand on one side
> not only [1] that all power should be derived from the people,
> but [2] that those intrusted with it should be kept in dependence
> on the people by a short duration of their appointments; and [3]
> that even during this short period the trust should be placed not
> in a few, but in a number of hands. (37, p. 227)

The second condition is contrary to stability, and both the second and third are contrary to energy, while the first condition is not said to be contrary to either. The suggestion that the "genius of republican liberty" is in opposition to the essential qualities of "good government" which serve the "chief blessings of civil society" poses an "arduous" problem indeed. *The Federalist* appears to agree with the views of Hobbes and Locke as to the proper ends of government; and to admit that the "genius of republican liberty" is in tension with those ends. *Federalist* 37 leaves unexplained both why republican liberty deserves inviolable attention despite this difficulty and how the difficulty can be overcome.

A third difficulty for the convention was the "arduous" "task of marking the proper line of partition" between federal and state authority. Madison's elaboration of this point must be ranked as the most astonishing passage in *The Federalist*. Rather than give examples of the practical political problem he has raised, Madison offers a short essay concerning human understanding, which explains the difficulty of "contemplat[ing] and discriminat[ing] objects extensive and complicated in their nature." Not merely the proper distinction between state and federal, but all kinds of distinctions are difficult to make with precision and assurance. While I will suggest how these theoretical speculations do indeed bear on *The Federalist*'s practical concerns, their rather lengthy intrusion into the argument may justify Madison's plea to be "indulged" (37, p. 224) by his readers.

Madison first explains the difficulty men have in distinguishing among *natural* phenomena which are in themselves distinguished in a "perfectly accurate" way. He gives two examples:

> [1] The faculties of the mind itself have never yet been distinguished and defined with satisfactory precision by all the efforts of the most acute and metaphysical philosophers. Sense, perception, judgment, desire, volition, memory, imagination are found to be separated by such delicate shades and minute gradations that their boundaries have eluded the most subtle investigations, and remain a pregnant source of ingenious disquisition and controversy. [2] The boundaries between the great kingdoms of nature, and, still more, between the various provinces and lesser portions into which they are subdivided afford another illustration of the same important truth. The most sagacious and laborious naturalists have never yet succeeded in tracing with certainty the line which separates the district of vegetable life from the neighboring region of unorganized matter, or which marks the termination of the former and the commencement of the animal empire. A still greater obscurity lies in the distinctive characters by which the objects in each of these great departments of nature have been arranged and assorted. (37, pp. 227–28)

Man's knowledge of nature is uncertain; even the wisest men cannot be confident that their understanding of the categories into which natural objects are divided is accurate. To identify the "distinctive characters" of each category is still more difficult; accordingly, Madison leaves it unclear whether animals constitute one of three great "kingdoms of nature," or have an "empire" in contrast to the vegetable "district" and mineral "region."

These uncertainties bothering natural scientists and metaphysicians might seem to be of dubious political relevance. But Madison's two examples of uncertain natural distinctions are linked by a further example to which both of them point. The "faculties of the mind" are parts of a part of man; and man is one of the provinces into which one of the great kingdoms of nature is divided. Our uncertainty about nature includes an uncertainty about man—about the parts of which he is composed (his "faculties") and about his place among the other parts of nature. Even if the "line" between man and other provinces of the animal kingdom is fairly clear, the "distinctive characters" of man may be more obscure. I find support for this interpretation in the introductory lecture of Professor Witherspoon's course on moral philosophy. Witherspoon there explains that "human nature" can be studied from two points of view: by considering the differences between the human species and other creatures; and by considering the "parts" which compose the nature of an individual man. In connection with the first approach, Witherspoon notes the difficulty of classifying certain species as belonging to the vegetable or animal kingdom; and among the "parts" of man Witherspoon lists various "faculties of the mind."³ Thus the "imperfection" of man's "eye" in "survey[ing]" the "works of nature" (37, p. 228) impedes a confident survey of human nature—both as a compound of certain faculties and as a part of the whole of nature.

Madison turns to a second difficulty men face in making distinctions. In the "institutions of man," the "obscurity arises as well from the object itself as from the organ by which it is contemplated." Thus while Madison is willing to assume that nature is ordered according to "perfectly accurate" (although imperfectly visible) "delineations," that assumption cannot be made about the things which men devise.

> Experience has instructed us that no skill in the science of government has yet been able to discriminate and define, with sufficient certainty, its three great provinces—the legislative, executive, and judiciary; or even the privileges and powers of the different legislative branches. Questions daily occur in the course of practice which prove the obscurity which reigns in these subjects, and which puzzle the greatest adepts in political science. (37, p. 228)

The institutions of man rely on categorical distinctions which prove in practice to be uncertain; thus, "daily," men may disagree about whether a given act is legislative or executive or judicial. Because this distinction is invented by man rather than found in nature, there is no guarantee that these branches are really delineated, i.e., separated by a specific (even if imperfectly known) line; it is possible that man has invented categories which overlap or which are not exhaustive. In *Federalist* 75, Hamilton says that the power of making treaties really does not fit into the distinction of three powers (p. 451).

Madison gives several other examples of institutions of man which are delineated by "indeterminate limits." The extent of different codes of laws (common, statute, maritime, ecclesiastical, corporations, other local laws and customs) and the jurisdiction of different courts (general, local, law, equity, admiralty, etc.) in Great Britain are imperfectly known, despite an industrious study for "ages" by "the most enlightened legislators and jurists." And even the most carefully formed new laws are "more or less obscure and equivocal" until they have been applied in a series of particular cases (37, pp. 228–29).

One might wonder why the works of man cannot be more accurately distinguished. Cannot men define their own works as they please, and stick by those definitions, just as a geometer makes and abides by his definitions? Madison's unusually abstract discussion was occasioned by his assertion that it is an arduous task to find the "proper line of partition" between the authority of the central government and that of the states. The problem is not just that *any* line which America might institute would be somewhat obscure. The task is to find the *proper* line—just as the adept political scientists and enlightened legislators and jurists seek the proper line dividing the powers of government, and the kinds of laws and courts. But the search for the proper line in the institutions of man encounters the obscurity of the works of nature, because the works of man are intended to fit man's natural faculties and his natural situation. For example, the proper respective jurisdiction of ecclesiastical, statute, and common law would depend upon the extent to which men are naturally subject to God and his assistants, the extent to which men can freely legislate for themselves, and the extent to which men must be bound by their history. Similarly, the proper line between federal and state power seems to depend on certain natural facts about which there is an inescapable uncertainty. Men wish to institute a central government because independent neighbors are natural enemies (6, p. 59); they wish to keep state governments because they have a natural trust of what they know most closely (17, p. 119). Man's natural tendencies and situation (the "natural . . . course of human affairs" [34, p. 207]) seem uncertain and even contradictory; the human institutions which attempt to make distinctions in accordance with these facts will also be uncertain.

The third difficulty in making distinctions is the "use of words." There is not a word for every "complex idea," nor does every word unequivocally convey a single complex idea. So even if we could understand the proper powers of the state and central governments, those powers could not necessarily be perfectly expressed. This difficulty supports *The Federalist*'s denigration of "parchment" barriers; not only are they too flimsy to restrain passionate men, they are subject to interpretations which may justify what the parchment's words were intended to prevent. Even God's "luminous" meaning, when expressed in man's language, is "dim and doubtful" (37, p. 229)—and may therefore be no clearer than man's own imperfect conceptions about natural and human things.

Federalist 37's discussion of the obstacles to man's theorizing is meant to moderate our expectations of what man's sagacity can achieve; we cannot expect a faultless plan even from a sage convention. But the reader might find his expectations for human sagacity positively depressed, inasmuch as Madison does not explain how men may have any confidence in the distinctions they make. *Federalist* 37 appears as a skeptical digression in the middle of a rather confident book. We must especially consider the grounds of the distinction Madison makes and insists on shortly thereafter, the distinction between republican and non-republican governments.

Republican Government

In *Federalist* 39 Madison raises the questions of whether the proposed government is "republican" and whether it is "federal." These are apparently man-made words which describe man-made categories, although the categories seem to have some relation to that "wor[k] of nature," man's own nature. In discussing whether the plan is federal Madison adopts his adversaries' definition of "federal" and shows that the plan is partly federal. In discussing whether the plan is republican he adopts his own definition of "republican" and shows that the plan is wholly republican. While the question of federalism is presented as the objection of an adversary (39, p. 242), the question of republicanism is said to be the "first question that offers itself" in a "candid survey" of the proposed Constitution; indeed *"The conformity of the proposed Constitution to the true principles of republican government"* (1, p. 36) is the official topic of *The Federalist's* entire second volume. *The Federalist* volunteers a discussion of this subject and goes rather far in stressing its importance:

> It is evident that no other form would be reconcilable [1] with the genius of the people of America; [2] with the fundamental principles of the Revolution; or [3] with that honorable determination which animates every votary of freedom to rest all our political experiments on the capacity of mankind for self-government. If the plan of the convention, therefore, be found to depart from the republican character, its advocates must abandon it as no longer defensible. (39, p. 240)

In contrast to Madison's acknowledgment that the federal form has been considerably modified by the plan, the republican character must be "strictly" adhered to. Madison's statement may seem extreme; are all nonrepublican governments utterly indefensible? It is not clear whether "defensible" means defensible in itself or defensible before the people. The reasons given are a bit sketchy. Only the republican form is "reconcilable" with three standards. The "genius of the people of America"— also cited at the Constitutional Convention as demanding republican government[4]—could mean the people's destiny, or their way of life, or simply their prejudices. The fact that for many years Americans had accepted the British monarchy would suggest that their genius is not unalterable. Perhaps, though, their genius has been fixed by the "fundamental principles of the Revolution." But, at least according to the letter of the Declaration of Independence, men are entitled to choose whatever form of government seems to them most conducive to their safety and happiness. Madison himself implies that the American Revolution's purpose was "that the people of America should enjoy peace, liberty, and safety" (45, p. 289). While "liberty" means that government must contain a popular element, that requirement could be satisfied by England's mixed monarchy—not only by a "strictly" "republican" form.

Yet Madison says that only the republican form is "reconcilable" with the Revolution's principles. He may therefore intend to move beyond the explicit revolutionary doctrine and assert a kinship between the Revolution's principle that the people are entitled to choose and judge their form of government, and the republican principle that the people are entitled to choose and judge their rulers. Only republican government with its scheme of elections puts into a form the necessarily informal principle of revolution. The operation of government with periodic consent is most reconcilable with the institution of government by consent. Even if such an argument is plausible, it is undoubtedly some steps beyond the Declaration of Independence's avowed principles, according to which the people's "Safety and Happiness" are the necessary end, and any particular form of government only a means.[5]

Madison's most expansive statement in defense of the republican form is that it is reconcilable with "that honorable determination which animates every votary of freedom to rest all our political experiments on the capacity of mankind for self-government." Men's capacity for self-government is here not an undeniable truth but a hypothesis on the basis of which votaries of freedom make governmental "experiments." Even if a contrary hypothesis could be inferred from considerable past experience, this hypothesis is adopted out of a certain "honorable determination." If political experiments relying on this hypothesis have failed, other aspects of the experiments can be modified, but this hypothesis must be preserved. Thus, as the word "votary" implies (by its resemblance to "devotion"), the experiment is not the work of open-minded scientists who are equally willing to test and reject all hypotheses, but of men devoted to an "honorable" hypothesis about human "capacity."

According to *Federalist* 37 there is a considerable lack of clarity about exactly what faculties or capacities men have. While naturalists and metaphysicians may continue disputing the nature of man—the faculties of which he is composed and his place among other natural phenomena—Madison bases his political science on an honorable interpretation of men's faculties. It is honorable because it treats men as beings capable of choosing intelligently and ruling; men are above the level of tame beasts moved by pleasure and pain and ruled by masters. Madison admits it is an "honorable determination," that is, it is a kind of prejudice or presupposition.[6] This prejudice is consistent with human "pride" (10, p. 84) and with *The Federalist*'s hope that Americans will "vindicate the honor of the human race" (11, p. 91).[7]

In order to judge whether the plan is "strictly republican," Madison must consider what the "distinctive characters of the republican form" are (39, p. 240). *Federalist* 37 had warned of the great difficulty of specifying the "distinctive characters" of anything (p. 228); they are even harder to specify than are the lines of division between one category and another. Madison says that previous political writers have used the term "republic" with "extreme inaccuracy," applying it to Holland, Venice, Poland, and England, which are "nearly as dissimilar to each other as to a genuine republic." The previous usages are not only defective in being contradictory, they are also defective according to some standard of genuineness. So Madison supplies his own definition of "republic," resorting "for a criterion to the different principles on which different forms of government are established."

> [W]e may define a republic to be, or at least may bestow that name on, a government which derives all its powers directly or indirectly from the great body of the people, and is administered by persons holding their offices during pleasure for a limited period, or during good behavior. (39, p. 241)

In light of *Federalist* 37's discussion of the problems of making distinctions and applying words to objects, Madison's statement that we "may bestow" the name "republic," or "may define" the word this way, admits that his usage is disputable. Indeed, one might find his definition rather relaxed in comparison to the account in *Federalist* 37 of the "genius of republican liberty," which seemed to require short terms and a large number of officers (37, p. 227). But this definition is based on the "principles on which different forms of government are established." Madison implies a typology of forms according to two criteria: (1) from whom the powers of government are derived, and (2) the terms of its officers. The first criterion resembles the traditional distinction between governments by one, few, and many, but departs from that tradition by referring not to those who rule but to those from whom powers are derived. The disjunctive formulations—"directly or indirectly" and "for a limited period, or during good behavior"—indicate that the category Madison creates by this definition could easily have been further subdivided. But even if it appears to be an inclusive definition in theory, it does in practice exclude the four regimes others have called republics.

What justifies this definition? Madison elaborates by specifying the limits between which republics are found:

It is *essential* to such a government that it be derived from the great body of the society, not from an inconsiderable proportion or a favored class of it; otherwise a handful of tyrannical nobles, exercising their oppressions by a delegation of their powers, might aspire to the rank of republicans and claim for their government the honorable title of republic. It is *sufficient* for such a government that the persons administering it be appointed, either directly or indirectly, by the people; and that they hold their appointments by either of the tenures just specified; otherwise every government in the United States, as well as every other popular government that has been or can be well organized or well executed, would be degraded from the republican character. (39, p. 241)

The *"essential"* condition separates republican government from less popular forms; if the electors are not "the great body of the society," the election only mimics republican elections. Madison's reference to the "honorable title" of republic echoes his statement of the "honorable determination" in favor of self-government. It would appear that the minimum requirement for a republic is that it honor the great body of the people by respecting their capacity to choose. This characteristic of a "genuine" republic was absent from the four examples of specious republics. England has "one republican branch only, combined with an hereditary aristocracy and monarchy" (39, pp. 240–41). To derive only part of the government from the people and institute a separate claim to a share in rule by a favored few is to dishonor the people. Even this relatively benign mixed regime gives scope to the "arrogant pretensions" to "superiority" by a few which affront "the honor of the human race" (11, pp. 90–91).

Madison's definition of republic is not merely justified by being clear and consistent. It is justified insofar as it takes into account the reasons for which men insist on a republic in the first place. "Republic" may be a category men can invent, but its inventors must make their definition compatible with the natural phenomena of human impulses which lead men to distinguish such a category and be devoted to it.

One might think that an insistence on the republican form as a matter of the people's "honor" is somehow wrong-headed. Ought not regimes be justified by their substantive results, and cannot republics be fully defended by their superior protection of men's security and pursuit of happiness? Whatever the merits of this position in retrospect, it cannot quite be ascribed to *The Federalist.* That work takes a stand for popular government, and explains how to improve it; and perhaps praises of popular government's results rely on those improvements. But *The Federalist* itself presents a paradox: popular government "has so long labored" under "opprobrium" (10, p. 81); yet "republic" is an "honorable title" (39, p. 241). The opprobrium is due to its record of instability, injustice, and disregard for the public good. England's nonrepublican government has a relatively good record of securing private rights and security (see 9, p. 72 and 56, p. 350). Given the difficulty of combining republican liberty with the ingredients of good government, England's mixed government might seem preferable to republican government if men sought only to enjoy the private fruits of good government.[8] Instead England's government must be abandoned as "no longer defensible" because it does not deserve the "honorable title of republic."

Madison's statement of what is *"sufficient"* for a government to deserve the title of republic indicates that a fairly wide range of arrangements is acceptable. At the limit, all officers could be appointed by indirect elections for a term of good behavior; and since "persons" must administer it, the government apparently must consist of more than one officer but not necessarily more than two. It is worth noting that this definition is compatible with the plan of government that Alexander Hamilton proposed to the Constitutional Convention.[9] While this definition may strain the adherents of the republican "genius" (short terms and multiple offices), it does exclude some institutions. Even officers chosen by indirect elections—in which the people elect electors who elect officers— are far different from "self-appointed" officers (51, p. 324). And "good behavior" is not the same as a life term (not to mention hereditary offices) since the officer's commission can be revoked—either by the people or by some person(s) whom they directly or indirectly choose. This is a crucial distinction, since it preserves the people's right to judge their rulers, and forbids the kind of permanently binding consent which Hobbes recommended and required. The people can choose to keep their own choice dormant while their officers behave, but they cannot choose to give up their future choice altogether.[10]

Madison seems to suspect that some may find his definition of "republic" too broad, but he replies that a more restrictive definition would degrade from the "republican character" both (1) "every government in the United States," and (2) "every other popular government that has been or can be well organized or well executed." Thus Madison relies on the respectability of the existing American governments (state governments and the Articles of Confederation) to vindicate the indirect elections and long terms which might seem problematic. The American insistence on republics is partly an insistence on the kind of governments

America has already instituted. Madison's strategy allows him to list impressively the existing institutions which in each state require his expansive definition. All states have some indirect elections and officers with a "definite period" of tenure—the latter provision suggesting that a more extreme popularly elected government could operate by continuous recall. In the middle of Madison's accounts of how "all" or "most" states have institutions which require his definition, he declares confidently that "according to one [state constitution], this mode of appointment [indirect] is extended to one of the co-ordinate branches of the legislature" (39, p. 241)—as if this one example were frosting on the cake rather than a lonely precedent for the U.S. Senate.

Defining "republic" by its "principles" permits a recombination and extension of certain features of the state governments. As Madison proceeds to demonstrate, the proposed Constitution fits his definition "in the most rigid sense" (39, p. 242); and each element of the Federal Constitution has at least one state precedent. But no state has *all* the elements of the proposal. Madison's point is that the principles of indirect election and long terms or good behavior have been accepted as not being serious affronts to the people's honorable right to choose.

Perhaps more important in Madison's own view than the state precedents is the concern that the definition of republic not rule out "every . . . popular government that has been or can be well organized or well executed." To degrade those good governments from the dignity of being called republics would at the same time degrade republics from the possibility of being good governments. In his recitation of the features of the proposed plan, Madison lists the mode and tenure of appointment for each office and likens it to those existing state institutions which it most resembles. He departs from this pattern in one case:

> The tenure by which the judges are to hold their places is, as it unquestionably ought to be, that of good behavior. (39, p. 242)

While he had in the previous paragraph adduced the fact that "most" states follow this procedure, Madison now emphatically appeals to the standard of what "unquestionably ought to be" as a measure of the proper definition of republican. In *Federalist* 37, Madison posed the conflicts between stability and energy, and the "genius of republican liberty." To institute the republican genius in a "form" requires its principles to be understood as open to the elements which all forms of government need but which the republican genius might seem to oppose. Men honorably determined to vindicate their capacity for self-government would be frustrated if the form of their self-government were poorly organized and poorly executed, and led to injustice and instability rather than repose and confidence. Such a result would rather manifest men's incapacity for self-government. This was the conclusion sometimes drawn from the gloomy histories of the ancient Greek republics, whose defective structures "pervert[ed] the direction and tarnish[ed] the luster" of their people's talents (9, pp. 71–72.).

Madison finds a "further proof" of the system's "republican complexion" in its guarantee that states shall preserve the republican form, and in the absolute prohibition of titles of nobility (39, p. 242). Hamilton later emphasizes the great importance of the latter as the "cornerstone" of republican government (84, p. 512; see p. 511). To deprive the great body of the people of their right to choose would require the institution of some formal distinctions among the people. If "republic" is the most "honorable title," the people are honored as a whole; no special titles give a smaller number a superior right to choose.

Madison's definition of republic is devised to be compatible with three opinions: (1) republics honor the people's capacity to choose; (2) the existing American governments are republics; (3) republics can be good governments.

The Federalist's republicanism departs from the view made famous by Montesquieu that a patriotic and self-sacrificing "virtue" is the principle of republican government.[11] *The Federalist* honorably determines that human beings are capable of opining and choosing, but does not look for a "happy empire of perfect wisdom and perfect virtue" (6, p. 59) which would guarantee the public-spiritedness of those opinions and choices. Not the expectation that political life will be an arena of self-lessness, but the attractiveness of political life as an occasion for an honorable self-assertion underlies *The Federalist*'s defense of republican government. While Montesquieu apparently requires that virtuous citizens passionately forget their private good in their devotion to the public, other authors of the "classical republican" tradition describe man's political nature in terms closer to *The Federalist*'s. In Aristotle's account, men's political nature consists fundamentally not in an instinctive sociability but in a capacity to think and speak, i.e., to express and act upon disputable opinions about good and bad, just and unjust. That capacity would be in vain if men were not political, and nature makes nothing in vain.[12] While expressing some doubt about how clearly men can understand nature's intentions, *The Federalist* honorably determines to respect the political capacity which naturally or assertedly distinguishes human life from animal life.

Thus man's political nature cannot be reduced to the concern (detected by an "interest-group" analysis) which "each individual would have in his own self-interest and personal freedom."[13] Men's proud determination to rule, rather than merely be ruled well, makes England's mixed government unacceptable. On the other hand, *The Federalist*'s republican argument does not issue in a defense of the "pure" (direct) democracy of ancient republics. Among the most evident reasons for this are the inability of even small republics (like the states), let alone direct democracies (cities), to survive in the modern world of nations, and the inability of direct democracies to secure men's private rights (10, p. 81). In defending modern improvements in the "science of politics" (9, p. 72) *The Federalist* attempts to preserve the spirit of republican political life while modifying its practice so as to make it compatible with other human aims. In a representative republic a man can be both a private citizen (24, p. 161), generally absorbed in the pursuits of gain (8, p. 69) and spared the vexing and perhaps risky task of continually making political decisions, and a political partisan, entitled to take his own opinions seriously because of their equal share in the ultimate authority of a republican regime.

Federalist 39 is thus in agreement with *Federalist* 10: government must be both good government, which can successfully serve the proper ends of government, and republican government, in which men's honorable insistence on their faculty of opining is respected.[14] In discussing *The Federalist*'s essays on the "particular structure" of the proposed Constitution, I will consider more precisely how man's political nature is manifested in this form of government—a theme to which I will return especially in the Conclusion. Those essays on the government's particular structure also elaborate the meaning of and requirements for "good government." Because "in every political institution, a power to advance the public happiness involves a discretion which may be misapplied and abused" (41, pp. 255–56), the goodness of government consists both in its contributions to the public happiness and in its refraining from abusively causing the public unhappiness. Good government must, to borrow terms from later essays (72, p. 437; 53, p. 336), have both the "negative merit" of being "safe" and the "positive merit" of being "useful." The former requirement is the subject of Madison's analysis of separation of powers (chapter 5), and of his assertion that the arrangement of the House of Representatives will be "safe to the liberties of the people" (chapter 6, first section). The latter requirement is the subject of the argument that the House will be "useful to the affairs of the public" (chaper 6, second section), and especially of the papers on the "more permanent branches" of the government which can contribute the "requisite" "stability and energy" (chapter 7).

·[Five]·

Separation of Powers

In *Federalist* 47 Madison turns to the "particular structure" of the proposed government, its "distribution" of its "mass of power" among its "constituent parts" (p. 301). Power is not an undifferentiated whole by which government rules; the mass of power can be assigned to "distinct departments" in a "regular distribution" (9, p. 72). But before Madison even explains how power can be distributed and what departments are appropriate, he pauses to discuss an objection by the Constitution's opponents:

> One of the principal objections inculcated by the more respectable adversaries to the Constitution is its supposed violation of the political maxim that the legislative, executive, and judiciary departments ought to be separate and distinct. In the structure of the federal government no regard, it is said, seems to have been paid to this essential precaution in favor of liberty. (47, p. 301)

Madison goes rather far in endorsing the significance of this objection. He says the "political truth" "on which the objection is founded" has great "intrinsic value" and the authority of "enlightened patrons of liberty." The political truth on which the objection is founded is that

> [t]he accumulation of all powers, legislative, executive, and judiciary, in the same hands, whether of one, a few, or many, and whether hereditary, self-appointed, or elective, may justly be pronounced the very definition of tyranny. (47, p. 301)

·[126]·

The "truth" is that accumulation of all powers is tyranny; the "maxim" deduced from this truth (and perhaps less certain than this truth) is that separation of powers is essential to liberty. If the Constitution really accumulates or tends to accumulate all powers, "no further arguments would be necessary to inspire a universal reprobation of the system."

Separation of powers—the "celebrated maxim which has been so often mentioned, and seems to be so little understood" (66, p. 402)—appears as a "precaution" to prevent "tyranny" by a government which accumulates all powers. As Madison's later summary statement indicates, the section of *The Federalist* on separation of powers concerns how "to guard the society against the oppression of its rulers" (51, p. 323). This precautionary or negative approach to the government's structure leads some to conclude that the Founders devised a government characterized by "deadlock" out of a fear that an active government would act badly. However, this section on separation of powers precedes but does not preview the book's positive account of the government's structure. *Federalist* numbers 47–51 do not discuss "energy" or "stability," or even say much about the particular functions of the different departments.

This chapter will first discuss what separation of powers meant to those who made it such a celebrated "political maxim"; and then consider how Madison transforms that maxim into his own related but broader maxim: "Ambition must be made to counteract ambition" (51, p. 322). Madison's analysis pays less attention to the scope of each department's function than to the opportunity which each department's situation gives it to indulge the human passion of ambition, i.e., the love of power. Precisely in a wholly popular government—where one might think that society could easily guard itself "against the oppression of its rulers" by the fact that it chooses its rulers—ambition is of great importance. Some men's love of power—together with the complementary susceptibility of other men to the charms of the ambitious—preserves the danger of oppression by rulers which the popularization of government might seem to have abolished.

Rule by Law

Because Madison is merely agreeing with respectable opponents who insist on the necessity of separation of powers, he does not really explain why separation is of such importance. But he does refer to Montesquieu as the "oracle" who has displayed and recommended separation of powers most effectually to mankind's attention, and quotes part of Montesquieu's explanation.

"When the legislative and executive powers are united in the same person or body," says he, "there can be no liberty, because apprehensions may arise [on peut craindre] lest *the same* monarch or senate should *enact* tyrannical laws to *execute* them in a tyrannical manner." Again: "Were the power of judging joined with the legislative, the life and liberty of the subject would be exposed to arbitrary control, for *the judge* would then be *the legislator*. Were it joined to the executive power, *the judge* might behave with all the violence of *an oppressor*." Some of these reasons are more fully explained in other passages. . . . (47, p. 303)[1]

Most commentators have found these remarks cryptic at best. Does Montesquieu consider liberty secured if reasonable laws are executed in a tyrannical manner, or if tyrannical laws are executed in a reasonable manner? Montesquieu's repeated assertion that there would be "no liberty" without separation of powers depends on his explanation of liberty which precedes the passage Madison quotes:

Political liberty in a citizen is that tranquillity of spirit which proceeds from the opinion which each has of his safety; and for one to have this liberty, it is necessary that the government be such that a citizen cannot fear another citizen.[2]

Separation of powers dispels men's fears. If the legislature and executive were united, "on peut craindre" that they would tyrannically apply tyrannical laws; thus a citizen could fear the other citizen or citizens who exercised those powers. And by separating the power of judging from the other rulers, and giving it to men temporarily drawn from the people, it appears less "terrible" to men, who then fear only the office of judge rather than the citizens who are judges.[3] Montesquieu does not say that liberty is sufficiently secured if the three powers are separate, but only that there is no liberty if they are not. Thus even if the three powers are separated, a citizen might fear other threats to his safety. There might also be threats to his safety which he does not fear.

The distinction between these three powers is made possible by the view that governments can and should govern by laws. Ruling need not be a series of particular decisions about particular cases but can be done by general enactments, announced in advance, which apply to all cases. Locke argued that unless men are "govern'd by *declared Laws*," "their Peace, Quiet, and Property will still be at the same uncertainty, as it was in the state of Nature."[4] Laws allow men to "know their Duty," i.e., they allow each man to "know what is his."[5] In addition, the quality of rule may be improved if men are ruled by laws. Rulers will be

kept within their due bounds, and not . . . be tempted, by the
Power they have in their hands, to imploy it to such purposes,
and by such measures, as they would not have known, and own
not willingly.[6]

Ruling by announced laws is publicly visible and therefore less likely to
be sinister. Montesquieu too emphasizes rule by law in a remark which
precedes his discussion of separation of powers:

A constitution can be such that no one will be constrained to do
the things which the law does not require of him, and to not do
those which the law permits him.[7]

While there could be no separation of the powers of legislating, executing, and judging without rule by law, there could be rule by law
without such a separation. A lawgiver could rule the subjects in accordance with the laws he himself makes. But Locke proposes separation
as a means of preventing the "temptation" such a ruler might face:

And because it may be too great a temptation to humane frailty
apt to grasp at Power, for the same Persons who have the Power
of making Laws, to have also in their hands the power to execute
them, whereby they may exempt themselves from Obedience to
the Laws they make, and suit the Law, both in its making and execution, to their own private advantage, and thereby come to have
a distinct interest from the rest of the Community, contrary to the
end of Society and Government: Therefore in well order'd Com-
monwealths, where the good of the whole is so considered, as it
ought, the *Legislative* Power is put into the hands of divers Persons who duly Assembled, have by themselves, or jointly with others, a Power to make Laws, which when they have done, being
separated again, they are themselves subject to the Laws, they
have made; which is a new and near tie upon them, to take care,
that they make them for the publick good.[8]

Thus the "tie" by which the publicity inherent in *"declared Laws"* encourages respectable purposes and measures is considerably supplemented by a separation of powers which makes the laws apply to the
lawmakers. This is probably the meaning of Montesquieu's statement
concerning tyrannical laws tyrannically applied; if the legislators cannot
ensure a tyrannical execution, i.e., one which favors themselves, they
will be less likely to make tyrannical laws for fear that they themselves
will be tyrannically ruled by them. Each legislative enactment is in effect
a new commission of power for the executive, a permission or instruction
to commit certain acts. If the legislature executed, it could use "all the
power it gave itself."[9] Citizens will not fear government if the executive

who uses power uses only what is given to him, and if the legislature can give power but not use it itself.

If a separate executive will enforce the law even against the lawmakers, the lawmakers will not have a "distinct interest from the rest of the Community." W. B. Gwyn has called this doctrine the "rule of law version" of separation of powers. He notes that it is the only version of the several he detects in the history of thought which actually requires a separation between legislature and executive and he notes the congruence on this point between Locke and Montesquieu.[10] While I suggest that this is the fundamental meaning of separation of powers as such, scholars have noted considerable "confusion" about the doctrine's true meaning. Much of the confusion can be traced to the fact that the three most famous accounts of the separation of powers—in Locke, Montesquieu, and *The Federalist*—all move beyond this primary meaning of the doctrine. Locke's discussion of *"Prerogative"* expands the role of the "executive" beyond what that term would literally imply.[11] Montesquieu insists that the executive must be able to "stop" the legislature by vetoing its laws; distinguishes (as Locke did not) a "judicial" power separate from the executive; then substitutes the House of Lords for the judiciary as one of the three powers; and finally suggests that the "distribution" of powers need not be a separation in the sense first suggested.[12] Neither of these authors regarded separation of powers as a complete solution to the problem it addresses; and we shall see that this is also true of *The Federalist*.

Legislative Vortex

Federalist 47 attempts to assure the Constitution's critics that the proposed government does not violate separation of powers. To this end, Madison explains that according to Montesquieu's theory and in British and American practice, separation of powers means not that a total separation is required but rather "no more than this,"

> that where the *whole* power of one department is exercised by the same hands which possess the *whole* power of another department, the fundamental principles of a free constitution are subverted. (47, pp. 302–3)

Thus branches which are separate can still have some *"partial agency"* in" or *"control* over" each other, as when (in Britain) the executive acts as a branch of the legislature, or (in American states) the legislature elects the executive. But Madison concludes that in fact some states have "violated" the "fundamental principle under consideration" "by too great a mixture, and even an actual consolidation of the different powers" (47, p. 307)—implying that the interpretation of the principle quoted above was too loose. Separation is consistent with some mixture, but not with too great a mixture.

Madison clarifies that difficulty by explaining what kind of partial agency or control is needed between the parts of government. Some such connections are necessary in order to maintain separation "in practice."

> It will not be denied that power is of an encroaching nature and that it ought to be effectually restrained from passing the limits assigned to it. After discriminating, therefore, in theory, the several classes of power, as they may in their nature be legislative, executive, or judiciary, the next and most difficult task is to provide some practical security for each, against the invasion of the others. What this security ought to be is the great problem to be solved. (48, p. 308)

Each power has a distinctive nature which may be discriminated (37, p. 228), but all powers share a common nature in being encroaching. Montesquieu's account of the excellence of separation was immediately followed by the statement that European monarchs have become despotic by "reuniting" all powers in their own person.[13] Separation is a desirable condition of the three powers, but it is always in danger, at least from the legislature and executive.[14] For this reason, the principle of separation of powers can be invoked by either branch in objecting that the acts of the other are encroachments. Montesquieu, in a nonpartisan spirit, catalogues ways in which each branch might destroy liberty by transgressing its natural boundaries.[15] But Madison says that in America's governments separation is more likely to be endangered by the legislature, which is "more powerful" and which "is everywhere extending the sphere of its activity and drawing all power into its impetuous vortex." Earlier Americans have been preoccupied with "the danger, to liberty, from the overgrown and all-grasping prerogative of an hereditary magistrate, supported and fortified by an hereditary branch of the legislative authority"; and have invoked separation of powers as an argument against monarchical domination. This caused them to neglect the other danger Montesquieu reported, and the one which Madison emphasizes, the "legislative usurpations, which, by assembling all power in the same hands, must lead to the same tyranny as is threatened by executive usurpations" (48, p. 309).

That the legislature is the more powerful branch is related to its control of the salaries of the other branches, and more importantly to its being "less susceptible of precise limits." The executive power is "within a narrower compass" and "more simple in its nature" (and the judiciary's function is "still less uncertain"). The legislature gives the law, and others follow the law; so encroachments by the legislature may be questions of "real nicety" (48, p. 310).

But Madison does not rely on this functional distinction in explaining the legislative "vortex." The legislature derives its strength less from the nature of legislation than from the nature of republican government. Encroachment by the executive is to be feared from a "hereditary monarch" with "numerous and extensive prerogatives," or in a democracy, where ambitious magistrates may "on some favorable emergency" take advantage of the people's "incapacity for regular deliberation and concerted measures."

> But in a representative republic where the executive magistracy is carefully limited, both in the extent and the duration of its power; and where the legislative power is exercised by an assembly, which is inspired by a supposed influence over the people with an intrepid confidence in its own strength; which is sufficiently numerous to feel all the passions which actuate a multitude, yet not so numerous as to be incapable of pursuing the objects of its passions by means which reason prescribes; it is against the enterprising ambition of this department that the people ought to indulge all their jealousy and exhaust all their precautions. (48, p. 309)

A representative republic is constructed with an eye on the dangers of kings, and thus carefully limits the executive's power. The representative legislature feels confident of its strength because of its "supposed influence over the people," a supposition the legislators may base on the fact that they influenced the people to elect them. A "multitude" of men can feel the passion of "enterprising ambition," and this multitude of legislators has the capacity to pursue that end. Precisely because the legislature seems closest to the people, it is most dangerous to the people; it sees its closeness as "influence" which it can use in the service of its own enterprising ambition.

Thus Madison shifts the subject from (1) separation of powers, to (2) practical security to preserve the separation of powers, to (3) practical security against legislative encroachments. But the danger under consideration is still "tyranny," i.e., a ruler who neither enforces the laws made by others nor relies on others to enforce his laws, but who can rule by himself for his own good and against the people's good. Madison points to a new potential tyrant, but he preserves separation of powers as a precaution taken by the people to prevent "oppression" by "rulers" (51, p. 323). He does not say separation should inhibit the people's wishes; it should rather protect them from the "enterprising ambition" of a few. This presentation justifies those who assert that separation of powers is not an undemocratic device,[16] although what follows in *Federalist* numbers 49 and 50 and later in the book must qualify that verdict.

The People

In *Federalist* 51, Madison outlines his own suggested "practical security" against legislative encroachments; but he first pauses in *Federalist* numbers 49 and 50 to consider a proposal by "[t]he author of the *Notes on the State of Virginia*" which "ought not to be overlooked" (49, p. 313). Jefferson's plan for Virginia's Constitution "appears ultimately to rely as a palladium to the weaker departments of power against the invasions of the stronger" on occasional conventions of the people. This proposal is hardly conspicuous in Jefferson's own text, was made some years before, and does not explicitly refer to preserving separation of powers but only to correcting "breaches of" the Constitution.[17] Madison's expansive discussion is thus on his own initiative, and addresses the question: Should the people be relied on to preserve separation of powers? Such a reliance seems "consonant" to "the republican theory":

As the people are the only legitimate fountain of power, and it is from them that the constitutional charter, under which the several branches of government hold their power, is derived, it seems strictly consonant to the republican theory to recur to the same original authority, not only whenever it may be necessary to enlarge, diminish, or new-model the powers of government, but also whenever any one of the departments may commit encroachments on the chartered authorities of the others. (49, pp. 313–14)

The "theory" that the people are the "fountain" of the "charter" is Lockean; Montesquieu did not suggest that separation comes from a charter granted by the people. Madison's response distinguishes alterations of the Constitution from enforcements of it. Certainly on "great and extraordinary occasions," the people should act as the "legitimate fountain of power" by the "constitutional road" of the amending process— just as on the *most* extraordinary occasions they may need to act on the unconstitutional "road" of revolution. But Madison suggests that questions about encroachments by one department or another will be quite "frequent" rather than extraordinary, and sees "insuperable objections" to relying on the people to decide them.

Madison first makes an objection which "may be thought to lie rather against the modification of the principle, than against the principle itself"; that is, that if (as in Jefferson's plan) two-thirds of two departments are required in order to call a popular convention, then one department can by the support of one-third of another protect its encroachments. The "modification" of the "principle" is the mechanism by which a convention is called. While Madison's objection "may be thought" to be remediable by a different mechanism, perhaps that objection in fact touches the principle itself. Advocates of the principle that the people shall judge may overlook the importance of when and by whom the people are called upon to judge.

Madison's second and third objections are general warnings of the dangers of frequent reconsideration by the people of their form of government (see p. 33 above), and restate *Federalist* 10's explanation of the connection between opinion and passion. Government rests on opinion, apparently the people's opinion that it is a good government. But their opinion will not be the "enlightened reason" of a "nation of philosophers." Madison does not refer here (as he did in *Federalist* 10) to the fallibility of men's reason, but to the fact that men are too "timid and cautious" to reason by themselves as a philosopher does. Opinions are fortified by a kind of group solidarity; this can take the form either of passionate partisanship in alliance with a group of living men, or of a "veneration" encouraged by numerous and ancient examples of men with the same opinion. To open constitutional questions arouses the "public passions" to take opinions on both sides in a "spirit of party." It also disrupts the prejudice of those who have assumed that all Americans have thought this a good government. Because men's opinions are not simply rational, "the most rational government will not find it a superfluous advantage to have the prejudices of the community on its side."

Madison applies the same understanding of men's passionate opinions when he says that the "greatest objection" to Jefferson's proposal is

> that the decisions which would probably result from such appeals would not answer the purpose of maintaining the constitutional equilibrium of the government. (49, p. 315)

Although the people may (*The Federalist* hopes) be willing to choose a government with a regular distribution of powers into the separate departments, they are unlikely to preserve the evenhanded spirit with which they chartered the government. Because of the "different situations" of the different departments, the people will be more likely to side with the legislature. The executive and judiciary are few and far from the people.

The members of the legislative department, on the other hand, are numerous. They are distributed and dwell among the people at large. Their connections of blood, of friendship, and of acquaintance embrace a great proportion of the most influential part of the society. The nature of their public trust implies a personal influence among the people, and that they are more immediately the confidential guardians of the rights and liberties of the people. With these advantages it can hardly be supposed that the adverse party would have an equal chance for a favorable issue. (49, p. 316)

The legislature will be more likely to prevail in an appeal to the people for the same reason that the legislature will be more likely to encroach in the first place. Its "confidence in its own strength" is not misplaced; its "supposed influence over the people" (48, p. 309) is often real influence. The legislators and their friends may even be elected by the people to the popular conventions which are to judge the legislature's conduct, and be the "leading characters, on whom everything depends in such bodies" (49, p. 316).

Madison's warning that the legislature's encroachments will have popular support may tempt those readers who remember *Federalist* 10 to conclude that he is really discussing the problem of a majority faction using legislative power to oppress the minority. But Madison himself does not mention that danger. His subject is the vulnerability of the *whole* people to the ambitious aims of political leaders who are able to "influence" them. One reason for this vulnerability is that the "tyrannical concentration" of power (48, p. 313) precedes the tyrannical exercise of that power, so that the danger of concentration may not be clear to the people at the time their trusted representatives are concentrating it. Madison also describes legislative encroachment stemming not from cleverly concealed ambition but from legislators "eagerly bent on some favorite object, and breaking through the restraints of the Constitution in pursuit of it" (50, p. 318). The object may also be a favorite of the people themselves, and its attractiveness may obscure the danger of concentrating power in pursuit of it. While separation of powers as a general arrangement protects the people, it may in particular cases frustrate their aims (if it is effective); thus Madison does not rely on the people to enforce separation.

But even if, in a constitutional dispute submitted to the people, a particularly flagrant legislature and particularly popular executive tipped the scales the other way, the question would not be decided on its "true merits." Madison says the spirit of pre-existing parties or of parties arising out of the question would dominate any popular convention's decision.

The heart of the problem is that the people are not a dispassionate "fountain" of authority which can judge according to the charter it grants. The people themselves retain enough authority under their charter to be partisans; they elect with varying degrees of immediacy those who exercise the authority specified in the charter, and will have passionate opinions about the men in office. The people assert their opinion when they vote and are encouraged by their authority as voters to form or hold opinions between elections as well; "an extinction of parties" "ought to be neither presumed nor desired" (50, p. 320). Thus when they act as the fountain of authority, the people's verdict on the authority of the departments will be tainted by their own part in the dispute; "The *passions*, . . . not the *reason*, of the public would sit in judgment" (49, p. 317). Republican political life stirs the passions of partisanship, and cannot hope to preserve the government's structure by a nonpartisan decision of the people. In *Federalist* 50 Madison reports Pennsylvania's experience with its Council of Censors; that attempt to have a popular judgment of a partisan struggle merely replicated the partisan struggle.

"Ambition Must Be Made to Counteract Ambition"

In *Federalist* 51 Madison presents his account of how the "necessary partition of power" can best be maintained. Because "exterior provisions" are inadequate, the government's "interior structure" must be such that its "constituent parts" can keep each other in their "proper places." Madison says this idea is "important" but that he will present only a "few general observations," not a "full development" of it.

To secure the "separate and distinct exercise of the different powers," "each department should have a will of its own," meaning that (insofar as possible) branches should not appoint each other or control each other's salaries. As to the former,

> Were this principle rigorously adhered to, it would require that
> all the appointments for the supreme executive, legislative, and
> judiciary magistracies should be drawn from the same fountain of
> authority, the people, through channels having no communication
> whatever with one another. Perhaps such a plan of constructing
> the several departments would be less difficult in practice than it
> may in contemplation appear. (51, p. 321)

This argument adheres not only to the principle that each department should have a will of its own but to the principle that the people are the "fountain of authority." Montesquieu, unconstrained by that principle, found that a hereditary monarch whose person is sacred has a sufficient will of his own to act separately. Montesquieu also insisted that different magistrates not be "of the same body [corps]."[18] Madison avoids uniting all three powers in the body of the people by "draw[ing]" each official from the people. Each department somehow has a "will of its own" rather than merely the will of the people which, one might think, could be transmitted through each of the separate channels. It seems that one drawn from the people necessarily differs from the people in having his own will; an example of this distinct will is the "enterprising ambition" Madison attributed to the popularly elected legislature. The people as a body exercise none of the three powers, but no power is assigned to a body independent of the people. Thus Madison's interpretation of separation of powers differs from theories of mixed government according to which the people's rule was mixed with ruling elements independent of them.

Madison admits that the proposed Constitution departs to some extent from the method he suggests; he also implies that not all of the departures were advisable. Thus "in practice" it might have been feasible to avoid the role of Congress in deciding close presidential elections.[19] The only departure Madison defends involves the judiciary, in which case a method of selection which involved the people rather than the other branches (1) might not have secured the "essential" "peculiar qualifications"; and (2) is largely unnecessary because the judiciary's permanent tenure destroys any sense of dependence on the appointing branches. He thus implies (1) that the "primary consideration" in the mode of appointment of the other branches is not simply the "qualifications" of their members, and (2) that each of those other branches with its impermanent tenure feels a dependence on its appointers which modifies the "will of its own."

If each branch has a will of its own, it will not be subject in making its decision to the "overruling influence" of another branch (48, p. 308), but it still might be annihilated against its will by the usurpations of a more powerful branch. Thus

> the great security against a gradual concentration of the several powers in the same department consists in giving to those who administer each department the necessary constitutional means and personal motives to resist encroachments of the others. (51, pp. 321–22)

Constitutional means of resistance must be *given* because not all of the departments possess such means as part of the functions naturally assigned to them by the separation of powers.[20] Thus, paradoxically, their powers can only be protected by being altered. Departures from the strict, functional separation of powers implied by the "maxim" are not only supported by precedent (as *Federalist* 47 argued), they are necessary to preserve any separation in practice. The "political truth" that concentration of all powers is tyranny requires modification of the "maxim" that these three specific powers must be separated (see p. 126 above).

Because resistance against encroachments requires effort, officers must be given "personal motives" to use the constitutional means they are given; and Madison's elaboration especially stresses the motives:

> The provision for defense must in this, as in all other cases, be made commensurate to the danger of attack. Ambition must be made to counteract ambition. The interest of the man must be connected with the constitutional rights of the place. (51, p. 322)

The danger of attack comes from ambition; the commensurate defense can therefore also come from ambition. The most likely danger of attack in republican government is, according to *Federalist* 48, from the enterprising ambition of the legislative department. This must be "counteract[ed]" by the creation of an ambitious executive. An unambitious executive might think his interest most prudently served by ingratiating surrenders to the legislative vortex. For this reason the "constitutional rights of the place" must be impressive enough that the executive's interest is to ambitiously defend and extend them. A constitution which enlarges the executive's powers thus both increases his means to resist and alters his motives. A more powerful office may attract more ambitious men or stimulate the ambition of its occupant or both. Because ambition is a love of power rather than a mere defensive tactic, the executive's ambition not only frustrates the legislature's ambition, it gives the legislature's ambition a useful function—frustrating the executive's ambition. There is a connection between the principle of ambition counteracting ambition and Madison's republican premise. Ambitions of popular representatives are not checked by a king or aristocracy secure in their power; they are checked by other ambitious men who are also striving for a power which they incompletely possess.

Madison appears to anticipate later critics who see in this principle a bleak, "Hobbesian" view of man: [21]

> It may be a reflection on human nature that such devices should be necessary to control the abuses of government. But what is government itself but the greatest of all reflections on human nature? If men were angels, no government would be necessary. If angels were to govern men, neither external nor internal controls on government would be necessary. (51, p. 322)

As the "greatest of all reflections on human nature," "government itself" surpasses Madison's proposals as a reflection on human nature. This is because Madison's view could be based on the premise that power corrupts; whereas the very fact of government suggests that men are corrupt even without power. Madison's language implies that the same nonangelic human quality which makes rulers dangerous—"ambition"—makes men need government in the first place.[22] Those who would like to adopt a more flattering view of human nature should not merely reject Madison's plan for "controls on government"; they must also deny the necessity of government altogether.

There is a further sense in which the necessity of "such devices" is a reflection on human nature. The need for "internal controls" reflects not only the need for controls but the failure, or insufficiency, of external controls, that is, controls by the people themselves.

> A dependence on the people is, no doubt, the primary control on the government; but experience has taught mankind the necessity of auxiliary precautions. (51, p. 322)

The "honorable determination" that men are capable of self-government might be thought to imply that a vigilant people armed with the power of elections could control the "abuses of government"; "experience" teaches a different "reflection on human nature." The ambition of rulers makes them "enterprising" in their encroachments; the people may not feel the personal motives to use their own means of resistance as strongly as ambitious men feel their personal motives to encroach. And encroachments in pursuit of a "favorite object" by their trusted legislators may not seem to the people to pose a danger of "assembling all power in the same hands."

Madison likens his suggestion to examples throughout the "whole system of human affairs, private as well as public." It is a "policy of supplying, by opposite and rival interests, the defect of better motives." Thus subordinate offices are arranged so that each will check the other. While their superiors might in theory be in a position to control these subordinates (just as the government in principle has a "dependence" on the people), the superiors may be otherwise occupied and can make their supervision easier by relying on these "inventions of prudence." Prudence tells a man or a people to expect other men to have interests of their own and to pursue them. In private affairs, for example, a buyer's economic interest will "counteract" and thereby moderate the effect of a seller's economic interest, to supply the "defect of" the "better motives" which would, if they existed, restrain the latter's greed. In public affairs, the Constitution's framers prudently invent and the people can prudently adopt arrangements which employ different ambitious men to resist one another's ambitious enterprises, and which do not rely on the people's prudence to detect and resist the danger in each case.

Because the legislature's natural functions and popular character make it "necessarily predominat[e]" (51, p. 322), its encroachment must be prevented not by other departments in the exercise of their natural functions, but by the division of the legislature and the fortification of the executive. The judicial branch is not mentioned in this discussion of ambition counteracting ambition, just as Montesquieu omitted it as "en quelque façon nulle"[23] in his account of the political struggles among the powers of government. It should be noted that a bicameral legislature is not required by the principle that the "legislative, executive, and judiciary departments ought to be separate and distinct" (47, p. 301); and an executive who is "fortified" by a power to veto legislation seems positively forbidden by a literal understanding of that principle. Madison says the legislature's two houses should be rendered

> by different modes of election and different principles of action, as little connected with each other as the nature of their common functions and their common dependence on the society will admit. (51, p. 322)

This means that *some* connection is the inevitable result both of the insistence on the republican principle and of the fact of a common function. If the two branches must agree in order to pass a law, the conduct and opinions of each clearly influence the other. Even if each has a "will of its own," it cannot exert its will on its own, and this fact will modify its will. More upsetting to the principle of separation of powers is that the share in legislation which the fortified executive's qualified veto gives him makes lawmaking a "common functio[n]" of the executive and legislature which makes them "connected with each other." The executive is no longer a neutral outsider who evenly applies laws made by a separate body; he has a hand in the making of those laws, so the laws reflect his own wishes to some degree. Since the veto probably does not give the executive enough influence over the legislature to dictate the laws altogether, there remains a functional separation which discourages enactment of tyrannical laws. But while the veto gives the executive the "constitutional means and personal motives" to defend himself against legislative encroachments—and thereby protect the public from the eventual consequences of a tyrannical concentration of power—it also gives him the means to do much more than that. He has a direct voice in lawmaking; and we must consider later whether the personal motives which encourage resistance to legislative usurpations are supplemented by personal motives to use well the considerable additional power conferred by this "constitutional means" (see chapter 7, below).

Agreeing with the "truth" that "the accumulation of all powers . . . in the same hands . . . may justly be pronounced the very definition of tyranny," Madison transforms the maxim of separation of powers into the maxim that "[a]mbition must be made to counteract ambition" by focusing on the inability of prescribed powers to sustain themselves against the human passion of ambition. In a republican government, the legislature is inherently best situated to formulate ambitious enterprises. Giving the executive a share in the legislative function (i.e., the veto) would be a more convincing solution to the problem of the legislative vortex if the legislative function were the cause of the legislative vortex. But the legislature's primary advantage is in the principle of republican government, which makes the legislators close to the people and justifiably confident of popular support. Must the executive imitate that closeness to be a match for the legislature's strength? That conclusion is suggested by proponents of a more popularized executive. An alternative conclusion would be that what the executive lacks in popularity and hence in confidence about his prospects of success, he might make up in the greater incentive which the possibility of succeeding *by himself* would offer (see below, chapter 7, section on "Responsibility and Reputation"). Because he is in a position to be ambitious by himself, the president is less tempted to join in the collective enterprises of the legislature.

Minorities

Madison concludes *Federalist* 51 with "two considerations" which place America's system "in a very interesting point of view"—i.e., which bear no obvious relation to what has just been discussed. Because of these "considerations" *Federalist* 51 is often considered a synopsis of the book. The first consideration develops a parallel between the division of power into departments of the government, and the division of power between the state and federal governments. Ambition can be made to counteract ambition both within and between the two governments, offering a "double security" to the rights of the people (51, p. 323).

The second consideration is a long paragraph in which Madison recapitulates some major arguments from *Federalist* 10. He begins:

It is of great importance in a republic not only to guard the society against the oppression of its rulers, but to guard one part of
the society against the injustice of the other part. (51, p. 323)

The preceding discussion has been concerned with oppression by rulers.
Constructing departments in which ambition will counteract ambition
will make the government less likely to act, as a government, in a manner
oppressive to the people considered as a whole. But because all departments are "dependent" on "the society," which Madison tells us means
in practice "the majority," the rulers might still unitedly serve a majority's
unjust inclinations. While this subject had been treated impressively in
Federalist 10, Madison's recapitulation makes explicit the contrast between his approach ("Extend the sphere") and a traditional nonrepublican approach to the same problem—that is, mixed government or
monarchy.

I suggest that this last paragraph of *Federalist* 51 is related to the
preceding discussion of the separation of powers in the following way.
Madison had given separation of powers a purely republican interpretation, as if that doctrine's intentions were fully consonant with popular
government. And insofar as a fortified republican executive can be given
the "ambition" sufficient to replace the monarch's power, the republi-
canization of separation of powers seems plausible. But Montesquieu's
presentation argues that the separation of legislative, executive, and
judicial powers is not by itself enough to make men feel safe; and indeed
by the end of the long chapter in which Montesquieu explains England's
separation of powers, when he refers to the "three powers" he means
the king, House of Commons, and House of Lords.[24] A House of Lords
is necessary because

> There are always in a State men distinguished by birth, riches or
> honors; but if they were mingled among the people, and if they
> had but one voice like the others, the common liberty would be
> their slavery, and they would have no interest in defending it, be-
> cause most of the resolutions would be against them. The part
> that they have in legislation must therefore be proportioned to
> the other advantages which they have in the State; which will oc-
> cur if they form a body which has the right to stop the enter-
> prises of the people, as the people have the right to stop theirs.[25]

Only if this minority controls a separate house by which to stop the
people's (i.e., the majority's) enterprises can it enjoy the tranquillity of
spirit and feeling of safety which all men deserve.

Madison's coda to *Federalist* 51 addresses this issue which the repub-
licanized separation of powers does not address. Madison states the prob-

lem more generally; rather than an aristocracy being at the mercy of the people, any minority's rights will be insecure. "There are but two methods of providing against this evil. . . ." The second is that of *Federalist* 10, which I have already discussed; the first is "by creating a will in the community independent of the majority—that is, of the society itself." Society *is* its majority in that society's will can only be the majority's will. An "independent" will is found

> in all governments possessing an hereditary or self-appointed authority. This, at best, is but a precarious security; because a power independent of the society may as well espouse the unjust views of the major as the rightful interests of the minor party, and may possibly be turned against both parties. (51, p. 324)

By saying this independent will would "espouse" certain views rather than that it would impose them, Madison suggests that the government would "posses[s] an hereditary or self-appointed authority" in the sense of including it among its parts, rather than in the sense of having it as its foundation. "The government of England, which has one republican branch only, combined with an hereditary aristocracy and monarchy" (39, pp. 240–41) fits this description. The hereditary (and ultimately self-appointed) authority of the king and House of Lords can secure the rights of the minority against the enterprises of the republican branch. But this security is "precarious"; the independent authority might "espouse the unjust views of the major . . . party." One explanation for that appears in *Federalist* 58, where Madison describes the "continual triumph of the British House of Commons over the other branches of the government" (p. 359). While an independent branch might be awed by the major party, it might also turn against "both parties," presumably in support of its *own* unjust views. The one or few who are the independent authority may not always be the same minority as the one whose rights are endangered. For this reason,

> In a free government the security for civil rights must be the same as that for religious rights. It consists in the one case in the multiplicity of interests, and in the other in the multiplicity of sects. (51, p. 324)

England has a "free government" (see 9, p. 72); but while its mixed government may protect the aristocracy, it cannot be counted on to protect religious minorities. English religious rights are secured, if they are, by a multiplicity of sects. Because there is no single vulnerable group in need of protection, mixed government is a "precarious" security for minority rights.

Even so, Madison proceeds to warn the "sincere and considerate friends of republican government" that in a contracted sphere even that precarious security would be necessary. Because "the best security, under the republican forms, for the rights of every class of citizens, will be diminished," the "stability and independence of some member of the government, the only other security, must be proportionally increased." This statement leaves beautifully ambiguous whether stability and independence are an inferior security "under the republican forms" or are a security inconsistent with the republican forms; the context suggests that the friends of republican government will only reluctantly accept those qualities. But while republicans reject the stability of hereditary rulers and the independence of self-appointed ones, Madison states the matter as one of proportion, as if stability and independence can be found in different degrees, and not only in the (intendedly) unqualified stability of heredity and unqualified independence of self-appointment. Later in the book, a case is made for the "stability" of the Senate (62, pp. 380–81; 63, p. 385), the "independence of the judges" (78, p. 469), and a president able to resist a "transient" popular "impulse" (71, p. 432).

While Madison expects that republicans would rather accept an extended sphere than accept governmental stability and independence, some might accept neither. In explicit support of the former, and implicitly in support of some portion of the latter, Madison emphatically states the end which both of them serve:

> Justice is the end of government. It is the end of civil society. It
> ever has been and ever will be pursued until it be obtained, or
> until liberty be lost in the pursuit. (51, p. 324)

Justice, meaning the protection of each man's faculties, is the end of civil society because men leave the state of nature so as to protect their faculties. Men use their natural liberty to seek protection for their faculties by forming a civil society and instituting a government; and if the justice they seek is not "obtained," they use whatever political liberty they have to seek a more efficacious protection. Madison's use of the passive voice conceals who it is who is pursuing justice; is it not the "society," "that is," by Madison's admission, "the majority"? One might think the pursuit would end when the majority has used its liberty to secure *its* faculties, by enlarging its own authority.[26] But

> In a society under the forms of which the stronger faction can
> readily unite and oppress the weaker, anarchy may as truly be
> said to reign as in a state of nature, where the weaker individual

is not secured against the violence of the stronger; and as, in the latter state, even the stronger individuals are prompted, by the uncertainty of their condition, to submit to a government which may protect the weak as well as themselves; so, in the former state, will the more powerful factions or parties be gradually induced, by a like motive, to wish for a government which will protect all parties, the weaker as well as the more powerful. (51, pp. 324–25)

Just as Locke likened absolute monarchy to a state of nature, because there is no judge between the monarch and the people,[27] Madison says that unimproved popular governments are like a state of nature, because there is no judge between the majority and the minority. The most successful majority faction will—like the strongest man in the state of nature—feel an "uncertainty" about its condition, stemming from the fear that the weaker will find a way to fight back.

Because the majority cannot rest secure with unjust majority rule, society's majority and minority will pursue the justice of a "government which will protect all parties." Men need liberty to pursue justice, and therefore the pursuit ends if "liberty be lost in the pursuit." Liberty would be lost if men chose an unfree government which they thought would protect them; or if their pursuit of justice inadvertently gave occasion for a forcible or fraudulent usurpation. The former case would exhibit the "folly" Madison spoke of in *Federalist* 10: abolishing liberty so as to extinguish factious oppression. Yet, Madison says, if Rhode Island were by itself, factious rule in that small sphere would lead men to call for "some power altogether independent of the people" (51, p. 325). Men's attempt to secure themselves against injustice might lead them to institute not just the precarious security of a mixed government which combines liberty with stable and independent members of the government, but perhaps even an "altogether independent" government, one in which "liberty" was altogether "lost."[28]

Surrendering liberty in pursuit of justice has the disadvantage that if the unfree government chosen turns out badly, the further pursuit of justice is foreclosed by lack of liberty (except if a "lost" liberty can be reclaimed in revolution).[29] But *Federalist* 10 called abolishing liberty "folly" for a more fundamental reason. If justice means the protection of men's faculties, and those faculties properly understood include the political faculties which men exercise in political life, then liberty is part of justice and cannot be sacrificed to it. By invoking the "state of nature" Madison calls attention away from men's honorable political capacities toward men's unexalted necessities. Weakness makes men vulnerable to violence and strength does not dispel uncertainty. Madison does not, as Hobbes does, urge men to swallow their pride, look to their necessities, and choose an independent government; he rather warns them that those necessities will ultimately make themselves felt and "gradually" induce men to "wish for"[30] such a government.[31] The honorable determination that men are capable of self-government, if it rejects as a matter of honor the improvements and auxiliary precautions of modern political science, is a pride which precedes a fall. The extended sphere proportionally diminishes the necessity for the governmental stability and independence which offend republican pride. But republicans who both befriend the extended sphere and can live with some degree of stability and independence as "auxiliary precautions"[32] will avoid the mortification of a later resort to more permanent and more independent innovations or even an "altogether independent" government.

The explicit point of *Federalist* 51's last paragraph is the importance of the extended sphere in protecting against oppressive majorities, as distinguished from the protection against oppressive government offered by the separation or distribution of powers. These are two different issues, but the analysis is similar. In each case the problem is that a society of men cannot act as a whole in ruling itself; it is divided into majority and minority, and into rulers and ruled—however much the principles of popular government might mean to soften the latter distinction, and however much theorists of republican simplicity might hope to eradicate the former. The remedy for the problems posed by those ineradicable divisions is a further division of the more dangerous part—multiplying interested or passionate groups in society, and multiplying ambitious men in government. In both cases the effect intended is a negative one, the prevention of mischief.

But because *Federalist* 51 focuses on the prevention of "tyranny" (47, p. 301) or "oppression" or "injustice" (51, p. 323), it cannot be considered a summary of the whole book. *Federalist* 51's final paragraph restates *Federalist* 10's argument that a multiplicity of parties discourages injustice, but omits *Federalist* 10's more positive suggestion that representatives who are fit characters can serve the public good. Similarly, its discussion of the branches of government considers their relative dangerousness but abstracts from the qualities and even, for the most part, the powers of those branches. The Constitution's arrangement of the government's branches has a positive intention which is developed in the later numbers of the book: to contribute "energy" and "stability," so as to constitute a "good" or "useful" government rather than merely a safe one.

·[Six]·

Representation

Madison's principle that ambition must be made to counteract ambition does not by itself give much indication of what sort of "departments" the government's power should be distributed among. *Federalist* 52 begins the "particular examination" of the government's parts with the least controversial part, the House of Representatives. The House is the branch which is most consonant with the "genius of republican liberty" according to which power must be derived from the people and held for a short duration by a number of hands (37, p. 227). But the Anti-Federalists charge that two years and sixty-five pairs of hands are too long and too few, and the main theme of *The Federalist*'s account of the House is that these arrangements are indeed "safe to the liberties of the people." A second claim is that these arrangements are "useful to the affairs of the public" (53, p. 336).

"Safe to the Liberties of the People": Representation of the Whole

I should first reiterate the meaning of "liberty" as that word is used by *The Federalist*. The fundamental meaning of liberty is what is today usually called "political liberty," as distinguished from the "private liberty" or "civil liberty" which governments may secure for their citizens. Men are free when they engage in political life—not when they are merely benignly neglected. Liberty exists in a government in which the people or their elected representatives have at least a share in rule. Thus both republican government—in which *all* power is derived from the people—and England's mixed monarchy—in which one branch of the legislature is derived from the people—are "free" governments.

This association of "liberty" with a form of government rather than with a government's protection of individual men was criticized in advance by both Hobbes and Montesquieu. The latter said that one should not confuse the people's "power" with their "liberty."[1] It is true that in discussing Montesquieu's account of the separation of powers, Madison seemed to adopt temporarily a Montesquieuan view of the "liberty" being secured as the individual's freedom from fear of his rulers (see p. 128 above)—although one might, in a less Montesquieuan spirit, read the danger which the "accumulation of all powers" poses to "liberty" as a danger from a usurping branch of government to the people's *political* role as electors.

The liberty which requires that the people or their elected representatives have at least a share in rule should ensure that government will act not for its own good but for the public good. In a "pure democracy" the people may be expected to pursue the public good (see p. 92 above); "the people commonly *intend* the PUBLIC GOOD" (71, p. 432). If the people can be considered as a whole, as a "great body" (57, p. 351), the public good is their own good. Representation, as a "substitute for a meeting of the citizens in person" (52, p. 327), is intended to replicate the people's concern with their own good. Even in England's mixed monarchy, the fact that one branch of the legislature is representative of the people means that the government as a whole has "a common interest with the people" (52, p. 327), because the government as a whole cannot govern the people without the consent of its representative part.[2] A free government—a government wholly or in part composed of or representative of the people—can therefore be expected to be what Aristotle called a "right" form of government, which rules in the interests of the ruled.[3]

As we have already seen, and will see again, this requirement of "liberty" does not solve all the problems of government. Even if a free government feels a "common interest" with the whole people and intends to serve the public good, it is not necessarily capable of wisely carrying out its good intentions (see below, chapter 7). And the people or their representatives might be divided in ways which permit a free government to work in the interest of only the larger part of the people, or even to deliberately abuse the smaller part (see above, chapter 3). But while these are important difficulties, one should not skip too rapidly over the problem of preserving liberty in a representative government, a problem taken very seriously by both *The Federalist* and its opponents. Representation is a "substitute" for an assembled people seeking its own good, which means that it is not quite the original thing. The rulers are dependent on the people, but no matter how short the leash of dependence they are still only a few of the people. For the same reasons that the people intend the public good, these few might be expected to intend their own good. Most self-serving policies by this few (for example, taking bribes or embezzling public revenues) could be detected and punished at the next election. But one self-serving policy in particular would evade this control: cancel the next election, and "boldly resolve to perpetuate themselves in office by one decisive act of usurpation" (60, p. 372). Election fraud or other policies might be devised to accomplish the same result. And, of course, once the representatives were freed entirely from their "dependence," other policies in the interest of the rulers would easily follow.

For this reason, the most important claim the Anti-Federalists make about the proposed Constitution's scheme of representation is that it is unsafe to the liberties of the people. This means not that particular private liberties ("rights") are in danger from particular policies, but rather that the representatives will be unfaithful, betray the people, and attempt "innovations" which will put them in control of an "unlimited" government, that is, a government unlimited by popular elections (53, p. 332; 55, p. 344; 57, pp. 351–52). While one might think the extremism of those Anti-Federalists who claim that the plan will result in "tyranny" makes *The Federalist*'s task too easy, *The Federalist* suggests that such extreme complaints may be the most respectable opposition position, since the admitted urgency of America's situation under the Articles of Confederation requires that this proposed improvement either be adopted or be shown to be, not imperfect, but positively pernicious (66, p. 401). And Madison's extensive arguments that the proposed institutions are safe to liberty, that is, that they will not altogether escape from popular control and thereby extinguish their "common interest" with the people, were not as modest in their claims as they might appear in light of their retrospective vindication. That America's popular elections have not been abolished or fixed or ignored is a success too obvious to be admired today, but that result could not be taken for granted in 1787.

Madison defends both the two-year term and the relatively modest size of the House of Representatives as safe to liberty. Contrary to the maxim that where annual elections end tyranny begins, "the period within which human virtue can bear the temptations of power" is not naturally connected with the sun or seasons, but "lies within extremes," and varies according to other circumstances (53, pp. 330–31). Power tempts rulers to enlarge their own power at the people's expense, but past experience shows "human virtue" withstanding the temptations of even a seven-year term—as in the case of American "representatives of the people" who prior to the American Revolution showed a "spirit and conduct" favorable to the public liberties (52, p. 329).

Similarly, there is no "precise solution" (55, p. 341) possible to the question of how many representatives are needed for "safety"; history shows that fewer than the House's initial sixty-five have sufficed. Moreover, Madison emphasizes that the proposed House of Representatives has less power than the legislatures he compares it with, and will be more "watched" by the state legislators than those legislators are by anyone else. And the House will not face those means of seduction which diverted Britain's popular representatives from the proper spirit (52, p. 330). Madison thus implies that the House's "temptations of power" might lead the House, not to attempt a spontaneous assertion of its own oligarchic rule, but to enlist in the cause of other men better situated to gain absolute power. These would include foreigners, but Madison says the House is less in a position to be bribed by foreign gold than was the Continental Congress, which had a spotless record. As to American seducers, no private citizens are wealthy enough to bribe the House with their personal fortunes. Those who might be most suspected are the "more permanent branches" (52, p. 330) of the new American government—just as the king in England corrupted the Commons. But the Senate and president have no real means of seduction because of the Constitution's separation of powers and particularly its exclusion of Congressmen from most appointed offices. To suppose that the small number of offices to which Congressmen could be appointed "would be sufficient to purchase the guardians of the people, selected by the people themselves, is to renounce every rule by which events ought to be calculated, and to substitute an indiscriminate and unbounded jealousy, with which all reasoning must be vain."

> The sincere friends of liberty who give themselves up to the extravagancies of this passion are not aware of the injury they do their own cause. As there is a degree of depravity in mankind which requires a certain degree of circumspection and distrust, so there are other qualities in human nature which justify a certain portion of esteem and confidence. Republican government presupposes the existence of these qualities in a higher degree than any other form. Were the pictures which have been drawn by the political jealousy of some among us faithful likenesses of the human character, the inference would be that there is not sufficient virtue among men for self-government; and that nothing less than the chains of despotism can restrain them from destroying and devouring one another. (55, pp. 345–46)

Human nature is a mixture of "qualities." *Federalist* 37 described the difficulty of specifying precisely what qualities characterize any object as extensive and complicated as man; thus human nature cannot be known with great precision. Republican (i.e., representative) government must presuppose some grounds for "confidence" in human nature because it must assume that those elected will have "virtue" enough to withstand whatever temptations are offered by whatever power they have. If men are utterly depraved, there would be no one worthy of being elected to any office, that is, trusted with any power however widely shared, closely watched, or limited in time. But Madison extends this point to refer not only to the virtue or depravity of the representatives but also to the virtue or depravity of the people as a whole. A depraved people is incapable of "self-government," a term which emphasizes the role of the electors rather than of the elected; they need the "chains of despotism" to restrain them from "destroying and devouring one another." The view that elected representatives will be depraved implies that the people are not able or not inclined to elect good men, or that there are no good men at all. A despot can be depraved while restraining the depravity of others, since he may take anything he wants for himself. An "honorable determination" about man's nature underlies the attachment to republican government.

But how can reason discriminate the proper boundaries of jealousy so as to avoid "indiscriminate and unbounded" jealousies? Only a few papers earlier, Madison called attention to the "defect of better motives" which reflects unfavorably on human nature (51, p. 322). That analysis is indeed what underlies some of the safeguards Madison cites to show that the House is safe to liberty. The unreasonable, extravagant jealousy which occasions Madison's rebuke is the fear that the House can be seduced by the Senate's or president's offer of a few offices. Madison does not say it is unreasonable to think men can be bought, but that it is unreasonable to think they can be bought cheaply. The division of branches was intended to make "[a]mbition . . . counteract ambition." It may be precisely the ambition of Congressmen which makes them immune to the paltry seductions which their would-be corruptors can offer. This suggestion is supported in the course of Madison's systematic account of five sources which secure the "fidelity" of representatives to the people. After noting that a representative may be "somewhat distinguished" by the qualities which the voters thought he had when selecting him, and will probably feel "grateful," Madison turns for his third point to a motive "of a more selfish nature."

His pride and vanity attach him to a form of government which favors his pretensions and gives him a share in its honors and distinctions. Whatever hopes or projects might be entertained by a few aspiring characters, it must generally happen that a great proportion of the men deriving their advancement from their influence with the people would have more to hope from a preservation of the favor than from innovations in the government subversive of the authority of the people. (57, p. 352)

For most men, the prospect of a personal ascendancy does not exist, and their "pride and vanity" will resist being the ill-paid tool of another man's usurpation. The same ambition which calls for "circumspection and distrust" is grounds for "confidence" because those who are ambitious will be circumspect regarding the ambitions of others.[4]

Madison lists two more motives to fidelity. Fourth is the "restraint of frequent elections," which reminds representatives of their "dependence on the people." As time erodes their grateful sentiments, it engenders sentiments anticipating reelection or rejection.[5] Finally, the House is restrained from "oppressive measures" by the fact that

they can make no law which will not have its full operation on themselves and their friends, as well as on the great mass of the society. (57, p. 352)

This is the contribution Locke said the separation of powers makes to the quality of laws. This "has always been deemed one of the strongest bonds by which human policy can connect the rulers and the people together." This connection does not result from the scheme of representation as such, but from the scheme of the separation of powers, according to which the executive applies the laws to all. Locke observed that the legislators "themselves" are bound by the laws,[6] while Madison here refers to "themselves and their friends," and *Federalist* 35 refers to themselves and their "posterity" (p. 216). These additions make the legislator's motive not simply selfish, while at the same time showing that sympathetic ties of family and friendship are not "bonds" with "the people," unless it can be ensured that the laws which apply to the people also apply to those few.[7] But Madison senses that it might be asked what prevents the legislature from exempting "themselves and a particular class of the society" from the law as part of the law (which exemption the simply separate executive could not prevent but only enforce).

I answer: the genius of the whole system; the nature of just and constitutional laws; and, above all, the vigilant and manly spirit which actuates the people of America—a spirit which nourishes freedom, and in return is nourished by it. (57, p. 353)

If the people's manly spirit can manage to prevent this specific abuse, the mechanism of separation of powers can ensure that other laws will reflect a "communion of interests" between rulers and ruled (57, p. 352). The people's freedom to elect is not merely a fact for the representative to keep in mind but an influence on the people's own "spirit." The spirit of republican liberty is the honorable assertion by the people that they and no one else can claim a right to rule. This spirit should make the people alert to a "discriminatio[n]" by the legislature in favor of itself and its friends, which smacks of a claim to rule by a few. Madison had said that the representatives will tend to support a government which favors their "pretensions." He also says that the proposed scheme of representation is impartial to the "pretensions" of all classes of citizens (57, p. 351). A pretension, as *The Federalist* seems to use the word, is a claim to rule. The people—like the representatives—find representation favorable to their "pretensions." Elective representation, even while avoiding the direct rule by the people of a pure democracy, keeps the people's pretensions very much alive—which means the people will be "vigilant and manly" if the representatives visibly abandon their "communion of interests and sympathy of sentiments" with the people.

Madison concludes his account of the motives to fidelity with a summary list—"Duty, gratitude, interest, ambition itself"—and then cautions:

> It is possible that these may all be insufficient to control the caprice and wickedness of men. But are they not all that government will admit, and that human prudence can devise? (57, p. 353)

These motives may be of insufficient strength or found in too small a supply to control human wickedness. Madison's admission is consistent with the fact that the "existence of . . . qualities" necessary to republican government is a "presuppos[ition]," an "honorable determination." Even if the "unbounded jealousy" Madison criticizes might seem to be warranted by evidence of human depravity together with man's inability to see precisely the characters or boundaries of natural objects, that skepticism leads to despair of the possibility of self-government.[8] Experience leads Madison to distrust human motives and to devise institutional checks; an "honorable determination" supplies the boundary to that distrust which reason alone cannot supply. The "human prudence" which thinks of all the checks it can is guided by a human pride which asserts rather than deduces and therefore hopes rather than knows that self-government is possible.

"Useful to the Affairs of the Public": Representation of the Parts

Besides being "faithful" and "safe to the liberties of the people," the House of Representatives meets another standard; it is "useful."[9] While its safety is a matter of embodying the people's own intentions, its usefulness depends on its own qualities which distinguish it from the people. Madison summarizes both elements:

> The aim of every political constitution is, or ought to be, first to obtain for rulers men who possess most wisdom to discern, and most virtue to pursue, the common good of the society; and in the next place, to take the most effectual precautions for keeping them virtuous whilst they continue to hold their public trust. (57, p. 350)

The rulers' wisdom cannot be enforced by the precautions which attempt to preserve their virtue, and both virtue and wisdom need to be "obtain[ed]" in the first place. Thus election is an attempt to select "rulers" with these useful qualities. Madison cautiously specifies that "the elective mode of obtaining rulers is the characteristic policy of republican government," without assuring us that this mode does indeed obtain the "most wisdom" and the "most virtue." It will obtain those "whose merit may recommend [them] to the esteem and confidence of [their] country," and thereby win the people's "judgment" and "inclination" (57, p. 351). The constitutional qualifications for Congressmen are deliberately relaxed so that the House will be "open to merit of every description, whether native or adoptive, whether young or old, and without regard to poverty or wealth, or to any particular profession of religious faith" (52, p. 326). The litany of alternatives should not distract us from the word "merit." "[M]erit of every description" means that no particular assumptions about who is meritorious will be imposed on the electors; but however the people's judgment or inclination may diverge from obtaining the most wisdom and virtue, the people will be seeking some merit which distinguishes the representative from a citizen chosen at random.

Madison also defends as "useful" the two-year term and the size of the House of Representatives. A two-year term is better than one year because it makes travel easier and successful election fraud more punishable, thereby encouraging "fit men" to seek office and discouraging the sinister (53, p. 335). Above all, it is useful in improving the representatives' "knowledge":

No man can be a competent legislator who does not add to an upright intention and a sound judgment a certain degree of knowledge of the subjects on which he is to legislate. (53, p. 332)

This knowledge is most obtained by experience in office. While a state legislator's one-year term may be sufficient, given the natural acquaintance men have with local affairs, a member of the House will need to learn about the other states and about foreign affairs. Madison also raises the question of "knowledge" when he states an Anti-Federalist objection to the *size* of the House as follows:

that they will not possess a proper knowledge of the local circumstances of their numerous constituents. . . . (55, p. 341)

Madison's reply is that the House is sufficiently large to be properly knowledgeable, because there is not so much diversity within each state relevant to federal legislation as to require a more numerous representation. Each representative can be well "acquainted with the interests and circumstances of his constituents" (56, p. 346), and communicate that knowledge to the other representatives.

In this argument, Madison displays what was invisible in his argument that the House is safe to the liberties of the people: that is, that neither the House nor the people is simply a whole. Representatives are not simply representatives of "the people," of "the United States," or of "their numerous constituents"; each representative has "his constituents," who have "interests and circumstances" peculiar to them (56, p. 346). Madison's presentation treats the diversity of the people as raising a problem of knowledge. Each representative can bring with him a knowledge of his constituents' circumstances and interests, and communicate it to all of the representatives (56, p. 348), with the result that the "House of Representatives" as a whole will "possess a due knowledge of the interests of its constituents" (56, p. 346). To wisely pursue the public good requires a knowledge of the country's diversity. Thus in Madison's account a "proper representation" of particular "interests" means to *report* those interests to other representatives who will need knowledge of them in order to act competently as "impartial guardians of a common interest" (46, p. 297).

But, as Madison admits, such guardians will at least be tempted to be less than impartial. The problem did not appear with reference to the safety of liberty, because liberty is an object favorable to the rights and pretensions of the people as a whole. The problem of liberty arises because representative government divides the whole people into electors and elected, a division that must be bridged by the motives to "fidelity" felt by the latter. But when the representatives do something useful, they reveal that the people are not a whole to begin with. The "great body" of the people consists of many bodies, and the legislative body reflects that fact.

> There is sufficient diversity in the state of property, in the genius, manners, and habits of the people of the different parts of the Union to occasion a material diversity of disposition in their representatives towards the different ranks and conditions in society. (60, p. 367)

If representatives have an "immediate dependence" on the people (52, p. 327), they will be safe to the liberty the people as a whole want, but may also be partial to what is useful to the part of the people they depend on. This would seem to detract from the "merit" which makes them useful to the people as a whole.

Hamilton discussed the relation of representation to the people's diversity in *Federalist* 35. He began with a beautifully constructed statement of an Anti-Federalist complaint against the small size of the House:

> that the House of Representatives is not sufficiently numerous for the reception of all the different classes of citizens in order to combine the interests and feelings of every part of the community, and to produce a true sympathy between the representative body and its constituents. (35, p. 214)

The two alleged purposes of a large House reflect the two problems of representation I have discussed. The second is the "sympathy" between the representative body—considered as a whole—and "its constituents"—considered as a whole. The first recognizes that the constituents are not a whole but are a "community" with "part[s]," and that the parts have different "interests and feelings." Representation must somehow "combine" these parts.

The Anti-Federalist objection is "specious and seducing" and "well calculated to lay hold of the prejudices of those to whom it is addressed." It is addressed to the people, who may think the House of Representatives should resemble the people's own largeness and diversity. But Hamilton says the argument is erroneous:

> The object it seems to aim at is, in the first place, impracticable, and in the sense in which it is contended for, is unnecessary. (35, p. 214)

It is "impracticable" to receive all classes, and it is unnecessary "in the sense . . . contended for," i.e., in the sense in which Hamilton stated the

Anti-Federalist objection. If a scheme of representation need only "combine" the community's parts and ensure "sympathy" between representatives and constituents, a reception of all classes is unnecessary. But if representation is understood in a different "sense"—as creating an accurate replica of the people meeting in person—then a reception of all classes would be necessary.

Hamilton's argument for the impracticality of all classes being received in the House is not based on the most obvious objection—that there will be too many classes to fit (a point Hamilton saves for *Federalist* 36)—but on a recognition of certain major classes and an analysis of their likely voting behavior. Where the people's votes are "free,'" three types of men will generally be elected: merchants, elected by merchants, manufacturers, and mechanics; landed men, elected by a united bloc from the wealthiest landlord to the poorest tenant; and members of the learned profession, chosen by their peers and by others. Hamilton's account of voting resembles Madison's later emphasis on the people judging and inclining to "merit," but admits that the voters seek more than merit. Mechanics and manufacturers, because their businesses are intimately related to commerce and because they see that merchants have certain "acquired endowments" useful in a "deliberative assembly," "are aware that . . . their interests can be more effectually promoted by the merchant than by themselves." Thus they seek a kind of merit which can "promot[e]" their interests and combat any "spirit which might happen to infuse itself into the public councils, unfriendly to the manufacturing and trading interests." Landed owners and tenants will elect some "landholder" "in whom they have the most confidence," who will "know and feel whatever will promote or injure that species of property" (35, pp. 214–16).

The electors' search for "merit", i.e., the merit of being able to protect or promote their interests, reduces the variety of representatives. Mechanics and manufacturers seem to overlook the very real "rivalships" among themselves (36, p. 218) when they vote for merchants, apparently because they cannot find the requisite "acquired endowments" among men who share their narrower interest and might be expected to prosecute their rivalships. Similarly, landholders of all kinds will seek a landholder in whom they have "confidence," rather than insisting on one with a particular quantity of land (35, p. 215). The shortage of talented proponents for interests more narrowly understood may contribute to the possibility of "combin[ing]" interests.

Hamilton then describes how these likely representatives will serve the interests which elected them. But he suggests that the elected may moderate the impulses of their electors. The landed representative will "from his own interest in that species of property, be sufficiently prone to resist every attempt to prejudice or encumber it" (35, p. 216). While he knows and feels what will "promote or injure" the landed interest, Hamilton says he will resist injuries but does not say he will sponsor promotion. And the elected merchant will "understand and be disposed to cultivate, as far as may be proper, the interests of the mechanic and manufacturing arts to which his commerce is so nearly allied." In describing the impulses of the merchant's electors, Hamilton did not mention the limits of propriety.

Representation can combine the people's interests if those interests are broadly conceived—e.g., as "the mechanic and manufacturing arts" (35, p. 216), rather than as "the linen manufacturer" (36, p. 218)—and if representatives can moderate the impulses of those interests. Hamilton's rather optimistic account of this moderation in *Federalist* 35 may be due to his charitable assumption that the Anti-Federalist complaint is on behalf of interests which seek only their "proper" promotion or protection. The question of why representatives of interests are not more aggressively partisan recalls Madison's account in *Federalist* 10, according to which (1) among a large variety of interests, any interest is more likely to be a minority and therefore unable to have its way, and (2) in the best case, representatives will be "fit characters" who can "refine and enlarge" the public views. Hamilton later reports that the mercantile class in America is a clear minority (60, p. 369); this would enforce circumspection in its representatives' attempts to promote it.[10] As to the landed majority, which might be more capable of causing an "improper bias" in the legislature,[11] Hamilton echoes Madison's suggestion about "fit characters." Men who are "accustomed to investigate the sources of public prosperity upon a large scale" will be "convinced of the utility of commerce."

> The importance of commerce, in the view of revenue alone, must effectually guard it against the enmity of a body which would be continually importuned in its favor by the urgent calls of public necessity. (60, p. 370)

Hamilton shows some confidence that interests can be reconciled by representatives who think about public "prosperity" or at least public "necessity." This reconciliation is possible because enlightenment teaches that commerce is beneficial to all interests (12, pp. 91–92), and also that the most productive tax is the least burdensome (35, p. 217). Hamilton's prediction that some men of "the learned professions" will be elected to the legislature and act as "impartial arbiter[s]" between the other interests according to their view of the "general interests of the society" provides some basis for expecting enlightened representatives. These learned men "form no distinct interest in society," probably because there are so few of them that "little need be observed" about them (35, pp. 215–16). Furthermore, in "occasional instances," "strong minds in every walk of life" will overcome their disadvantageous situations and "command the tribute due to their merit, not only from the classes to which they particularly belong, but from the society in general" (36, p. 217). More ordinarily relevant than these few strong-minded or learned representatives is Hamilton's suggestion that interested men will elect men of ability so that their representatives will be at least "equal to" contests with the men who represent other interests.[12] If intelligent representatives (see 36, p. 218) can be expected to recognize certain truths about the utility or necessity of commerce (or can be brought to recognize them by some especially intelligent man who makes reports and proposals to them),[13] then the representatives' abilities will have beneficial consequences which transcend the motives of the electors. The man an interest thinks smart enough to protect it from other interests may be smart enough to learn about economics.

Federalist 10 presented the prospect of "fit characters" as a hopeful possibility, and Hamilton does not predict that intelligence will yield impartiality (as distinguished from a modicum of moderation).[14] Whatever the prospects for avoiding an "improper bias" in the legislature, the immediate point is that to "combine" interests is a more difficult and more important task than to receive them into the legislature. *The Federalist* suggests that the best an interest's representative can do is "resist" unfriendly measures, and contribute "knowledge" of the interest which other intelligent representatives will need to learn. But even the task of resistance will only be an attempt, because most interests will be in the minority. What interests really need in the legislature is not a lonely partisan spokesman but rather men who understand them and attempt to combine them with other interests. The "reception" of all interests into the legislature would not suffice to combine them, and might even make an intelligent combination more difficult.

The other aspect of combining that Hamilton referred to was the task of combining the "feelings of every part of the community." Once again, to receive all classes with all their feelings does not combine those feelings into a whole. According to Hamilton's statement, what is necessary is that the feelings of all parts be "understood" and "attended to" (35, p. 215). Attention to the people's feelings requires that the representatives not be "inattentive" to "the momentary humors or dispositions which may happen to prevail in particular parts of the society"; that is, they must be attentive to the fact that some apparent "feelings" of the people may be only momentary or felt by only "parts" of society. Thus a good representative must be a "competent judge of [the] nature, extent, and foundation" of the people's feelings; he *judges* them rather than replicates them.

> Is it not natural that a man who is a candidate for the favor of the people, and who is dependent on the suffrages of his fellow-citizens for the continuance of his public honors, should take care to inform himself of their dispositions and inclinations and should be willing to allow them their proper degree of influence upon his conduct? (35, p. 216)

Hamilton leaves open what the "proper degree" would be, but we may infer that it is something less than a fully compelling influence. The people's feelings are not a whole which the representative can easily share. He could not reflect all the different feelings of all his constituents, even if that were desirable, and even if he had a considerably smaller district. This explains Hamilton's rather modest requirement that the representative be "acquainted with the general genius, habits, and modes of thinking of the people at large" (35, p. 217) rather than with their specific opinions. One may wonder whether modern survey-research has much changed this situation, given the imprecision and nonunified quality of public opinion. Hamilton implies that a man "whose situation leads to extensive inquiry and information" can better judge the people's feelings than can a local man who merely shares his neighbors' feelings.

Those who contend for a more minute representation of society on the grounds that society has many diverse parts overlook representation's purpose of combining those parts into a whole. Madison explains the difficulties of confederations ruled by assemblies of "deputies," each of whom spoke for his own part (18, p. 123; 19, p. 131; 46, pp. 296–97). If the people "*intend* the PUBLIC GOOD," then the "will" of this "political body" which representation is supposed to "concente[r]" (14, p. 100) is a will for the public good. The representative body is of most significance when it speaks for the people as a whole—when it defends the people's right to rule against ambitious usurpers. But its usefulness in other cases where the people are not a whole depends on its taking a broad view of what is useful and of the people's feelings or likely feelings about what is useful. This requires intelligence and knowledge more than local attachment. The best House may possess these useful qualities, but in any case their absence could not be compensated for by a kind of representation which more minutely reproduced the people's interests and feelings. *The Federalist*'s most important claim for the House is that it can always "bring back" the Constitution to its "primitive form and principles," the people's right to rule (63, p. 390). Whether that will be necessary depends on the trustworthiness of those "more permanent branches" (52, p. 330) designed to raise the quality of government.

·[SEVEN]·

Good Government
The More Permanent Branches

The Federalist's claims about the House of Representatives' usefulness to the public good, as distinguished from its safety to liberty, shifted the subject to the proposed government's "positive merit." A good government serves the public good, in addition to refraining from doing the public ill. In this chapter, I will first recapitulate *The Federalist's* view of the proper ends of government; and then consider the "more permanent branches" of government designed to serve those ends.

Ends

Federalist 10 was concerned with two related but distinct objects of government: "justice" or "private rights," and "the public good." In two later passages, each of those objects appears as the fundamental end of government.

[T]he public good, the real welfare of the great body of the people, is the supreme object to be pursued; and . . . no form of government whatever has any other value than as it may be fitted for the attainment of this object. (45, p. 289)

Justice is the end of government. It is the end of civil society. It ever has been and ever will be pursued until it be obtained, or until liberty be lost in the pursuit. (51, p. 324)

The terms and the contexts of these passages suggest how we should understand the relation between them. Justice is a more fundamental end; it is not only the end of government, it is "the end of civil society." This is because justice means the protection of each individual's faculties, which is the object each man seeks when he joins civil society. Madison's distinction between "government" and "civil society" recalls Locke's account of men's original, *unanimous* choice to form a society, which is the foundation for the *majority's* right to choose a form of government.[1] If society is created by a unanimous choice of men seeking security for the right to exercise their faculties, then it must above all secure that right for all of its citizens. But government need not plan elaborate ways of meting out justice, if justice means protecting men's faculties in a manner that respects their free choice (see pp. 84–85 above). Rather, government need only prevent certain well-known injustices (i.e., crimes) by private men, and refrain from committing injustices itself. Thus the context of Madison's assertion that "[j]ustice is the end of government" is an argument that men will not accept a government which causes injustices, and will pursue a just government as long as they are free to do so.

The public good, rather, is the "supreme object to be pursued"[2] *by government* because it requires the more active attention of a "good government." When a form of government is chosen, the majority tries to choose one which will serve the "real welfare of the great body of the people." The choice is not unanimous, and the real welfare sought is an "aggregate." Madison notes in this context that certain individuals (state officers) may be unhappy with a form which detracts from their own importance (45, p. 289). But disappointed individual interests are not an objection to a plan which serves the interests of the "great body of the people." A violation of *rights* would be an objection; and unless the great body of the people interprets its real welfare as including protection for minorities, it will endanger "civil society" by stimulating insurrection. But while private rights must be respected by government, it is the public good which is to be "pursued" by government. While justice may sometimes require active measures by government (see 58, p. 361), for the most part government shows "negative merit" in refraining from committing injustices on behalf of either selfish rulers or factious majorities, and shows its "positive merit" in its service of the public good. The language of the Constitution's Preamble reflects this distinction; while "Justice" is to be "establish[ed]," the "general Welfare" is to be "promote[d]."

The object of "safety" is the dominant element in *The Federalist's* understanding of the public good. We recall that "the common defense of the members [and] the preservation of the public peace, as well against internal convulsions as external attacks" were those of the "principal purposes to be answered by union" which Hamilton argued required an "energetic" government (23, p. 153). And in *Federalist* 37 Madison wrote of the "requisite stability and energy in government." "Stability" was said to be "essential . . . to that repose and confidence in the minds of the people, which are among the chief blessings of civil society," and "energy" appeared to be a necessary means of assuring stability (p. 226). Good government allows men repose and confidence. One might say that to qualify as a good government, a nontyrannical government need only avoid allowing by its own error or negligence that which its benignity prevents it from causing deliberately, i.e., attacks on men's lives and properties. Government must be energetic to stop others from committing the oppressions it refrains from, and it must have a "certain portion of . . . stability" (62, p. 382) so that its well-intentioned rule does not upset the repose and confidence which it is trying to protect.

But in addition to safety or repose and confidence, *The Federalist* clearly points to a further object which good government should serve. Hamilton's list of purposes to be answered by union also included "the regulation of commerce with other nations and between the States [and] the superintendence of our intercourse, political and commercial, with foreign countries" (23, p. 153). These tasks are, surely, partly means to the end of safety, in that they are means of preventing disputes between states and with foreigners which could lead to war (see 4, pp. 46–47 and 7, pp. 62–63). But the regulation of commerce has a further purpose: to benefit America's prosperity. For example, by showing Britain a united front we can "negotiate, with the fairest prospect of success, for commercial privileges of the most valuable and extensive kind in the dominions of that kingdom" (11, pp. 85–86). In this and other ways, a national government can serve the "prosperity of commerce," which "is now perceived and acknowledged by all enlightened statesmen to be the most useful as well as the most productive source of national wealth" (12, p. 91).

Thus good government can contribute to "national wealth." It does so by opening prospects for men to exercise their acquisitive faculties. The promotion of commerce has this effect:

> By multiplying the means of gratification, by promoting the introduction and circulation of the precious metals, those darling objects of human avarice and enterprise, it serves to vivify and invigorate all the channels of industry and to make them flow with greater activity and copiousness. The assiduous merchant, the laborious husbandman, the active mechanic, and the industrious manufacturer—all orders of men look forward with eager

expectation and growing alacrity to this pleasing reward of their toils. (12, p. 91)

Government's promotion of commerce stimulates "all orders of men," moved by the "eager expectation" of "reward," to exercise their acquisitive faculties. This policy is consistent with justice, because it impartially benefits those who exert their faculties, and it also contributes to the aggregate interests of the community. Commercial policies are therefore one field in which government may devise and pursue "enlarged plans" for the public good (30, p. 191).

While a certain "structure" of government may make government unlikely to be tyrannical, it is harder to see how a structure can cause government to be "good" in intelligently securing the public safety and encouraging national prosperity. In part, this goodness is made possible simply by the grant of the useful powers to the new government. Thus *The Federalist*'s pleas for a more adequate defense and the promotion of commerce came in the book's first section, advocating "union"—implying that *any* national government would do something toward these ends. The book's third section insisted on granting the necessary powers to that government. But beyond that, one might think that the quality of the government will depend on the quality of those who hold its powers. Hamilton did say that the prosperity of commerce is known to be important by "all enlightened statesmen" (12, p. 91). But Hamilton modifies Pope's famous maxim:

> Though we cannot acquiesce in the political heresy of the poet who says:
> "For forms of government let fools contest—
> That which is best administered is best,"—
> yet we may safely pronounce that the true test of a good government is its aptitude and tendency to produce a good administration. (68, p. 414)

Contrary to the political "heresy" which denigrates the importance of the form of government—and thereby denigrates the significance of the people's ability to choose a form of government—Hamilton suggests that the form can have a "tendency" toward a certain quality of rule. The proposed Constitution forms several of its branches in a way which is intended to contribute to an aptitude and tendency toward energy and stability.

Federalist 37 suggested a conflict between energy and stability on one hand, and republican liberty on the other. While the government's "more permanent branches" (52, p. 330)—the Senate, executive, and judiciary—are "strictly" republican according to *Federalist* 39's definition, they stray from the "genius of republican liberty" identified in *Federalist* 37, according to which power should be delegated to large numbers for short terms. These branches are technically republican attempts to introduce the elements which are partly opposed to, and must be blended with, "republican liberty."

The more permanent branches all take their character from the "situation"[3] in which their occupants are placed by their number and their term in office. *The Federalist* devotes a lengthy and separate section to each branch, but one can see the importance of these facts by an inspection of the outline of each of those sections. Madison's account of the Senate is divided into five subjects: qualifications, appointment, apportionment, number and term, and powers. Only when he reaches the fourth subject, number and term, does he find it "proper to inquire into the purposes which are to be answered by a senate" (62, p. 378). Thus the Senate's distinctive nature is located in those features, rather than in the fact of equal representation for all states, or election by state legislatures (both of which Madison had opposed at the convention as intrusions on the original intention of the institution), or in the Senate's special powers.

Similarly, Hamilton builds the discussion of the executive around the assertion that "[e]nergy in the executive is a leading character in the definition of good government" (70, p. 423). His discussion follows an outline of "the ingredients which constitute energy in the executive," that is, unity, duration, adequate provision for support, and competent powers. But the discussion of the executive's powers is more precisely a discussion of why those powers are assigned to an energetic executive, not an account of how those powers contribute to energy. The essence of the executive—his energy—is primarily constituted by his number ("unity") and term ("duration"). Hamilton divides his presentation of the judiciary into four subjects: appointment, tenure in office, support, and extent of authority. The second subject—the judiciary's remarkable tenure of "good behavior"—is the occasion for Hamilton's analysis of the purposes of a judiciary altogether. The number of men in these branches and their term in office are the quantitative details which give the government its form. Men are placed in certain situations in which they may be expected to contribute certain qualities to government. Because republican government forbids any self-appointed rulers, the qualities of government do not derive from the qualities of the class of men who rule. While republican government, because it is wholly popular, might be said to take its essential character from human nature, its blending of qualities derives from the ways in which human nature may be expected to behave in certain prescribed circumstances.

Senatorial Stability

Madison refers to the proposed Senate as "a senate," meaning an institution belonging to a classification which is named after the Roman senate and which includes Britain's House of Lords. Some ancient senates had members who served for life, and even filled their own vacancies. Those examples are "as unfit for the imitation as they are repugnant to the genius of America" (63, p. 385)—or (otherwise stated) they are fit for imitation except insofar as they offend America's "genius" (see p. 118 above). But America needs an "institution that will blend stability" with the "liberty" of a republic, and the longest and central of Madison's seven arguments for the Senate defends it as a "stable institution in the government" (62, p. 380).

The republican spirit favors frequent elections, but experience in the states indicates that half of the representatives are replaced at each new election.

> From this change of men must proceed a change of opinions;
> and from a change of opinions, a change of measures. But a con-
> tinual change even of good measures is inconsistent with every
> rule of prudence and every prospect of success. (62, p. 380)

Madison does not explain why the people so often elect new men. But the new men seem to act from a desire to put their own stamp on affairs, rather than prudently retain the old policies. The men ambitious enough to be elected are ambitious enough to insist on opinions and measures of their own. The Senate's six-year term assures fewer changes of men, so that branch can blunt the House's likely tendency to adopt new measures. Likewise, the president's four-year term is a stabilizing influence (although not as much of one as a probably preferable longer term would provide); and his re-eligibility leaves the people the "option" of preserving a stable administration even longer, thereby avoiding "the fatal inconveniences of fluctuating councils and a variable policy" (72, p. 439). The "option" of reelecting the same man allows the people to choose stability, but the constitutional imposition of longer terms enforces stability without the people's choice. While Madison does not say that the people themselves are seeking new measures when they choose new men, at least the people do not appreciate the advantages of stability enough to deter them from the change.

A "mutable government" has various "mischievous effects." First, it "forfeits the respect and confidence of other nations," just as a man with no plan or with a plan he abandons is pitied or perhaps exploited by his neighbors.

CHAPTER SEVEN

One nation is to another what one individual is to another; with
this melancholy distinction, perhaps, that the former, with fewer
of the benevolent emotions than the latter, are under fewer restraints also from taking undue advantage of the indiscretions of
each other. (62, pp. 380–81)

Madison's analogy is interesting in its own right; "perhaps" individual
human beings have more "benevolent emotions" than nations do. Men's
benevolent emotions are possibly, although not necessarily, the basis of
the "patriotism" and "virtue" *The Federalist* describes elsewhere (see above,
pp. 24, 70). This passage does not specify how numerous, widespread,
or powerful these emotions are[4] but does suggest that they restrain men's
taking advantage rather than inspire philanthropy, and that they only
restrain "undue" advantage. Men who exert their unequal faculties of
acquisition are due a certain advantage by their avoidance of those indiscretions of their competitors by which they profit. In any case, the
benevolent emotions either do not extend so far as to cross national
boundaries,[5] or are overcome by the cooler heads who rule nations.

Every nation, consequently, whose affairs betray a want of wisdom
and stability, may calculate on every loss which can be sustained
from the more systematic policy of its wiser neighbors. (62, p.
381)

While Madison also suggests that the Senate can contribute "wisdom"
(see below), stability is one element of wisdom, or at least of what looks
to foreigners like wisdom. To adhere to one's plan appears "systematic,"
while to change plans implies that one's plans were unwise. "Wiser neighbors" who can cause the nation "loss" provide one clear standard for
judging how good America's government is. Men honorably determined
to rule themselves, unless they can contrive to have no neighbors, must
rule themselves through a government wise and stable enough to sustain
them against those neighbors.

Madison turns, second, to the "internal effects" of a mutable policy,
which are worse. "It poisons the blessings of liberty itself" (62, p. 381).
Liberty exists where "the laws are made by men of [the people's] own
choice." But these laws cannot be what law should be, a "rule of action,"
if they are "little known, and less fixed." According to Locke, the security
of living under fixed, promulgated laws is a principal advantage of civil
society over the state of nature.[6] Even if frequent elections are in the
spirit of republican liberty, they may be unfavorable to the "blessings of
liberty," i.e., that benign and secure rule which men expect will result
from liberty. Madison's third and fourth points make this problem more
specific:

Another effect of public instability is the unreasonable advantage
it gives to the sagacious, the enterprising, and the moneyed few
over the industrious and uninformed mass of the people. Every
new regulation concerning commerce or revenue, or in any manner affecting the value of the different species of property, presents a new harvest to those who watch the change, and can trace
its consequences; a harvest, reared not by themselves, but by the
toils and cares of the great body of their fellow-citizens. This is a
state of things in which it may be said with some truth that laws
are made for the *few*, not for the *many*. (62, p. 381)

We should recall in this context *Federalist* 10's statement that government's first object is the protection of men's faculties. The "industrious"
should be able to reap the harvest of their own "toils and cares"—even
if they are "uninformed." While Madison implies that the sagacious,
enterprising, or moneyed few (the repetition of "the" may mean these
are not all the same few) will have some *reasonable* advantage under a
government which protects men's naturally unequal faculties of acquiring property, they should not have the unreasonable advantage of spec-
ulating on governmental policy's effects, an unproductive source of
undeserved profit. Madison does not go so far as to suggest that these
enterprising few might stir up the policy changes they profit from; he
reports that sharp speculators can merely "watch" the instability which
naturally results from the people's propensity to elect new men who have
a propensity to choose new measures. The *"many"* are "industrious and
uninformed," and can profit from their toils and cares unless sudden
changes in circumstances alter the natural "harvest" which normally flows
from those efforts.

But Madison's next complaint against instability is on behalf of the
"enterprising" "few."

What prudent merchant will hazard his fortunes in any new
branch of commerce when he knows not but that his plans may
be rendered unlawful before they can be executed? What farmer
or manufacturer will lay himself out for the encouragement given
to any particular cultivation or establishment, when he can have
no assurance that his preparatory labors and advances will not
render him a victim to an inconstant government? In a word, no
great improvement or laudable enterprise can go forward which
requires the auspices of a steady system of national policy. (62,
pp. 381–82)

Thus stability is vital not only to the slow but steady industrious men,
but also to the few men who take risks and undertake "great" enterprises.
Mutable government corrupts the few by causing them to "watch" and

speculate on mutable laws, rather than "lay [themselves] out" and exert their faculties in laudable enterprises. A "steady system of national policy" is admirably impartial in protecting the faculties of both the slow and industrious, and the quick and enterprising.

Finally, the "most deplorable effect" of mutability is "that diminution of attachment and reverence which steals into the hearts of the people" towards a government which is not "truly respectable" (62, p. 382). A "certain portion of order and stability" is necessary to respectability. The people will despise an unstable government for the same reason that foreign nations will, and will be less ready to obey and more open to replacing it. But it must be said that the people despise precisely what they seem to cause. The spirit of republican liberty is most embodied in the least stable institutions; the people's exercise of their "option" brings on the changeableness they do not respect. One might instead blame the instability on the ambitious men who run for office and insist on displacing incumbents and upsetting their policies. But the success of those ambitions depends on the people's propensity to vote for new men. Perhaps this tendency can be explained by the political opinionatedness which is inevitable in a free country (see 10, pp. 78–79). The people's partisanship parallels and supports the ambitions of a few, and opposes their own interest in stability.

Human beings exercising their faculties are constantly making or attempting to make changes, and the "mutability" Madison complains of is not the fact of change but rather the rapidity of change. Men rely on stability even when they disrupt it by their attempts to change things. Toils and cares of laboring men, laudable enterprise by entrepreneurs, the new measures of ambitious men, and the votes for new men by partisan men are all human exertions designed to make changes. But all these changes depend on the assumption that other things will not change: that crops will not be confiscated or trade outlawed or the government overthrown. Even those who corruptly speculate on governmental policy changes, or who hope for political confusions by which to aggrandize themselves—they too assume some sort of stability, at least after the favorable change of policy or government. For ambitious politicians and opinionated partisans, stability is a source of frustration— because new men and measures must slow down—but with some compensation perhaps in the prospect that one's own measures, when adopted, will not be so quickly reversed. For individual private citizens, political stability is a condition under which men may exert their own faculties in making changes for themselves.

Executive Energy

Hamilton's defense of the proposed presidency is largely composed of an argument for "[e]nergy in the executive."

> There is an idea, which is not without its advocates, that a vigorous executive is inconsistent with the genius of republican government. The enlightened well-wishers to this species of government must at least hope that the supposition is destitute of foundation; since they can never admit its truth, without at the same time admitting the condemnation of their own principles. Energy in the executive is a leading character in the definition of good government. (70, p. 423)

The advocates of the idea that an energetic executive and republican government are "inconsistent" might look for support to Madison's statement in *Federalist* 37, according to which the "genius" of republican liberty assigns power to many hands for short terms, while energy requires "a certain duration" and "a single hand." According to Montesquieu, monarchies are prompt in execution, while democracies execute poorly (see p. 91 above); and Hamilton seems to agree that monarchy does indeed have an energetic executive (see 77, p. 463). But the people have an "aversion" to monarchy, which the Constitution's opponents have appealed to; so Hamilton goes to great lengths to show that the president is not a monarch. He attacks the opponents' exaggerations partly by exaggerating their exaggerations:

> He [the president] has been shown to us with the diadem sparkling on his brow and the imperial purple flowing in his train. . . . We have been almost taught to tremble at the terrific visages of murdering janizaries, and to blush at the unveiled mysteries of a future seraglio. (67, pp. 407–8)

The president will be without the monarch's pomp (diadem, purple) and without certain of his powers (see *Federalist* 69); but he must nonetheless be energetic. Hamilton does not define "energy." The word is perhaps free of the monarchical resonances of words like "power" and "prerogative," and its scientific flavor suggests less the awe-inspiring omnipotence of a king or god than the application of a certain quantity of force to create a specific motion. In *Federalist* numbers 23–36, government's energy was said to depend on its quantity of power and on "upon whom" that power is exercised (see chapter 2, above). Now energy appears also to depend on by whom the power is exercised.

Hamilton explains why good government requires an energetic executive:

It is essential to the protection of the community against foreign attacks; it is not less essential to the steady administration of the laws; to the protection of property against those irregular and high-handed combinations which sometimes interrupt the ordinary course of justice; to the security of liberty against the enterprises and assaults of ambition, of faction, and of anarchy. (70, p. 423)

In all four cases, energy is the necessary means to stability. Foreigners, criminals, criminal conspiracies, and political conspiracies can all interrupt and even destroy the tranquillity of a people living under stable laws.

A feeble execution is but another phrase for a bad execution; and a government ill executed, whatever it may be in theory, must be, in practice, a bad government. (70, p. 423)

The stability encouraged by the stable institution of a senate is only a "theory" unless supplemented by the "practice" of execution. The men who attack stability do not attack feebly with theories; they attack in practice, using their hands ("high-handed") and weapons. One might say that these men are themselves energetic in their attacks on the laws, and that for this reason the laws need an energetic defense.

Having gone to some pains to dissociate the American president from the British king, Hamilton invokes the bold but ancient example of the Roman dictator as a case of an "energetic executive." Rome took refuge in the "absolute power of a single man." Hamilton uses this example to show that a "feeble executive" is insufficient, but does not specify whether the president goes as far beyond feebleness as the Roman dictator did. The crucial ingredients of energy are unity and duration, and Hamilton explains each of them at some length.

That unity is conducive to energy will not be disputed. Decision, activity, secrecy, and dispatch will generally characterize the proceedings of one man in a much more eminent degree than the proceedings of any greater number; and in proportion as the number is increased, these qualities will be diminished. (70, p. 424)

The quality of "secrecy" is presumably valuable in taking by surprise those criminals and conspirators whom the executive must defeat. The other three qualities emphasize the importance of speed, perhaps even at the expense of accuracy. To show how unity is conducive to those qualities, Hamilton discusses some historical examples of plural executives, but no American examples (e.g., of experience of an executive who is bound by a council), and then turns from the "dim light of historical research" to the "dictates of reason" (70, p. 425). If two or more men must act together, they may have different opinions and may passionately insist on their own opinion from motives of "personal infallibility." Hamilton here echoes the psychology of *Federalist* 10, according to which men divide themselves in the passionate defense of their own fallible opinions. Such dissensions "lessen the respectability, weaken the authority, and distract the plans and operations of those whom they divide" (70, p. 426). One man can decide more quickly than many men can agree, and his decision will be more impressive to those it addresses because it will always be, so to speak, unanimous. This is of particular importance in time of war (70, p. 427, and 74, p. 447).

Quickness and decisiveness are bought by a sacrifice of certain other qualities. Hamilton cites approvingly the view that a "numerous legislature" is "best adapted to deliberation and wisdom, and best calculated to conciliate the confidence of the people and to secure their privileges and interests" (70, p. 424). But "energy"—not "deliberation and wisdom" —is the "most necessary qualification" of the executive; "vigor and expedition" are the "most necessary ingredients in its composition" (70, pp. 424, 427). Hamilton's previous statement—that a "feeble execution is but another phrase for a bad execution"—had implied that an energetic execution is by that quality alone a good execution. All of this suggests that execution does not really require much deliberation, perhaps because it does not present many choices. To execute well means to execute vigorously whatever laws there are against whatever lawbreakers there are. The choices which require deliberation are apparently made by the legislature. Precisely to the extent that the executive's function is dictated by necessity, the executive's most necessary quality is something other than an ability to deliberate and choose.

But this conclusion—that the executive must act quickly rather than deliberate—must be modified in light of *The Federalist*'s presentation of his power to negotiate treaties and his power to pardon criminals. Jay's argument concerning the treaty power claims that the power demands both the senatorial stability which will give "system" to our foreign arrangements, and the executive's *"secrecy"* and *"dispatch"* in negotiation (64, p. 392).

They who have turned their attention to the affairs of men must have perceived that there are tides in them; tides very irregular in their duration, strength, and direction, and seldom found to run twice exactly in the same manner or measure. To discern and to

profit by these tides in national affairs is the business of those
who preside over them. . . . (64, p. 393)[7]

The executive's quickness in this case is his ability to *think* quickly, to
"discern" so as to "profit." The existence of "tides" shows the limitation
of a senatorially stable "system" for dealing with other countries; systems
must by necessity be adjusted to any "new state of things." A system is
a "machine" which would run "into disorder" if not adapted (69, p. 420).
Thus, as Locke said about this *"federative"* (i.e., foreign policy) power, it
cannot entirely be directed by antecedent laws.[8] Jay presents tides as
opportunities for national profit; thus the executive's quick decisions will
be occasioned not only by the necessities of impending danger but by
his prudent discovery of opportunities for gain.

The executive's quick deliberation is also necessary in domestic policy
where "good policy" might require the exercise of the "benign prerogative" of pardoning. Some pardons are a matter of "humanity," to spare
"unfortunate guilt" from the usually "necessary severity" of a criminal
code (74, p. 447). In these cases, the executive's pardon quietly recognizes
that law cannot fully subject men to its dictates by its severe threats;
"unfortunate guilt" is possible, and the "humanity" which accepts human
imperfection pardons it. But in the case of treason—"a crime leveled at
the immediate being of the society"—Hamilton describes the pardoner
not as judging whether "humanity" or "vengeance" is fitting in each case,
but as deciding on "the *expediency* of an act of mercy" (74, p. 448, emphasis
added). Hamilton suggests that if the legislature had the power to pardon
treason, its sympathy for or antipathy toward the traitor might divert it
from a cool calculation of what is expedient. The president should decide
whether the "terror of an example" is *"necessary"* or whether *"policy"* demand[s] a conduct of forbearance and clemency" (74, p. 449, emphasis
added). Pardoning traitors is not a humanitarian correction of the law's
severity, but only an expedient concession which "good policy" might
make so as to preserve the law.

> [T]he principal argument for reposing the power of pardoning in
> this case in the Chief Magistrate is this: in seasons of insurrection
> or rebellion, there are often critical moments when a well-timed
> offer of pardon to the insurgents or rebels may restore the tran-
> quillity of the commonwealth; and which, if suffered to pass un-
> improved, it may never be possible afterwards to recall. (74, p.
> 449)

As in negotiations, a quick executive can "improve" critical moments (64,
p. 393). For Congress to occasionally delegate such a pardoning power
would "be likely to be construed into an argument of timidity or of

weakness, and would have a tendency to embolden guilt" (74, p. 449). The law must announce its commands in advance, and make threats of "necessary severity" so as not to encourage violation. But while it is necessary to threaten, it is not always necessary to carry out the threat, and (in "critical moments") may sometimes be necessary not to carry out the threat. A quick executive can prudently act on this fact which the law cannot prudently admit.

This account of pardoning might be applied to the task of execution generally. If a simply "vigorous execution" of all laws at all times is not possible, the executive must pick his spots. The likely importance of tides in men's affairs, and the possibility that not all recalcitrant offenders can be readily defeated, mean that the executive must deliberate, even if he does not have the leisure and diversity of views of a legislature.

Energy depends not only on the executive's unity, but on his "duration in office." Besides its advantages in producing a stable administration, duration encourages "the personal firmness of the executive magistrate in the employment of his constitutional powers" (71, p. 431). That is because men are more attached to, and risk more for, the things they hold by a more durable tenure. The executive's "firmness" seems to be part of energy; the executive will firmly resist the assaults of criminals, conspiracies, and foreign nations, even when those pose some "risk." But Hamilton gives the argument a different turn, and thereby shows that the executive's energy is not confined to his energetic execution. The risk of firmness is not in incurring the wrath of criminals, but rather in

> encountering the ill-humors, however transient, which may happen to prevail, either in a considerable part of the society itself, or even in a predominant faction in the legislative body. (71, pp. 431–32)

The executive's firmness against the legislature is familiar from *Federalist* 51; his firmness against "a considerable part of the society," so considerable as to constitute a "prevailing current" and even to appear as simply "the people" (71, p. 432), had not previously been suggested. The executive displays his firmness in these instances by using his qualified veto over legislation. This firmness of an energetic executive is very different in its effects from the quickness of an energetic executive. Rather than quickly defending a naturally slow form of government against the rapidity of the forces which threaten it, the president by his veto does the opposite; he slows down the government by his personal firmness against its more evidently popular part. The president's energetic quickness was justified as a necessary means of defending stability; and even if that quickness involves not merely vigorous application of the legislature's commands but a considerable scope for one man's deliberations, a partisan of republican government might reluctantly accept its necessity. But "firmness" needs a separate justification. An energetic "single magistrate" (69, p. 415) partly manifests his energy as a firm third branch of the legislature;[9] *The Federalist*'s argument for this parallels some of its arguments for the Senate, and I will consider them together.

Separation Revisited

The case for this tricameral arrangement of the power to legislate begins but does not end with *Federalist* 51's point: that additional branches can obstruct the House's attempts to accumulate all power. The Senate inhibits "schemes of usurpation or perfidy" because the concurrence of "two distinct bodies" is required (62, p. 379). And the executive must not be "dependent on the legislative body" (71, p. 433) if he is to enforce the laws against the legislators along with the other citizens, and use his veto to resist encroachments on his ability to do so (73, p. 442). But—and this goes beyond the argument of *Federalist* 51—the president's veto can prevent not only usurpations but also "the enaction of improper laws."

> It establishes a salutary check upon the legislative body, calculated to guard the community against the effects of faction, precipitancy, or of any impulse unfriendly to the public good, which may happen to influence a majority of that body. (73, p. 443)

The Senate has a similar ability to resist the "sudden and violent passions" of a "numerous" assembly like the House (62, p. 379). Not just usurpations but various passionate errors can be obstructed; and *The Federalist* makes very clear that those erring will sometimes be the people themselves. These passages contradict the simply "democratic" interpretation of separation of powers as a check only on representatives who might otherwise betray the people.[10] Regarding the Senate,

> To a people as little blinded by prejudice or corrupted by flattery as those whom I address, I shall not scruple to add that such an institution may be sometimes necessary as a defense to the people against their own temporary errors and delusions. (63, p. 384)

And in defending presidential firmness against prevailing popular currents, Hamilton says

> It is a just observation that the people commonly *intend* the PUB-LIC GOOD. This often applies to their very errors. But their good

sense would despise the adulator who should pretend that they always *reason right* about the *means* of promoting it. They know from experience that they sometimes err. . . . (71, p. 432)

The Federalist does not scruple to report to an uncorrupted people that the people have defects—although perhaps its scruples are visible in the gentle prefaces in each case. The people's errors are attributable partly to passion—"some irregular passion" (63, p. 384), a "sudden breeze of passion" (71, p. 432)—and (given more emphasis) partly to certain sinister individuals who mislead the people—"interested men" who employ "artful misrepresentations" (63, p. 384), or men who use "arts" to "flatter [the people's] prejudices to betray their interests" (71, p. 432). Parasites, sycophants, ambitious, avaricious, and desperate men all "beset" the people and victimize them by their "arts." The people are not altogether to blame for their errors, although their susceptibility to victimization is perhaps embarrassing in itself.

In these passages, *The Federalist* returns to the problem addressed by *Federalist* 10: popular impulses of passion or interest adverse to justice or the public good. We saw that the diversity of the extended sphere was suggested as a republican remedy to the impulses of injustice, and "fit" representatives were suggested as a possible remedy for the neglect of the public good. *Federalist* 51's final paragraph hinted that justice may gain an additional, though "precarious," security from the "stability and independence of some member of the government" (see p. 144 above). These later passages on the Senate and president elaborate that suggestion, although they focus primary attention on how these institutions serve the public good.[11] The popular errors which might divert the people from their true interests are presented as "sudden," "transient," "temporary." Presumably over a long enough period, the public will consider the permanent, aggregate interest of the whole rather than a temporary or illusory interest of the whole. Furthermore, if the delusion is not temporary, the obstructions posed by Senate and president will be inefficacious; they can only "suspend the blow," and "give [the people] time and opportunity for more cool and sedate reflection" (63, p. 384; 71, p. 432). While they are "more permanent branches" than the House, they are not simply permanent. The republican "genius" argues for short terms, on the honorable assumption that the people are capable of choosing well. But *The Federalist* honors the people's ability to reflect coolly and sedately over time, without assuming that every "inclinatio[n]" the people feel is in fact a "deliberate sense" (71, p. 432). Even if the people's deliberation will not be simply reasonable, they can come to a "deliberate sense" or "cool and deliberate sense" (63, p. 384). To honor (rather than flatter or adulate) the people's ability to choose requires one to understand choice as something distinct from inclination.

Senators and presidents are thus given the power to dampen the people's errors. But, in the spirit of *The Federalist* altogether, and in the language of *Federalist* 10, one can wonder if the effect might not be inverted. Might not these more permanent branches oppose the people's good? They have constitutional means and personal motives to protect their own authority, and constitutional means to protect the people; but what of their *motives* to protect the people? On the other hand, if one stresses that these branches are after all not permanent, but subject to the people's control, one might have to relinquish part of *The Federalist*'s claim about their value. We must therefore consider the grounds on which *The Federalist* expects salutary effects from putting these constitutional means in the hands of the Senate and president.

For one thing, the mere fact that the process of legislation is made to require the agreement of House, Senate, and president means that measures will be "oftener . . . brought under examination" by men in a "diversity" of "situations" (73, p. 443). The slowness of the process will encourage "due deliberation" and may even outlast a transient "passion." As I have noted, the president's "energy" in this case is in the service of slowness rather than quickness.

Another reason for expecting benefits from the senatorial and presidential role in legislation is the possibility that the mode of selection for these high offices, and their small number, will cause them to be filled by more excellent men. Hamilton praises the proposed method of electing presidents as creating "a constant probability of seeing the station filled by characters pre-eminent for ability and virtue" (69, p. 414). Jay—but not Madison—also praises indirect election of senators as likely to result in the choice of men "most distinguished by their abilities and virtue" (64, p. 391).[12]

A particular virtue which senators and presidents might contribute is wisdom. In arguing for a senate, Madison says that

> [i]t may be affirmed, on the best grounds, that no small share of
> the present embarrassments of America is to be charged on the
> blunders of our governments; and that these have proceeded
> from the heads rather than the hearts of most of the authors of
> them. (62, p. 379)

Madison points to the spectacle of continual repeals of state laws by succeeding legislative sessions as proof of "deficient wisdom"; each new session "impeach[es]" the wisdom of the last, nicely saving Madison from the awkwardness of himself arguing the stupidity of certain policies from the vantage point of superior wisdom. Madison defends the Senate's possible contribution not precisely as wisdom which can remedy "deficient wisdom" but as "knowledge" or a "due acquaintance with the objects and principles of legislation" (62, pp. 379–80). The House will be composed of men only briefly removed from the "pursuits of a private nature" which have occupied their thoughts, who are "led by no permanent motive to devote the intervals of public occupation to a study of the laws, the affairs, and the comprehensive interests of their country" (62, p. 379). Similarly, Hamilton argues for the president's re-eligibility, among other reasons, so as not to deprive the community of a man's "experience." The "wisest as well as the simplest" see that "experience is the parent of wisdom" (72, p. 438). The wisdom which might result from selection of men with superior ability is given less emphasis than the duration in office which permits experience and encourages study of the "means by which [the happiness of the people] can be best attained" (62, p. 380).

Wisdom, like "stability" and "energy," is more an effect of the "situation" of the officer than of his careful selection to begin with. The situation created for an officer by the length of his term and the number or absence of colleagues is meant to contribute the qualities which good government needs. A single president can be energetic, and senators with long terms can resist a rapid turnover of laws. But their situation also affects the behavior of senators and presidents by the specific manner in which it exposes them to rewards and punishments, that is, to being reelected or not, and to being praised or blamed. The number and terms of these officers make them "responsible" to the people in an important, although "paradoxical," way.

Responsibility and Reputation

Madison argues that the Senate remedies what would otherwise be the "want . . . of a due responsibility in the government to the people" (63, p. 383). Douglass Adair notes that the word "responsibility" appears to have been coined by Madison[13] although it clearly derives from the word "responsible," meaning "accountable," which has a longer history. Madison's association of "responsibility" with the Senate rather than the House is, he admits, a "new" and "paradoxical" view, since one would think a large number of representatives with short terms would be more responsible to the people than a small number with long terms. But

> Responsibility, in order to be reasonable, must be limited to objects within the power of the responsible party, and in order to be

effectual, must relate to operations of that power, of which a
ready and proper judgment can be formed by the constituents.
(63, p. 383)

Some objects of government depend "on measures which have singly an
immediate and sensible operation"; in those cases, the constituents can
judge those measures and hold their representatives responsible for
them.[14] But other objects of government depend "on a succession of
well-chosen and well-connected measures, which have a gradual and
perhaps unobserved operation." If the measures take a longer time to
succeed, the people might misjudge the goodness of the measures if they
must judge after a short time. And if the operation of the measures is
"unobserved," the constituents may not be able to judge the measures
at all. Madison's solution is a senate which,

> having sufficient permanency to provide for such objects as re-
> quire a continued attention, and a train of measures, may be
> justly and effectually answerable for the attainment of those ob-
> jects. (63, p. 384)

Thus the constituents cannot in these cases judge the "measures" themselves, since the measures have an unobserved operation; rather, they
judge the *effects* of the measures, that is, "the attainment of those objects"
for which the measures were designed. The people are at some remove
from policy making; they do not themselves devise or adopt measures,
but judge the measures their representatives devise (in cases where the
measures are judgeable), and judge the effects of measures their senators
devise (in cases where the measures are not immediately judgeable).
There would seem to be some imprecision in this judging of effects,
since the constituents could not be sure that the effects they judge were
really the results of the measures adopted. And if "[r]esponsibility, in
order to be reasonable, must be limited to objects within the power of
the responsible party," one must wonder if there will not be an element
of *unreasonable* responsibility. Do the people know what is "within the
power" of the Senate or of the government as a whole, and what is not?
If they are not sure how a certain object is attained, they cannot be sure
that a certain object *can* be attained. Thus representatives may be to
some extent rewarded for good luck or punished for failing to achieve
what is impossible. The people will have to judge claims by political men
of what objects are possible to achieve in order to judge those men
according to the visible results of their measures.

Just as new and paradoxical as the association of long terms with
responsibility is the association of small numbers with responsibility. Madison noted in passing that it is

> sufficiently difficult, at any rate, to preserve a personal responsi-
> bility in the members of a *numerous* body, for such acts of the
> body as have an immediate, detached, and palpable operation on
> its constituents. (63, p. 384)

Responsibility for even those measures which are most judgeable by the
people cannot easily be assigned to particular men. One can feel that
Congress is not doing a good job even while one continually reelects
one's own Congressman; he, after all, cannot be blamed for the deficiencies of his colleagues. This is the meaning of the charge (today) that
Congress is not sufficiently "responsible." No individual man can be held
responsible for its measures and for the results of those measures. The
attempt to bring one's representative closer to oneself has the effect of
making him less effectual; he is one of a greater number, and cannot
be responsible for any particular achievements or failures.

Accordingly, Hamilton argues that the executive's unity—apart from
its contribution to energy—is important in making the president responsible. "Responsibility is of two kinds—to censure and to punishment"
(70, p. 427). Both in quadrennial elections and in the possibility of impeachment, the president can be held responsible. If the executive con-
sisted of a number of men, each could plausibly shift the blame to others;
but a "single magistrate" cannot escape the blame for "pernicious measures." Hamilton refers here partly to ensuring that the president will
be "safe," i.e., that the dangers he might pose to liberty can be detected
and thwarted (70, p. 430); but also, more broadly, to his being held
accountable for his policies, e.g., bad appointments (70, p. 428; 77, p.
461). The single president's visibility makes him responsible, and a term
of some duration (Hamilton strongly implies that four years is too short)
helps make his responsibility reasonable, because it gives

> the officer himself the inclination and the resolution to act his
> part well [see "firmness" above], and to the community time and
> leisure to observe the tendency of his measures, and thence to
> form an experimental estimate of their merits. (72, p. 436)

The people's "experimental" judgment of the president's merits corresponds to their judging the *effects* of their senators' measures. With the
advantage of hindsight, they need not judge the measures themselves—
which, since the people may not be able to predict or even detect the
results of some measures, may be just as well. Hamilton elegantly outlines
the president's thoughts about the next election:

> Between the commencement and termination of [a four-year] pe-
> riod there would always be a considerable interval in which the

prospect of annihilation would be sufficiently remote not to have an improper effect upon the conduct of a man endowed with a tolerable portion of fortitude; and in which he might reasonably promise himself that there would be time enough before it arrived to make the community sensible of the propriety of the measures he might incline to pursue. Though it be probable that, as he approached the moment when the public were, by a new election, to signify their sense of his conduct, his confidence, and with it his firmness, would decline; yet both the one and the other would derive support from the opportunities which his previous continuance in the station had afforded him, of establishing himself in the esteem and good-will of his constituents. He might, then, hazard with safety, in proportion to the proofs he had given of his wisdom and integrity, and to the title he had acquired to the respect and attachment of his fellow-citizens. (71, pp. 434–35)

A successful president can establish a line of credit with the people. His ability to be audacious will depend on the visible results of his past audacity, although what I have said about the element of unreasonable responsibility affecting the Senate would apply to the president as well. Whether or not the people elect the best man in the first place, since wisdom is understood to conduce to proximate even if not instantaneous success, the president's exposed situation of responsibility gives him a motive to exercise his wisdom. Precisely the instability of public opinion and its concern for results may give the president enough hope to resist it.

The Federalist reinterprets responsibility by concentrating on what the responsible party is responsible for. It suggests that the people want a government they can hold responsible for choosing good policies, and even for achieving good results by policies whose effects they themselves cannot precisely detect. The visible and somewhat durable positions of president and senator encourage the people to do their judging from a distance.

When Hamilton speaks of responsibility to "censure" and to "punishment," punishment clearly refers to the aftereffects of impeachment, but censure is not confined to a rejected bid for reelection (see 70, p. 429; 77, p. 461). *The Federalist* suggests that the prospect of censure, or a sullied reputation, will be an independently effective motive in the case of senators and presidents. To some extent, or in some men, the desire for office can be subsidiary to the concern for reputation.

Thus Madison argues that the Senate's "sense of national character" is one of the advantages it has which the House lacks. This sense is a concern by individual senators for the reputation of the government and the nation in the opinion of the world. Such a sense is needed, because it is advantageous that other nations esteem rather than despise us. Our actions should appear to them as "the offspring of a wise and honorable policy" (63, p. 382). In addition, a sensibility to the "presumed or known" world opinion can help government choose just and proper measures. Here Madison seems to "[e]xtend the sphere" further, though only in thought, to take in the views of the "unbiased part of mankind." Whichever men have no passions or interests at stake in a particular decision constitute mankind's unbiased part. But since this part of mankind will not in fact control any bloc of votes, its effect depends on the government's concern for its own "character," that is, its reputation. This "sense of national character"

> can only be found in a number so small that a sensible degree of the praise and blame of public measures may be the portion of each individual; or in an assembly so durably invested with public trust that the pride and consequence of its members may be sensibly incorporated with the reputation and prosperity of the community. (63, p. 383)

The first half of Madison's sentence concerns the praise and blame which men may experience concerning "measures" the government chooses; the second half concerns their stake in the community's reputation and prosperity, i.e., in the *results* of their measures. One officeholder among a large number is too obscure to expect either praise or blame. A brief officeholder could stake his "pride and consequence" on other objects, such as private successes, and could expect others to consider the community's failures not his fault. We recall that *Federalist* 10 argued that "moral . . . motives"—which are or include a concern for reputation—are not an adequate control on individuals, and "lose their efficacy in proportion to the number combined together." The motive of reputation moves men most when they are few and visible. The republican genius of short terms and many men makes each man invisible and undermines whatever restraint a concern with reputation imposes. Madison defends the Senate's greater sensibility to reputation as a possible spur to good government, but does not rely on this often inadequate "control" to restrain abuses of government.

The "single" president is even more in a position to win a good or bad reputation, which he might care about either for its effect on his retaining his office, or for its own sake. Hamilton says those presidents with the "noblest minds" will have a "love of fame," a desire for a reputation which will extend across time and space. For this reason, it is important that such men not be excluded from running for reelection:

Even the love of fame, the ruling passion of the noblest minds,
which would prompt a man to plan and undertake extensive and
arduous enterprises for the public benefit, requiring considerable
time to mature and perfect them, if he could flatter himself with
the prospect of being allowed to finish what he had begun,
would, on the contrary, deter him from the undertaking, when he
foresaw that he must quit the scene before he could accomplish
the work, and must commit that, together with his own reputation, to hands which might be unequal or unfriendly to the task.
(72, p. 437)

Since not all presidents will have the "noblest minds," Hamilton also
discusses the effect which forbidding reelection would have on less noble
minds. The "generality of men," limited to one term, would at best display
the "negative merit of not doing harm, instead of the positive merit of
doing good." Almost all men would feel "less zeal" in doing their job if
they could not hope to continue by *"meriting"* continuance.

This position will not be disputed so long as it is admitted that
the desire of reward is one of the strongest incentives of human
conduct; or that the best security for the fidelity of mankind is to
make their interest coincide with their duty. (72, p. 437)

One could also have an interest in avoiding punishment, and that could
be another "one of the strongest incentives of human conduct." But
"zeal" is moved by the prospect of "reward," even if "fidelity" could be
secured by the prospect of punishment. The normal reward for a president would be "continuance" of the "advantage of the station." For an
"avaricious man who might happen to fill the office," the primary advantage of the station would be his salary. If a policy of honesty could
win his reelection and a continued salary, his avarice would guard against
his avarice's attraction to "peculation"; if no reelection were possible, he
would likely "make the harvest as abundant as it was transitory." Another
sort of man, moved by ambition, would also behave better if he could
hope for reelection; otherwise he might attempt to prolong his power
by a violent usurpation. It is noteworthy that Hamilton does not speak
of an ambitious man as one "who might happen to fill the office"; ambition will be a considerably more typical presidential characteristic than
avarice.

This catalogue of presidential motives shows the principle of responsibility from the standpoint of the one being held responsible. The people
bestow the carrot as well as the stick, and may therefore win zealous
rather than merely safe service. Hamilton's assertion that the passion
for fame rules the most noble minds may mean that all minds are ruled

by passion. Such a view of passion's prominence is congenial both to theorists who emphasize men's selfish passions, and to those who explain man's morality by his passions (e.g., "sympathy," "benevolence") rather than associating virtue with reason.[15] Hamilton thinks the noblest, i.e., most admirable or beautiful, minds are ruled by the love of fame. This implies either that men's minds are not ruled by reason or by moral passions, or that minds so ruled are less noble than minds ruled by the love of fame.

But love of fame is not the same as ambition; ambition is a love of power. The noblest mind is not discouraged by the prospect of loss of power as such, but by the loss of opportunity to continue the great works which will bring him fame. Such a man, faced with an exclusion after four years, would either not seek the presidency at all, or he might try to achieve great works which could be accomplished quickly (if such were possible). The job will not draw fully on the energy of either the fame-lover or the power-lover unless he has some prospect that he can continue.

The situations of senators and presidents put their minds at least on a future a few years away, and at best on a lasting fame. Their minds are however still on themselves; these are "personal motives." The people, in turn, can benefit *themselves* by putting a few men in situations in which those men can think of themselves in a way different from that in which the numerous representatives and multitudinous citizens are able to think of themselves. A responsibility for results which the people will approve, and even a concern for the reputation or fame which future people will bestow, preserves the people as judges and the people's own ends as the standard of judgment.[16] The quasi-permanence of senators and presidents does not allow them to mix their policy ends with the people's policy ends, as a mixed government would intend; they are only allowed a certain flexibility in devising "measures" to serve the people's ends. But if these few men's "personal motives" look to the ends of power or fame, rather than to benefits which government's policies can confer, their personal ends are indeed mixed with the people's ends. The people employ as means men who savor that employment as an end.

Independent Judiciary

Among the more permanent branches of the proposed government, the judiciary is clearly the most permanent. Hamilton justifies this extreme permanence—the tenure of "good behavior"—by the special function of the judiciary. Good behavior is the term in the "most approved" state constitutions, and is "one of the most valuable of the modern improvements in the practice of government" (78, p. 465). This permanence makes a considerable contribution to stability, because the judges can consistently give the law the same meaning in particular cases over a long period. But the judiciary's function also seems to detract from the energy of the executive's enforcements of the law. *The Federalist's* account of the judiciary stands somewhat apart from the rest of the book, just as the judiciary stands somewhat apart from politics. We recall that in Madison's explanation of the separation of powers in *Federalist* numbers 47–51 the judiciary was insignificant.

What is the judiciary's special function? In Locke's account of the separation of powers, the judiciary is not a distinct power, but seems to be included in the "power to execute" the laws.[17] Common usage suggests the difficulty of distinguishing "executive" from "judicial." We say that the executive "enforces" the law and the judiciary "interprets" the law; but the usual method of enforcement is a court proceeding, and any enforcement in a particular case requires an interpretation of how the law applies to that case. Hamilton speaks of the court's role in the "administration" of laws (78, p. 465) and in "execution" (81, p. 486). And today we speak of a "criminal justice system" of which prosecutors (executive) and judges are two parts.

A "judge" is one who judges a dispute. This is clear enough when two men dispute over a contract or tort, and take their dispute to court. But such judging might seem extraneous in the enforcement of the government's laws. The executive can decide how the law applies to particular cases, and impose the legal penalties on violators. To introduce a power of judging here is to allow private men to dispute with the executive's decision about their case. If a man disputes neither the executive's view of the facts of the crime, nor the executive's view of the appropriate punishment, the executive is free to execute. To allow men to dispute the executive before a judge is of considerable importance; certainly the executive cannot be quite so energetic with lawbreakers if those he tries to control are permitted to dispute with him. "In a monarchy," the judiciary's independence is "an excellent barrier to the despotism of the prince" (78, p. 465). If the judiciary is not independent of the executive, the judging is a charade; if it is independent, judging seems to undermine an energetic execution.

But we should recall in this connection the distinction between individual bodies and collective bodies (see pp. 37–38 above). The separate judiciary allows each man by himself to dispute the executive's enforcement as it respects him. The executive's difficult task is to control "combinations" of men (70, p. 423); they must be arrested or defeated. If the necessary energy is deadly force in a domestic or foreign war, the losers will be unable to dispute. If they are merely arrested or otherwise survive, they will be allowed to dispute, but *one by one.* When men are separated into individual bodies, the "courts of justice" can manifest the "majesty of the national authority" (16, p. 116).

But Hamilton goes beyond a defense of judicial independence as a check on the executive, already exemplified in Britain. He also argues that an independent judiciary can check the legislature by a process now known as "judicial review." The court can not only judge disputes between a citizen and the executive; it can judge disputes between a citizen and the legislature. The former dispute can be judged according to the laws which limit the executive; the latter can be judged according to a Constitution which limits the legislature.

America's Constitution "contains certain specified exceptions to the legislative authority":

> such, for instance, as that it shall pass no bills of attainder, no *ex post facto* laws, and the like. Limitations of this kind can be preserved in practice no other way than through the medium of courts of justice, whose duty it must be to declare all acts contrary to the manifest tenor of the Constitution void. Without this, all the reservations of particular rights or privileges would amount to nothing. (78, p. 466)

Hamilton's statement might seem extreme; after all, cannot the people enforce the limits by their electoral power, or even by a revolution appealing to the Constitution's text as a rallying point? But it may be that the people judge the government's general tendency, and are not sufficiently attentive to "particular rights or privileges" which may have been violated in particular cases; or they might even support particular violations in the service of the majority's good. Judicial review of legislation has the impressive object of protecting these particular rights or privileges not just in general but for each individual citizen.

Hamilton grounds his argument on the principle that the people are superior to their representatives and therefore the people's choice of a limited government must be enforced against those representatives. But he moves beyond this principle when he extends judicial review to cases where the legislature's acts are supported or instigated by the people. A majority moved by a "momentary inclination" or "ill humors" might oppress minorities or make dangerous innovations in the government (78, p. 469). But:

> Until the people have, by some solemn and authoritative act, annulled or changed the established form, it is binding upon themselves collectively, as well as individually; and no presumption, or

even knowledge of their sentiments, can warrant their representatives in a departure from it prior to such an act. (78, p. 470)

Thus Hamilton does not leave the matter with the proposition that the people's will is superior to their representatives, because the representatives may well reflect the living people's will in opposition to the will of people now dead. Rather, he insists on the superiority of a "solemn and authoritative act" by the people to a "momentary inclination" of the people. In choosing a government, the people choose to establish a specific form by which their future choices to change that government can be recognized as solemn. And their original choice is itself taken in a solemn form, even if that form must be improvised. The initial choice of a limited government must be understood as more than a momentary inclination.

Hamilton considers the objection that the courts may effectively become legislators by interpreting the Constitution to forbid measures which they oppose.

It can be of no weight to say that the courts, on the pretense of a repugnancy, may substitute their own pleasure to the constitutional intentions of the legislature. This might as well happen in the case of two contradictory statutes; or it might as well happen in every adjudication upon any single statute. The courts must declare the sense of the law; and if they should be disposed to exercise WILL instead of JUDGMENT, the consequence would equally be the substitution of their pleasure to that of the legislative body. The observation, if it proved anything, would prove that there ought to be no judges distinct from that body. (78, pp. 468–69)

Thus even the attempt to make application of the laws to particular cases separate from lawmaking involves the risk that the legislature's intentions will be thwarted by a separate authority. Judges can willfully misinterpret the legislature's intention as well as they can misinterpret the Constitution's intention. One might object to this analysis that the Constitution is much more vague than statutes are and therefore opens a wider door to judicial creativity. Perhaps this objection should not be addressed to Hamilton but to those who adopted later, vaguer provisions in the Constitution. I have already noted Hamilton's clear implication that judges would not limit the government to its "enumerated" powers (see p. 44 above). By suggesting only that the court prevent exercise of "specified exceptions" to the legislative power mentioned in the Constitution, Hamilton refers only to some rather clear clauses.[18] These exceptions he mentions again in *Federalist* 84, where he argues that the Constitution contains "a number of . . . provisions" which constitute as much of a "bill of rights" as can "reasonably . . . be desired" (84, pp. 510–11, 513). Other proposed provisions cannot reasonably be desired:

> What signifies a declaration that "the liberty of the press shall be inviolably preserved"? What is the liberty of the press? Who can give it any definition which would not leave the utmost latitude for evasion? I hold it to be impracticable; and from this I infer that its security, whatever fine declarations may be inserted in any constitution respecting it, must altogether depend on public opinion, and on the general spirit of the people and of the government. (84, p. 514)

In a footnote, Hamilton explains that some taxation of the press would not abridge its liberty, and that therefore the degree of taxation would be a matter for legislative discretion; which means that a constitutional assertion would not prevent the use of that discretion to impose prohibitory taxes. Since no one could interpret "liberty of the press" to require absolute immunity from all taxation, no unevadable definition is possible as a constitutional restraint on the legislature. It would seem that the limitations Hamilton defended are considerably more precise than those he opposed, not to mention later phrases of even more latitude.

While the role of judicial review may be limited by Hamilton's stress on "specified exceptions" to the legislative authority, and by the fact that the exceptions did not include the subsequent constitutional amendments, Hamilton expands the judicial role in an additional suggestion. Not only unconstitutional laws but "unjust and partial laws" can be controlled by the court, although not by a declaration that they are "void," but only by "mitigating the severity and confining the operation of such laws" (78, p. 470). Hamilton gives no argument that this practice is justified by the superiority of the people's will over their representatives' will, or of the people's solemn choice over their inclinations. While his previous argument was that the judges are bound by "laws" (including, especially, the constitutional law which is "fundamental" because adopted by the people), here he suggests that courts may be lenient against the lawmakers' intention. While the separate executive can discourage injustice by enforcing the law against its makers, the judiciary can discourage injustice by dragging its feet in applying the law to anyone. The fact that the courts may show "scruples" which the legislature lacks will be noted by the legislature; the legislators will be "in a manner compelled, by the very motives of the injustice they meditate, to qualify their attempts."[19] To "qualify" unjust intentions would be to settle for lesser injustices which might be less obstructed by scrupulous courts. This effect is "calculated to have more influence upon the character of our governments than but few may be aware of" (78, p. 470). Perhaps only a few are aware of this effect because the cynical would not expect the courts to be scrupulous and the naive would not expect the legislature to have unjust motives. Hamilton speaks of *moderating* injustice, which both assumes that unjust motives exist and admits that they will partly succeed.

A judiciary which shows such "integrity and moderation" will disappoint those with "sinister expectations" but win "the esteem and applause of all the virtuous and disinterested." Hamilton gives two reasons why "considerate men" should favor such a judiciary:

> [1] [N]o man can be sure that he may not be tomorrow the victim
> of a spirit of injustice, by which he may be a gainer today. [2]
> And every man must now feel that the inevitable tendency of
> such a spirit is to sap the foundations of public and private confidence and to introduce in its stead universal distrust and distress.
> (78, p. 470)

Injustice makes even the winners insecure, as Madison explained at the end of *Federalist* 51; and injustice is eventually destructive of the public good. An impartial government best serves the ends of government, but a "spirit of injustice" may lead a legislative or popular majority in a different direction. Madison had earlier argued that one cannot reliably insure impartiality by appealing to a "will in the community independent of the majority," such as a hereditary authority, since it may not be impartial either (51, pp. 323–24). In his case for the independent judiciary Hamilton comes close to recommending such an independent will; but it is neither simply independent nor characterized as a "will."

Hamilton argues for the judiciary's permanent tenure as an encouragement to the "firmness and independence" required to perform the tasks just described (78, p. 466). Its permanence is meant to offset its natural weakness. Of all the branches,

> the judiciary, from the nature of its functions, will always be the
> least dangerous to the political rights of the Constitution; because
> it will be least in a capacity to annoy or injure them. The executive not only dispenses the honors but holds the sword of the
> community. The legislature not only commands the purse but
> prescribes the rules by which the duties and rights of every citizen
> are to be regulated. The judiciary, on the contrary, has no influence over either the sword or the purse; no direction either of
> the strength or of the wealth of the society, and can take no active
> resolution whatever. It may truly be said to have neither FORCE
> nor WILL but merely judgment. . . . (78, p. 465)

Hamilton's "on the contrary" distinguishes the judiciary from only part of his descriptions of the executive and legislature; the judiciary does have influence over "honors," and over the "duties and rights of every citizen." But it cannot exert that influence by an "active resolution." These powers are significant—and Hamilton's elaboration of judicial review makes them more significant—but they are "least dangerous" in one respect, that is, "to the political rights of the Constitution." In other words, the judiciary is least in a position to usurp power by overthrowing the other branches and the periodic elections which the Constitution establishes. That is why it did not appear in *Federalist* 51's description of ambition counteracting ambition. The executive with his sword and the legislature with its purse, and both with the hope of popular favor, may attempt to concentrate all power in themselves. The judiciary cannot be ambitious in that sense. If it is ambitious, its love of power will be manifested in the broader exercise of the function it already has. In its independence from the people, and in the function Hamilton prescribes, its power is already very impressive. Still, it cannot "annoy or injure" the other parts of government, although it can quietly dampen their projects. It can enforce the Constitution's "manifest tenor" and it can obstructively interpret laws intended to be unjust. It cannot openly announce that its "judgments" are its own "WILL." It does remain subject to impeachment—which Hamilton calls "a complete security" by itself that the judges will avoid the "united resentment" of the legislature, although not necessarily that they will avoid "particular misconstructions" of the law (81, pp. 484–85).

This account of the judiciary is consistent with Madison's discussion of the separation of powers, according to which the legislative "vortex" is in need of control. And it is consistent with the importance of "stability" to good government; the judiciary can invalidate new laws which violate the oldest law, and can impede the operation of laws which would "sap the foundations of public and private confidence."

But the judicial function as described by Hamilton puts the court almost outside of government, as a kind of neutral observer. It is to "inflexibl[y]" protect men's rights (78, pp. 470–71), as if men did not need to be governed at all, but could be secure in their repose and confidence against any impositions, either private, or foreign, or political impositions attempting to prevent those other impositions. One need not simply obey, one can appeal to a neutral outsider according to a written standard: the law against the executive, the Constitution against the legislature. In contrast to representation's intention to protect the people as a whole or (more optimistically) to protect "every class" of citizens (57, p. 351), judicial independence has the impressive object of protecting each individual citizen. The separate judge is an "intermediate body" (78, p. 467) that seems to shield men from the harsh fact of rule.

The jury system is the epitome of a judicial "independence" by which each individual can feel protected against government's impositions by a nonpolitical outsider. A new group of private men considers each individual's case by itself, without regard to any larger context. Hamilton's defense of the Constitution's flexibility about appellate court review of fact-finding by juries suggests the limits of this judicial separateness. It might sometimes be necessary to the "public peace" for the Supreme Court to review juries' findings; and Congress is therefore left to regulate the appellate power "in such a manner as will best answer the ends of public justice and security" (81, p. 490). The judiciary remains a branch of government at the same time that it stands apart from the government; it can be checked, especially by impeachment. The judiciary is on a long leash at the edge of the strictly republican regime, reflecting the hope that good government can promise repose and tranquillity to every individual man.

For human beings to choose a good government seems to require that they be attracted by the services such a government can provide—safety, private rights, opportunities for prosperity—and that they be willing to accept branches of government which might seem to offend their own proud claim to rule. As we have seen from the beginning, *The Federalist* does not expect men's interest in the benefits of good government to overawe their honorable determination to be more than survivors and producers and consumers. But while men's republican spirit may have a passionate root, it must have a reasonable manifestation, at least reasonable enough to accept *The Federalist*'s reasonings. It must not take offense at the requirements of good government, especially if (as seems to be the case), good government is not only useful for national gain but a matter of necessity. *The Federalist* suggests that republican government cannot be sustained unless it is a good government—because a bad government could defend itself neither against wise foreigners nor against citizens who find their private rights insecure (see 51, p. 324). This result would of course humiliate the honorable determination which makes men want republican government (quite apart from its disappointing men's interest in the private fruits of good government). It is therefore not inconsistent with the spirit of the people's own honorable impulse for Madison to insist that the republican form be defined in a way which will not prevent its being a good government (see p. 123 above). That his definition is nonetheless controversial reflects the fact that honorable impulses are not always fully contented by reasonable arguments for moderation.

Conclusion
The Ambitious and the Partisans

The structure of the proposed regime is intended to place men in situations where their qualities can contribute to the public good. The people are left to choose the men directly or indirectly and sooner or later. The distance between people and rulers is not an unhappy effect of geography but the happy coincidence between the necessities of geography and the requirements of good government. That distance makes possible energy, stability, knowledge, lengthy projects, and a reputable face to the world. It even allows the people to be served contrary to their own specific inclinations—although that event would require "fortitude" by the rulers and only be temporary (78, p. 470; see 71, p. 432).

Both the usefulness and the possibility of this "wholly elective" (65, p. 396) form of popular government derive from the problem of human ambition. Ambition is the love of power, and it is a problem because at least some men feel it and especially because they can be successful in obtaining what they want. Men can be attractive enough to attract partisans, or clever enough to lull other men who are inattentive or foolish. These qualities mean that the love of power will not be a vain desire. All government involves the existence of power and thereby raises the possibility of ambition. A monarchy in principle makes ambition irrelevant, since the king has absolute power and need not be ambitious, and everyone else cannot attain power, and therefore should not be ambitious. But of course the familiar stories of ambition for the lesser offices the king can bestow, and the not unknown stories of ambitious attempts to replace a king, show the ubiquity of ambition. Perhaps a "pure democracy" could avoid some ambition if it chose its officers by lot, but it could not avoid ambition entirely unless it chose its policies by lot.

> In the ancient republics, where the whole body of the people assembled in person, a single orator, or an artful statesman, was generally seen to rule with as complete a sway as if a scepter had been placed in his single hand. (59, p. 360)

This results from the fact that the "body of the people" contains not only artful, or "cunning," or "sophist[ic]" types, but also men of "limited information and of weak capacities" susceptible to the "eloquence and address" of the former.

Republican government—"wholly elective" government—is the regime in which ambition has its clearest field. Men *run* for election; power is available to those who seek it, if they can prevail on enough other citizens' inclinations. No office has a natural or "self-appointed" or random occupant; all offices are open to aspiration. Wholly elective government tends to improve on pure democracy because it forces the ambitious, so to speak, to fight with someone their own size. The ambitious orators who try to dominate an assembly meet in a body composed of at least some who have comparable skills and intentions. The people are not so assembled and cannot be duped in precisely this way, at least. *The Federalist* adverts, however, to the likely inequalities even in a representative assembly; some men, by their talents or reputation, or by repeated reelection which enables them to become "thoroughly masters of the public business," may have particular influence on their colleagues (53, p. 335; 54, p. 340). For this reason, attempts to democratize the representative body—by enlarging its number and shortening its term— are ill conceived, because they move representative government in the direction of the democracies which were ruled by a single orator. The people are thus encouraged not to try to prevent outstanding men from entering the assembly, but to find their own outstanding men to match wits with those others who will be there.

Besides the assembled ambitious men of the House, there are other branches whose members' ambitions can "counteract" the House's ambitions. In particular, the executive's ambition can be promoted, so that his strivings will inhibit a "tyrannical concentration" of power in the legislature. And the Constitution attempts to arrange the situations of its ambitious men in ways which not only protect the people from oppression but also encourage "good government." Although ambitious men would naturally interrupt the stability of policy for the sake of making their own policies, the situation of senators with long terms discourages that effect. And ambitious men would compete with one another in a plural executive and undermine the energy which secures stability for the people. The situation of a single executive frees him from ambitious competition in doing his job.

Where does this leave the people? Madison points with some satisfaction to the fact that this "wholly popular" government (14, p. 100) is distinguished by its *"total exclusion of the people in their collective capacity"* (63, p. 387). All men are included in their individual capacities as voters. But this means a very rare participation, which seems intended to choose men according to "merit" and to judge their measures or sometimes only the results of their measures. This may be consonant with men's "honorable determination" to respect no claims to rule by a self-appointed one or few. But does it not less honorably, deferentially grant the right to rule for a time to a small number of individual men?

Such a conclusion would overlook the significance in *The Federalist* of the people's own partisanship. *Federalist* 10 described how men become passionately attached to certain opinions or leaders. Passionately opinionated men, as well as ambitious men, manifest man's political nature. Passionate partisans perhaps uneasily compromise the impulse of self-assertion with the desire for self-preservation or comfortable self-preservation; they want their opinions to prevail, but they avoid the personal risks faced by ambitious men who make politics their primary activity.[1] The partisan does not insist on exercising power himself, but only that his opinions rule, or that his favorites rule. Even though for most people political acts are infrequent, they are still regularly and permanently scheduled. The people can therefore constantly expect to exercise power, and continually have political opinions. Parties will always exist; an "extinction of parties" "ought to be neither presumed nor desired" because it "necessarily implies either a universal alarm for the public safety, or an absolute extinction of liberty" (50, p. 320). In a universal alarm for the public safety, the people would presumably unite on the necessary measures. But ordinarily the "liberty" which makes the people the "fountain" of the authority their agents exercise results in the people's being opinionated and divided. This partisanship was an important reason why the people could not be relied upon to preserve the separation of powers. While it might be good for the people to be able to judge dispassionately the controversies of their rulers, the people will in fact be partisans. What they thereby lose in accuracy they may gain in readiness.[2] Liberty preserves the "vigilant and manly spirit" (57, p. 353) evidenced in the people's claim to rule, a spirit which will rebel against clear usurpations by the government even if its partisanship might cause it to miss lesser offenses. A neutral people might be insufficiently assertive to resist usurpation; partisanship is a lesser form of ambition which helps the people to counteract ambition.

Just as *The Federalist* shows how the ambitious can be expected to rule better and more safely when placed in the situations which the structure of government creates, it suggests similar benefits from the situation in which the people themselves are placed. On *The Federalist*'s advice, the people reflect and choose a form of government which delegates certain powers to certain officers, and which delegates the power of electing certain officers to themselves. The well-defined series of occasions on which the people exercise the power they have committed to themselves affects their use of that power. That the people elect rather than assemble means that each man behaves as an individual less passionately than he would in a group; thus *The Federalist* distinguishes between an assembly of Socrateses, which would be ruled by passion, and a nation of philosophers, which would not (55, p. 342; 49, p. 315).[3] Similarly, the unassembled people cannot be "regulated in their movements by [a] systematic spirit of cabal and intrigue" in the way that an assembled group can (76, p. 455). The people's restricted political situation preserves them from certain temptations they would feel in exercising power directly, although it does not keep at least many of them from being passionately opinionated about politics.

In addition to the partisanship rather than neutrality of the people, and the spirited rather than deferential quality of elections, there is an additional way in which this popular government which excludes the people in their collective capacity nonetheless respects men's "honorable determination" about their capacity to rule. Men may feel this determination individually, and in varying degrees; and those most honorably determined about their ability to rule are allowed to try. At one point Hamilton speaks of the judges in an impeachment as disposing of a man's "most valuable rights as a citizen," meaning his opportunity to retain his political office (65, p. 399). This statement notably disparages by comparison the privilege of voting.[4] A wholly popular government makes all of the people in principle eligible to office; and this fact may be as important as the fact that the people may vote for officers. When Abraham Lincoln told some soldiers that any of their sons could become president,[5] he exaggerated their actual chances, but had he been the king of England no such statement would even have been possible. Republican government is "impartial to the rights and pretensions of every class and description of citizens" (57, p. 351). While it might seem difficult to be impartial to men's pretensions, if men's pretensions are not as equal as their rights, republican government solves this difficulty by assuming that all men have pretensions to rule, and allowing men of any "description" to try. Those less pretentious will not object to their op-portunity to be pretentious; and they will appreciate a government whose structure gives them some protection from and promises them some benefits from the more pretentious. *The Federalist* recognizes and defends the faculties men display in political life, but these faculties—like the other faculties of men—are "unequal" (10, p. 78). The ambitious men, who love power, carry further the passionate desire to have one's own opinion prevail which characterizes the partisan. And many private men may even be relatively unopinionated altogether. In this respect, elective government protects the unequal faculties of men by giving a place to those who are more and those who are less political.

NOTES

Introduction

1. Letter from Jefferson to Madison, November 18, 1788, in Adrienne Koch and William Peden, editors, *The Life and Selected Writings of Thomas Jefferson,* The Modern Library, Random House, New York, 1944, p. 452.

2. Citations in parentheses refer to *The Federalist* by number and by page in the readily available edition of Clinton Rossiter (*The Federalist Papers,* New American Library, New York and Toronto, 1961). Rossiter's text is the McLean edition of 1788 (the first publication in book form). The Rossiter edition modernizes spelling and punctuation. I have found and silently corrected a few insignificant errors in its transcription of McLean. Jacob Cooke's edition (*The Federalist,* Wesleyan University Press, Middletown, Connecticut, 1961) describes, and annotates variations among, the most important available texts of *The Federalist:* the original newspaper versions; the McLean edition; the Hopkins edition of 1802; and the Gideon edition of 1818. Variations are quite minor. There are no surviving manuscript versions of Hamilton's or Madison's contributions to *The Federalist.*

3. For the Gideon edition of 1818, Madison provided a careful account of who wrote which essays. Modern scholarship has confirmed his attributions. Disputes on this subject were caused by an apparently careless list Hamilton left with a friend. Hamilton wrote 51 essays (nos. 1, 6–9, 11–13, 15–17, 21–36, 59–61, 65–85), Madison 29 (nos. 10, 14, 18–20, 37–58, 62–63), and Jay 5 (nos. 2–5, 64). See Douglass Adair, "The Authorship of the Disputed Federalist Papers," in *Fame and the Founding Fathers: Essays by Douglass Adair,* edited by Trevor Colbourn, W. W. Norton, New York, 1974, pp. 27–74; and Adair, "The Federalist Papers," in *Fame and the Founding Fathers,* pp. 257–58.

4. The essay most thoroughly planned in advance is *Federalist* 10; see chapter 3, note 2, below. A rough idea of the rate of composition can be inferred from the timing of publication (see the Cooke edition for dates). If one assumes all

three authors began writing a week before *Federalist* 1 appeared and each wrote essays at a uniform rate, then the most pressing part of each man's publication schedule required Madison to write an essay every four and a half days, and Jay to write one every five days. Hamilton had about three days per essay for volume 1, closer to four days per essay for volume 2.

5. "William Duer was also included in the original plan; and wrote two or more papers, which though intelligent and sprightly, were not continued, nor did they make a part of the printed collection." Memorandum by Madison quoted from the J. C. Hamilton edition of *The Federalist*, volume 1, p. lxxxv, by Adair, "The Authorship of the Disputed Federalist Papers," p. 57, n. 76.

6. Letter from Madison to Thomas Jefferson, August 10, 1788, in Gaillard Hunt, editor, *The Writings of James Madison*, G. P. Putnam's Sons, New York and London, 1901–10, volume 5, p. 246.

7. Letter from Hamilton to Madison, April 3, 1788, in Harold C. Syrett, editor, *The Papers of Alexander Hamilton*, Columbia University Press, New York, 1961–79, volume 4, p. 644; emphasis added.

8. See chapter 6, note 11 and chapter 7, note 12, and text at those points.

9. Alpheus Thomas Mason, "The Federalist—A Split Personality," *American Historical Review*, volume 57, number 3, April 1952, pp. 625–43, is less misleading if one pays careful attention to the passages he cites on pp. 641–42 which admittedly contradict the thrust of his argument.

10. See Madison's concern for "future curiosity" about the American Constitution which influenced his decision to take scrupulous notes at the convention ("Preface to Debates in the Convention of 1787," in Max Farrand, editor, *The Records of the Federal Convention of 1787*, Yale University Press, New Haven, 1966, volume 3, p. 550). And the elder Madison agreed with Jefferson that *The Federalist* "may . . . be admissible as a School book, if any will be that goes so much into detail." Letter to Jefferson, February 8, 1825, in Hunt, *Writings of Madison*, volume 9, p. 219.

11. Hamilton's Preface to *The Federalist*, contained in the first book edition (J. and A. McLean, New York, 1788, volume 1, pp. iii–iv) but inexplicably omitted from recent editions. Reprinted in the edition of Paul L. Ford, Henry Holt, New York, 1898, p. lxxvii. It could be said that *The Federalist*'s immediate practical purpose was served by *impressing* its readers, by creating an aura of science and learning; this would be risky, however, unless *The Federalist*'s authors thought their less practical speculations were convincing.

12. John Marshall's opinion in *M'Culloch v. Maryland*, 4 Wheaton 316 (1819).

13. See, for example, Richard Hofstadter, *The American Political Tradition*, Vintage Books, New York, 1948, pp. 10–15.

14. Bernard Bailyn, *The Ideological Origins of the American Revolution*, The Belknap Press of Harvard University Press, Cambridge, Massachusetts, 1967; Gordon S. Wood, *The Creation of the American Republic, 1776–1787*, W. W. Norton, New York, 1972; J. G. A. Pocock, *The Machiavellian Moment: Florentine Political Thought and the Atlantic Republican Tradition*, Princeton University Press, Princeton and London, 1975.

15. Pocock, *Machiavellian Moment*, p. 522.

16. Paul F. Bourke, "The Pluralist Reading of James Madison's Tenth *Federalist*," *Perspectives in American History*, volume 9, 1975, p. 294. See also Douglass Adair, "The Tenth Federalist Revisited," in *Fame and The Founding Fathers*, p. 92.

17. See Martin Diamond, "Democracy and *The Federalist:* A Reconsideration of the Framers' Intent," *American Political Science Review,* volume 53, March 1959, pp. 52–68.

18. While Locke does not find England's regime indefensible, he quietly suggests that it might be improved upon. See John Locke, *Second Treatise,* chapter 19, section 223 (*Two Treatises of Government,* edited by Peter Laslett, revised edition, New American Library, New York, 1965, pp. 462–63); and Nathan Tarcov, "Locke's *Second Treatise* and 'The Best Fence Against Rebellion,' " *Review of Politics,* volume 43, number 2, April 1981, pp. 211–12.

19. See especially Thomas Hobbes, *Leviathan,* chapter 17 (edited by C. B. Macpherson, Penguin Books, Middlesex, England, 1968, p. 226), on how men differ from naturally sociable creatures such as bees and ants: "amongst men, there are very many, that thinke themselves wiser, and abler to govern the Publique, better than the rest; and these strive to reforme and innovate, one this way, another that way; and thereby bring it into Distraction and Civill warre." Hobbes's sovereign is supposed to prevent such dangerous strivings. The *"Liberty of Subjects"* of a monarchy does not mean a share in rule. See ibid., chapter 21 (pp. 264, 266).

20. Locke and Montesquieu recognize these impulses as well, and explain how they may be useful in securing men's private rights; but they do not insist on a wholly popular government. For example, in Locke, the political passions of some "busie head[s]" among the people lead them in exercising the right of revolution; see Tarcov, "Locke's *Second Treatise,*" pp. 213–14. In Montesquieu, the people's partisanship helps balance the legislative and executive powers; see Montesquieu, *De L'Esprit des Lois,* book 19, chapter 27 (in *Oeuvres Complètes,* edited by Roger Caillois, Bibliothèque de la Pléiade, Editions Gallimard, Paris, 1951, volume 2, pp. 575–76).

21. Hobbes, *Leviathan,* chapter 17 (p. 223). See Locke, *Second Treatise,* chapter 9, section 123 (p. 395).

22. *Federalist* 85 suggests that *Federalist* 1's "formal division of the subject" "would appear" to have been adhered to (p. 520).

23. While it might be thought that republican government is needed to make government "safe," we will see that the strictly republican government *The Federalist* insists on may not be necessary for that purpose; "one republican branch only"—as England has—could be enough to insure a common interest between rulers and ruled.

24. See the opening passages of the following papers: 37, 39, 41, 47, 52, 62, 67, 78, 84, 85.

25. Hamilton's Preface to *The Federalist,* McLean edition, p. iv, or Ford edition, p. lxxvii. Hamilton adds that this "defect has even been intentionally indulged, in order the better to impress particular arguments which were most material to the general scope of the reasoning." Ibid. It might be noted that the many similarities between Hamilton's papers on the necessity of energy and Madison's on the powers of government tend to undermine the "split personality" theory.

Chapter One

1. While the Declaration of Independence asserts the people's right to "institute new Government," it is not so strict about old governments. The Declaration says that governments are "instituted among Men, deriving their just powers

from the consent of the governed"; but does not claim that "the governed" are those who "instituted" the government. Governments which were "instituted among Men" by means other than popular consent (for example, England's) may nonetheless have succeeded in "deriving their just powers" from the subsequent, perhaps tacit, "consent of the governed."

2. Plato, *Republic*, book 9, 592a (*The Republic of Plato*, translated by Allan Bloom, Basic Books, New York and London, 1968, p. 274); and Hobbes, *Leviathan*, chapter 15 (p. 211). Hobbes suggests that the "conceit[ed]" men Aristotle recommends as natural rulers would probably be defeated in a contest of force.

3. Locke, *Second Treatise*, chapter 1, section 1 (pp. 307–8).

4. Locke argued (1) that one cannot expect historical examples of the institution of government by consent in times before historical records were kept; (2) that Rome, Venice, and America (i.e., American Indians) display at least "manifest footsteps" of consent; (3) that "an Argument from what has been, to what should of right be, has no great force"; and (4) that at least those governments "begun in Peace" were founded by consent, and those founded by conquest cannot support Filmer's view—although, we might add, they can support the view that "Men live together by no other Rules but that of Beasts. . . ." Locke's tentative examples would seem to be necessary to show that the "right" he asserts, if it does not correspond to what "has been" in many or most cases, at least corresponds to what is possible. *Second Treatise*, chapter 8, sections 100–104 (pp. 377–80).

5. "Of the Original Contract," in David Hume, *Essays Moral, Political, and Literary*, Oxford University Press, London, 1963, p. 457.

6. See ibid., pp. 472–73.

7. Ibid., pp. 458–59.

8. See John Rawls, *A Theory of Justice*, The Belknap Press of Harvard University Press, Cambridge, Massachusetts, 1971, pp. 12, 21.

9. From the point of view of the defrauder, fraud is a clever choice which can replace or overcome force.

10. See especially chapter 4, below.

11. "Of the Original Contract," in Hume, *Essays*, p. 465.

12. See *Federalist* 42, where Madison says it would be "dishonorable" for America to use England's laws as "a standard for the proceedings of this [nation], unless previously made its own by legislative adoption" (p. 266).

13. Jay's distinction between just and unjust causes of war suggests the possible efficacy of choice. America can choose a government which will be unlikely to injure other nations and which will abide by the treaties it has chosen to make. But even while showing how America can avoid injustice, Jay shows particular concern to avoid injustices against nations which are "maritime, and therefore able to annoy and injure us" and which have "the circumstance of neighborhood" (3, pp. 42, 43). And choosing to be just will not deter unjust attack (4, pp. 46–47). Compare *Federalist* 34, p. 208.

14. I refer here to Hobbes's recommendation of monarchy; according to Hobbes, it is possible, although imprudent, for the people to institute a democratic commonwealth which preserves their choice. See *Leviathan*, chapter 19 (pp. 239–47).

15. Hamilton's quiet transition from the obstacles to "the discovery of truth" (1, p. 33) to the "opposition" to the Constitution proposed (p. 34) leads to his admission that "[y]ou will, no doubt, . . . have collected from the general scope

of [these observations] that they proceed from a source not unfriendly to the new Constitution" (p. 35).

16. See no. 9, p. 74; no. 14, p. 100; no. 22, pp. 151–52; no. 29, pp. 183, 187; no. 31, p. 194; no. 37, p. 225; no. 59, p. 366; no. 67, p. 411.

17. See Hofstadter, *American Political Tradition*, p. 16. Enthusiastically patriotic sentiments are easily explained if "humanity or a fellow-feeling with others" is "a principle in human nature." See David Hume, *An Enquiry Concerning the Principles of Morals*, section 5, part 2 (*Enquiries Concerning Human Understanding and Concerning the Principles of Morals*, edited by L. A. Selby-Bigge, third edition revised by P. H. Nidditch, Oxford University Press, London, 1975, pp. 218–32). See also Adam Smith, *The Theory of Moral Sentiments*, part 1, section 1, chapter 1 (with an introduction by E. G. West, Liberty Classics, Indianapolis, 1976, p. 47); and Francis Hutcheson, *A System of Moral Philosophy*, book 1, chapter 1, section 5 (*Collected Works*, Facsimile Editions prepared by Bernhard Fabian, Georg Olms Verlagsbuchhandlung, Hildesheim, 1971, volume 5, pp. 8–9). But men's benevolent impulses were also noted by the infamous Hobbes. Included in the long list of human passions Hobbes defines are the following: "*Desire* of good to another, BENEVOLENCE, GOOD WILL, CHARITY. If to man generally, GOOD NATURE." "*Love* of Persons for society, KINDNESSE." *Leviathan*, chapter 6 (p. 123). The description "Hobbesian" applies more precisely to the view that those passions are insufficiently reliable for important political purposes. *The Federalist* shared that view with Hobbes, as indeed did many authors famous for elaborating man's "moral" passions.

18. *Plutarch's Lives*, Englished by Sir Thomas North in Ten Volumes, J. M. Dent, London, 1898, volume 1, pp. 171–76.

19. Ibid., p. 306.

20. A temporizing policy toward selfish motives is prudent because "in politics, as in religion, it is equally absurd to aim at making proselytes by fire and sword. Heresies in either can rarely be cured by persecution" (1, p. 34).

21. Thus Locke, in explaining the Law of Nature, carefully pairs religious arguments for the preservation of others with arguments based on a concern for one's own preservation. *Second Treatise*, chapter 2, section 6 (p. 311); also chapter 6, section 60 (p. 350) and section 66 (p. 354).

22. Hobbes, *Leviathan*, chapter 13 (p. 183); see *Federalist* 51, pp. 324–25. On the problem of foreign intervention, see no. 5, p. 53, and no. 18, p. 127.

23. *Plutarch's Lives*, volume 2, pp. 147, 150, 169–78.

24. Publius Publicola is the Roman whose life Plutarch pairs with the life of Solon. Publius "would frame himself to the good acceptation and liking of the people," taking steps to "cut off envy from him, winning again as much true authority, as in semblance he would seem to have lost. For this made the people more willing to obey, and readier to submit themselves unto him; insomuch as upon this occasion he was surnamed Publicola, as much to say, as the people-pleaser." *Plutarch's Lives*, volume 1, p. 359.

25. Compare *Federalist* 66, according to which "[t]here will, of course, be no exertion of *choice* on the part of the Senate" when that body exercises its power to accept or reject the president's choice of nominees (p. 405).

26. *Federalist* 68 emphasizes this distinction when describing the electoral college. The choice of president will be committed "not to any pre-established body, but to men chosen by the people for the special purpose, and at the particular conjuncture" (p. 412).

27. See above, p. 18, for the problem that a modern nation of nonsoldiers has in preserving its choice against professional armies. It seems that a nation of citizen-soldiers cannot be created by free choice but it can maintain its free choice, while a nation of industrious people can be voluntarily chosen but may not be able to preserve its freedom. See chapter 2, below, on reconciling the standing army with liberty.

28. "He who dares undertake to found a people must feel that he can change, so to speak, human nature. . . ." Rousseau, *Du Contract Social*, book 2, chapter 7 (*Oeuvres Complètes*, edited by Bernard Gagnebin and Marcel Raymond, Bibliothèque de la Pléiade, Editions Gallimard, Paris, 1964, volume 3, p. 381). "[E]ach individual having no taste for another plan of government than that which corresponds to his particular interest perceives with difficulty the advantages which must redeem the continual privation which good laws impose." Ibid. (p. 383). Rather than temporize, Rousseau says the great-souled legislator will use superstition.

29. Locke, *Second Treatise*, chapter 11, section 138 (p. 406).

30. Even in constitutional law, where courts show a kind of informal reverence for the wisdom of the framers, the formal, legal basis for enforcing that wisdom is that the people by their supreme authority adopted the Constitution. See no. 78, p. 467; and *Marbury v. Madison*, 1 Cranch 137 (1803).

Chapter Two

1. See also "firm Union" (9, p. 71); and the numerous, impressively frank but unelaborated references to a "national government" (2, p. 37; 3, p. 43; etc.).

2. This phrase candidly represents Hamilton's private views on the new Constitution; *Federalist* 34 (p. 211) suggests that a more energetic provision concerning taxation would be an improvement.

3. The word was used at the Constitutional Convention; see, e.g., Farrand, *Records of the Federal Convention*, volume 1, p. 65 (James Wilson) and p. 112 (George Mason). Two earlier but apparently isolated usages may be found in William Blackstone and Edmund Burke. See Blackstone, *Commentaries on the Laws of England*, book 1, chapter 8, near the end (Clarendon Press, Oxford, 1765–69, volume 1, p. 325); and Burke, "Thoughts on the Cause of the Present Discontents," quoted in Harvey C. Mansfield, Jr., *Statesmanship and Party Government*, University of Chicago Press, Chicago, 1965, p. 160. In both of those cases the word is used in regard to a monarch.

4. Hobbes, *Leviathan*, chapter 18 (pp. 232–33).

5. Locke, *Second Treatise*, chapter 11, sections 135 and 139 (pp. 402–3, 407–8).

6. Even David Hume, who is famous for having been skeptical of this principle, when he wrote about political science asserted that "[e]ffects will always correspond to causes. . . ." "That Politics May be Reduced to a Science," in Hume, *Essays*, p. 22.

7. While a citizen militia seems to be the most "natural" plan of defense, that natural approach fails to take account of the fact that "[w]ar, like most other things, is a science to be acquired and perfected by diligence, by perseverance, by time, and by practice" (25, p. 166).

8. The Constitution permits both governments to impose direct taxes. States may not tax imports, and neither government may tax exports; but either may impose other indirect taxes.

9. Hobbes also assigned government a very limited end, but one which he thought required unlimited means.

10. The "weapon" in question in this context is a poll tax, which Hamilton admits is generally disagreeable and to be avoided, but thinks still might in "emergencies" be an "inestimable resource." He explicitly points to its value as an emergency revenue source; it is not clear whether his reference to "critical and tempestuous conjunctures" implies a political usefulness as well. This emphatic concern for the "general defense and security" concludes volume 1's argument for the necessity of energetic government, and suggests that necessity may in emergencies clash with the republican principles which are the subject of volume 2.

11. *Federalist* 44 even suggests that each enumerated general power refers not just to one object but to a series of objects; see the following note.

12. The same interpretation is clear in the preceding paragraph: "for in every new application of a general power, the *particular powers*, which are the means of attaining the *object* of the general power, must always necessarily vary with that object, and be often properly varied whilst the object remains the same" (44, p. 285). A variety of "necessary" means pertains to each "general power" because different means are necessary in the different applications of that power. But there are in addition a variety of proper means for *each* application; these proper means, while not all necessary, are authorized. (Each "new application" of a general power is connected with a new "object"; thus the enumerated "general power" is not precisely an enumerated object, but points to a series of objects.)

13. John Marshall's opinion in *M'Culloch v. Maryland*, 4 Wheaton 316 (1819) interprets the necessary and proper clause to similar effect, but by a different line of reasoning. Marshall thought "necessary" must be understood to mean not "absolutely necessary" but "useful" or "convenient." Among other reasons, if it meant "absolutely necessary," Congress would have no "choice of means," and it would be superfluous to limit them to "proper" means. Madison interprets "necessary and proper" as "necessary or proper"; Marshall interprets it as "useful [and] proper," or "appropriate [and] not prohibited."

14. Madison's formulation in *Federalist* 44 (pp. 285–86) is different; he suggests that the executive's and judiciary's roles ("to expound and give effect to the legislative acts") permit them to interfere with "usurpations," i.e., with acts by a Congress which "shall misconstrue" the necessary and proper clause and "exercise powers not warranted by its true meaning." This judicial role is less impressive when one considers that the necessary and proper clause itself prevents a narrow judicial enforcement of the more specific enumerated powers, and when one considers Madison's view of the clause's true meaning. Still, Madison does suggest a judicial attention to Congress's respect for the Constitution's most elastic enumerated power, rather than (as Hamilton does) only to Congress's respect for constitutional denials of power. But he does not assert as clearly as Hamilton does that the court's attention will take the form of declaring unconstitutional laws void.

15. Locke, *Second Treatise*, chapter 14, section 160 (p. 422).

16. Montesquieu, *De L'Esprit des Lois*, book 9, chapter 1 (p. 369). Hamilton in *Federalist* 9 (pp. 74, 76) adopts the misleading Thomas Nugent translation of this phrase ("a kind of assemblage of societies") (*The Spirit of the Laws*, Hafner Publishing Company, New York, 1949, volume 1, p. 126). Minor changes in the rest

of the passage suggest that Hamilton was not simply guided by Nugent, but might reflect either a consultation of the French or the policy of approximation evident in other of *The Federalist*'s quotations.

17. Hamilton wisely fastens on Montesquieu's praise of the Lycian federation to support his own more relaxed definition (9, p. 76). Montesquieu's judgment of Lycia suggests that he, like *The Federalist*, did not see federation simply as a means of securing the "internal advantages" of small republics; *De L'Esprit des Lois*, book 9, chapters 1–3 (pp. 369–72).

18. On *Federalist* 9 and on the entire issue of "federalism," see Martin Diamond, "The Federalist's View of Federalism," in *Essays in Federalism*, edited by George Benson, Institute for Studies in Federalism, Claremont, California, 1962, pp. 21–64.

19. Those theories of sovereignty which deny the possibility of two governments also deny the possibility of limited government. See Bailyn, *Ideological Origins*, pp. 228–29.

20. When Hamilton was secretary of the treasury, his policies were intended to win such respect for the government. See Syrett, *Papers of Hamilton*, volume 8, p. 223.

21. It is revealing that when the leading student of *The Federalist* wrote on the "ends" of federalism, he turned not to *The Federalist* but to Alexis de Tocqueville. Compare Diamond, "The Federalist's View of Federalism," and Martin Diamond, "The Ends of Federalism," *Publius*, volume 3, number 2, Fall 1973, pp. 129–52.

22. The importance of these leaders even according to Locke is explained in Harvey C. Mansfield, Jr., *The Spirit of Liberalism*, Harvard University Press, Cambridge, Massachusetts, 1978, p. 79.

23. Hamilton's emphasis on the people's much greater ability to exercise their right of revolution in a federal system may explain the otherwise puzzling asymmetry of his remark in *Federalist* 34: "If individuals enter into a state of society, the laws of that society must be the supreme regulator of their conduct. If a number of political societies enter into a larger political society, the laws which the latter may enact, *pursuant to the powers intrusted to it by its constitution*, must necessarily be supreme over those societies and the individuals of whom they are composed" (p. 204, emphasis added).

24. See Kenneth M. Stampp, "The Concept of a Perpetual Union," *Journal of American History*, volume 65, number 1, June 1978, p. 18.

25. Locke, *Second Treatise*, chapter 19, especially sections 219–20 (pp. 459–60).

Chapter Three

1. See Benjamin F. Wright, "*The Federalist* on the Nature of Political Man," *Ethics*, volume 59, number 2, part 2, January 1949, p. 17; Robert A. Dahl, *A Preface to Democratic Theory*, University of Chicago Press, Chicago and London, 1956, p. 5; and Ralph L. Ketcham, "Notes on James Madison's Sources for the Tenth Federalist Paper," *Midwest Journal of Political Science*, volume 1, number 1, May 1957, p. 20.

2. The previous versions of the argument are in Madison's memorandum "Vices of the Political System of the United States," April 1787 (in *The Papers of James Madison*, edited by William T. Hutchinson, William M. E. Rachal, Robert A. Rutland, Charles F. Hobson, and others, University of Chicago Press, Chicago

and London, 1962–, volume 9, pp. 354–57); his speech on June 6, 1787 to the Constitutional Convention (in Farrand, *Records of the Federal Convention,* volume 1, pp. 134–36); and his letter to Jefferson of October 24, 1787 (in *Papers of Madison,* volume 10, pp. 212–14). See also a letter to Washington, April 16, 1787 (in *Papers of Madison,* volume 9, pp. 383–84) and a letter to Lafayette, March 20, 1785 (in *Papers of Madison,* volume 8, pp. 250–54). Particular issues which Madison evidently considered in developing his argument include religious toleration, paper money, taxation, British oppression of colonial America, control of the Mississippi River, the apportionment of war debts, and slavery, as well as historical examples.

3. Unannotated quotations in this chapter are from *Federalist* 10 (pp. 77–84), and will generally follow its sequence.

4. Madison's letter to Jefferson of October 24, 1787 (see note 2 above) states "some of the ideas which have occurred to me on this subject" (the proper size for a republic), and says that a "full discussion of this question would, if I mistake not, unfold the true principles of Republican government. . . ." *Papers of Madison,* volume 10, p. 212.

5. For this meaning of "character," which I infer primarily from the immediate context, see especially *Federalist* 44's reference to the "loss which America has sustained . . . from the pestilent effects of paper money . . . on the character of republican government" (p. 281). See also no. 63, p. 382; "respect for character" in the June 6 speech and letter to Jefferson cited in note 2; and *Papers of Madison,* volume 4, p. 218; volume 5, pp. 141, 420; volume 8, p. 474; volume 9, p. 179. By contrast, no. 37, p. 228 ("distinctive characters") and no. 39, p. 243 ("real character") seem to mean the "aggregate of the distinctive features of any thing" (*Oxford English Dictionary,* volume 2, p. 280, definition 9). See also Hamilton's *Federalist* 70, p. 423.

6. See especially Madison's repeated specifications of the objects endangered by faction: "the rights of other citizens, or . . . the permanent and aggregate interests of the community" (p. 78); "justice and the public good" (p. 80); "both the public good and the rights of other citizens" (p. 80); "the public good and private rights" (p. 80). See also no. 51, p. 325; no. 58, p. 361; and no. 79, p. 474.

7. In connecting "liberty" with a popular share in rule, *The Federalist* departs from Montesquieu, according to whom "liberty" is associated more with safety and what is now called "civil liberty" than with sharing in rule, or what is now called "political liberty." Hamilton explicitly defined "freedom" in his tract during the Revolution, "A Full Vindication of the Measures of the Congress" (1774). "[A free] man is governed by the laws to which he has given his consent, either in person or by his representative. . . ." Syrett, *Papers of Hamilton,* volume 1, p. 47. Either a popular government or a mixed government with one popular part ensures that there will be such "consent." See p. 147–48, below.

8. One of those ends—justice—is also important to the friends of popular government. See below.

9. The "declamations" by "adversaries to liberty" are called "specious" by Madison. This could be because the vices of popular governments should not be held against "liberty" altogether, i.e., against a free government like England's (a point made in *Federalist* 9, p. 72). Or the declamations could be specious because Madison's argument in *Federalist* 10 will show them not to apply to an extensive republic.

10. These would seem to include some but not all of those modern improvements over ancient republics listed in *Federalist* 9 (p. 72).

11. This concession lends support to historians who interpret the problems of the 1780s as predictable difficulties of a postwar economy. But Madison thought that the political abuses which *Federalist* 10 is concerned with "were evils that had more perhaps than any thing else, produced [the Federal] convention." Farrand, *Records of the Federal Convention*, volume 1, p. 134; see also *Papers of Madison*, volume 10, p. 212.

12. Montesquieu, *De L'Esprit des Lois*, book 11, chapter 6 (p. 397).

13. See Aristotle, *Politics*, book 5, chapter 1, 1301b (translated by H. Rackham, Loeb Classical Library, Harvard University Press, Cambridge, Massachusetts, 1932, p. 373).

14. See Adair, "James Madison," in *Fame and the Founding Fathers*, p. 128.

15. Hutcheson, *An Essay on the Nature and Conduct of the Passions*, section 2, part 3, definition 11 (*Collected Works*, volume 2, p. 37).

16. Strictly speaking, either of these possibilities would justify Madison's "or."

17. On the relation between rights and the public good, see below, pp. 85–88, 91–92, 109, 162–63.

18. In 1781 Madison had attributed Necker's removal from the French monarch's court to "[s]ome of those little intrigues which prevail more or less in all Courts." *Papers of Madison*, volume 3, p. 223. Only absolutely unchallenged rule by one man would completely prevent faction; perhaps this cannot be considered "political life."

19. See James P. Scanlan, "The Concept of Interest in *The Federalist*: A Study of the Structure of a Political Theory," Ph.D. dissertation, University of Chicago, 1956, p. 30: "[T]he speculations of the authors are dominated by political principles which, for their purposes, are primitive. These principles state political ideals to which the authors are committed. . . ." Republicanism is one of those principles, according to Scanlan (p. 31). Gordon S. Wood implies that the Federalists' democratic rhetoric was largely determined by the view of their audience; Wood, *Creation of the American Republic*, pp. 562–63.

20. Dahl, *Preface to Democratic Theory*, p. 11.

21. Madison's immediate point is only the folly of abolishing "liberty"; men could live a political life with a partly popular government like England's. A wholly popular government most fully indulges the proud spirit of liberty which a partly popular government fosters. According to *Federalist* 52, the American colonies enjoyed a "sufficient portion of liberty" to cause a "zeal for its proper enlargement" (p. 329).

22. Hutcheson, *Essay on the Nature and Conduct of the Passions*, section 4, part 1 (*Collected Works*, volume 2, p. 88).

23. John Locke, *An Essay Concerning Human Understanding*, book 2, chapter 21, sections 47–48 (edited by Alexander C. Fraser, Dover Publications, New York, 1959, volume 1, pp. 344–45).

24. See Adair, "James Madison," p. 127.

25. According to Madison's *Federalist* 62 (pp. 380–81), "perhaps" men have "benevolent emotions" which restrain taking "undue advantage" of others; see p. 168 below. For Hume, Smith, and Hutcheson, see books cited in chapter 1, note 17; for Witherspoon, see John Witherspoon, *Lectures on Moral Philosophy*, edited by Varnum L. Collins, Princeton University Press, Princeton, N.J., 1912.

26. Hobbes, *Leviathan*, chapter 13 (p. 188); and chapter 6 (pp. 124–25): *"Joy, arising from imagination of a mans own power and ability, is that exultation of the mind which is called* GLORYING. . . ."

27. This interpretation is supported by my suggestion that men's fallible reason must be diversely, i.e., unequally, fallible. See above, pp. 68–69.

28. Locke, *Second Treatise*, chapter 5, section 44 (p. 341); emphasis in the original.

29. Ibid., section 28 (pp. 329–30).

30. Ibid., sections 40–43 (pp. 338–40).

31. Ibid., section 39 (p. 338).

32. Hunt, *Writings of Madison*, volume 6, p. 103; see Genesis 3:17–19, and Locke, *Second Treatise*, chapter 5, section 32 (pp. 332–33).

33. Locke, *Second Treatise*, chapter 5, section 48 (p. 343).

34. Ibid., section 28 (p. 330).

35. Ibid., section 27 (p. 329).

36. Ibid., chapter 2, section 4 (p. 309); emphasis added.

37. Ibid., chapter 5, section 44 (p. 341); emphasis in the original.

38. This paradox—that men are naturally equal enough to be their own masters but unequal in their acquisitive abilities—could perhaps be resolved by a Hobbesian interpretation of those "faculties" in which men are equal, i.e., men are equally vulnerable to murder and equally proud of their own intelligence; therefore each must be considered his own master. But might not consideration of these qualities make men unwilling to respect the unequal property claimed by the superior men in the same way they are unwilling to respect a claim to rule by superior men? The equal protection of unequal faculties then appears as a kind of compromise by the superior: Forego the exercise of unequal faculties in ruling, and keep the exercise of unequal faculties in acquiring. Perhaps this compromise is made likely by the possibility that more men feel they can gain by protecting unequal acquisitive ability than by respecting unequal ruling ability.

39. See *Papers of Madison*, volume 5, p. 83, and volume 8, pp. 78, 300; and *Federalist* 51, pp. 324–25.

40. This "perfectly" expresses Locke's thought, according to Leo Strauss, *Natural Right and History*, University of Chicago Press, Chicago and London, 1953, p. 245. Madison's statement avoids any embarrassment about taxation, which might otherwise seem to infringe on "property."

41. The broader implications of the "faculties of men" are especially suggested by this comma, although they are plausible without it. The comma appears in the 1818 Gideon edition of *The Federalist* ("The Numbers written by Mr. Madison corrected by Himself"), as well as in the 1802 Hopkins edition. It did not appear in the newspaper version (*New York Daily Advertiser*, November 22, 1787), or in the first book edition (the 1788 McLean edition, supervised by Hamilton). With the exception of the Jacob Cooke edition, most editions now in print include the comma, not always accurately reflecting the text they claim to follow.

42. Thomas Jefferson, *Notes on the State of Virginia*, Query 17 (edited by William Peden, W. W. Norton, New York, 1972, p. 161).

43. Witherspoon, *Lectures on Moral Philosophy*, pp. 5, 10–14. Hutcheson speaks in a similar way about the "several powers and dispositions of the species" in *A System of Moral Philosophy*, book 1, chapter 1, section 1 (*Collected Works*, volume 5, p. 2).

44. See also p. 72 above, on the phrase "not less."

45. See Aristotle, *Politics*, book 1, chapter 3, 1256a–b (p. 35).

46. See "Parties," an essay in the *National Gazette*, January 23, 1792, in Hunt, *Writings of Madison*, volume 6, p. 86.

47. Ibid.

48. See *Papers of Madison*, volume 9, p. 76.

49. Hutcheson, *A System of Moral Philosophy*, book 2, chapter 7, section 3 (*Collected Works*, volume 5, p. 326).

50. See Hamilton's *Federalist* 34, which contrasts the "fiery and destructive *passions* of war" with the "mild and beneficent *sentiments* of peace" (p. 208, emphasis added).

51. Hume, *Essays*, pp. 58–59.

52. See citations in note 2, above. In "Vices," Madison referred to "members of different religious sects" (*Papers of Madison*, volume 9, p. 355); in his Constitutional Convention speech he referred to "disciples of this religious sect or that religious sect" (Farrand, *Records of the Federal Convention*, volume 1, p. 135); finally, in the letter to Jefferson (*Papers of Madison*, volume 10, p. 213) he referred to religion as an example of opinion and mentioned the other kinds of opinions which were elaborated in *Federalist* 10 but not mentioned in the two earliest versions.

53. See Hamilton's *Federalist* 76: "There is nothing so apt to agitate the passions of mankind as personal considerations, whether they relate to ourselves or to others, who are to be the objects of our choice or preference" (p. 456).

54. See below, p. 103–4.

55. A very young Madison found interesting enough to summarize in his notes some pages of the Abbé de Bos's *Critical Reflections* explaining why men like to watch blood, battles, and shipwrecks. "The mere emotion of the mind . . . is the attraction. Even Gentlemen of Sense & Honour are fond of Gaming, & chiefly of Hazard, not from Avarice, but merely from the violent Emotion of the Passions; which gives such an enchanting Pleasure, as makes them undervalue the Ruin & Poverty into which they are running." *Papers of Madison*, volume 1, p. 20.

56. See *Papers of Madison*, volume 9, p. 76.

57. See above, pp. 17–18.

58. Montesquieu, *De L'Esprit des Lois*, book 3, chapter 3 (p. 251) and book 4, chapter 4 (p. 266).

59. Aristotle, *Politics*, book 3, chapter 4, 1278b (p. 201); and Aristotle, *Nicomachean Ethics*, book 1, chapter 7 (translated by Martin Ostwald, Bobbs-Merrill, Indianapolis, 1962, p. 17).

60. Compare James Wilson's remark at the Constitutional Convention that "the cultivation & improvement of the human mind was the most noble object" of government and society (Farrand, *Records of the Federal Convention*, volume 1, p. 605). But Wilson seems to have meant that this would be made possible by "civil liberty" rather than directly encouraged by government; see *The Works of James Wilson*, edited by Robert G. McCloskey, The Belknap Press of Harvard University Press, Cambridge, Massachusetts, 1967, volume 2, pp. 765, 767.

61. For the divisive effect of religion, see *Federalist* 19, p. 133.

62. In his letter to Jefferson (*Papers of Madison*, volume 10, p. 213), Madison had distinguished between the "natural" divisions based on property and the "artificial" divisions based on opinion and attachment. *Federalist* 10 does not make

that distinction, thereby emphasizing that it is "the nature of man" which leads him to create even the unnecessary divisions.

63. The corollary to this situation in international politics is stated by Hamilton in *Federalist* 6. Commerce has in modern times become the "prevailing system of nations," but "Has commerce hitherto done any thing more than change the objects of war?" (p. 57).

64. Locke, *Second Treatise*, chapter 7, section 87 (p. 367).

65. Montesquieu, *De L'Esprit des Lois*, book 11, chapter 6 (p. 398).

66. Witherspoon, *Lectures on Moral Philosophy*, p. 139.

67. Locke, *Second Treatise*, chapter 11, section 136 (p. 404).

68. Although this sentence appears to equate "party" with "faction," Madison does not always use "party" with the precisely defined meaning he gave to "faction"; thus perhaps he means only that the larger party in this example will necessarily have a factious motive.

69. *Papers of Madison*, volume 9, p. 141.

70. Farrand, *Records of the Federal Convention*, volume 1, p. 135, and *Federalist* 46, p. 298.

71. See Clinton Rossiter, *Seedtime of the Republic*, Harcourt, Brace and World, New York, 1953, p. 336.

72. The continuity suggested here between the principles of 1776 and *Federalist* 10 is an exception to Gordon Wood's interpretation of the trajectory of American thought. "Americans had begun the Revolution assuming that the people were a homogeneous entity in society set against the rulers. But such an assumption belied American experience, and it took only a few years of independence to convince the best American minds that distinctions in the society were 'various and unavoidable'. . . ." Wood, *Creation of the American Republic*, p. 606. At least those best minds who took to task not merely the king but the parliament and especially the *people of England* in the 1770s showed an appreciation of the dividedness of the people of the empire. See Syrett, *Papers of Hamilton*, volume 1, pp. 46 and 151; the Declaration of Independence, which complains that "our Brittish brethren" "have been deaf to the voice of justice and of consanguinity"; and especially Jefferson's draft of the Declaration in Julian P. Boyd, editor, *The Papers of Thomas Jefferson*, Princeton University Press, Princeton, N.J., 1950–, volume 1, pp. 318–19. See also Wood, *Creation of the American Republic*, pp. 177–78; and compare ibid., p. 503.

73. *Papers of Madison*, volume 8, p. 267; and Hamilton's *Federalist* 35, p. 213.

74. "Republican Distribution of Citizens," an essay in the *National Gazette*, March 5, 1792, in Hunt, *Writings of Madison*, volume 6, p. 99, emphasis added. Aristotle, *Politics*, book 1, chapter 4, 1258b (pp. 53, 55) contains a comparable discussion, but denigrates activities which require bodily labor.

75. Jefferson, *Notes on the State of Virginia*, Query 19 (pp. 164–65).

76. "Republican Distribution of Citizens," in Hunt, *Writings of Madison*, volume 6, pp. 96–97, 99.

77. Ibid., p. 96.

78. See also no. 12, p. 96, and no. 24, p. 161.

79. This may also be a difficulty in judicial proceedings. See *Federalist* 83 (p. 504) on the danger that juries will not "pay sufficient regard to those considerations of public policy which ought to guide their inquiries" in prize cases, where "reprisal and war" are possible results. See below, p. 192.

80. In his convention speech (Farrand, *Records of the Federal Convention,* volume 1, p. 135), Madison gives as examples of unjust laws the fact that the "landed interest has borne hard on the mercantile interest" and "[d]ebtors have defrauded their creditors." The phrase "borne hard on" as compared to "defrauded" suggests the greater difficulty of precisely specifying justice and injustice in the former case.

81. "Republican Distribution of Citizens," in Hunt, *Writings of Madison,* volume 6, p. 98.

82. "Parties," in Hunt, *Writings of Madison,* volume 6, p. 86; emphasis in the original.

83. See no. 51, p. 324, and below, pp. 162–63.

84. See *Federalist* 43: "Nothing can be more chimerical than to imagine that in a trial of actual force victory may be calculated by the rules which prevail in a census of the inhabitants, or which determine the event of an election!" (p. 277).

85. This statement is subject to the qualification on p. 72 above.

86. Hobbes, *Leviathan,* chapter 13 (p. 200).

87. "Of the Independency of Parliament," in Hume, *Essays,* pp. 42–43. Hamilton makes this point in *Federalist* 15 (pp. 110–11); see also no. 63, p. 383.

88. Farrand, *Records of the Federal Convention,* volume 1, p. 135, and *Papers of Madison,* volume 10, pp. 213–14.

89. Montesquieu, *De L'Esprit des Lois,* book 2, chapter 2 (p. 241).

90. Ibid., book 5, chapter 10 (p. 289).

91. Ibid., book 8, chapter 16 (p. 362).

92. Ibid., book 3, chapter 3 (pp. 251–53).

93. Perhaps Rousseau is meant, although Rousseau's own formulations express considerably more awareness of the obstacles to human homogeneity than does the erroneous supposition Madison recounts. Rousseau is close to the "theoretic politicians" when he speaks of "a true Democracy where everything [is] equal, as well in mores and talents as in maxims and fortune." But, he immediately adds, "I have already said that there has been no true Democracy at all." *Du Contract Social,* book 4, chapter 3 (p. 443). In book 2, chapter 3 Rousseau warns that "partial associations" (p. 371) can distort the people's will so that it is not general. It is important "that there be no partial society in the State. . . . Such was the unique and sublime institution of the great Lycurgus." But "if there are partial societies," Rousseau's suggestion is closer to Madison's: "it is necessary to multiply their number and prevent their inequality, as did Solon, Numa, and Servius" (p. 372). Madison's phrase "theoretic politicians" and the prospect of men "perfectly equalized and assimilated" reminds also of some passages of Plato's *Republic,* although that prospect results not from a perfect equality of political rights but from education and property arrangements contrived by a few.

94. *Papers of Madison,* volume 10, p. 212.

95. John Adams complained in 1819 that "Mr. Madison's . . . distinction between a republic and a democracy, cannot be justified. A democracy is really a republic as an oak is a tree, or a temple is a building." Quoted in Gerald Stourzh, *Alexander Hamilton and the Idea of Republican Government,* Stanford University Press, Stanford, California, 1970, p. 55.

96. We should recall that the most "considerate and virtuous citizens" are concerned with both justice and the public good; and note that "fit characters" both love justice and are patriotic (see below).

97. During the Revolutionary War, Madison often referred to the "arts of seduction" which Britain applied to the American people; see, for example, *Papers of Madison*, volume 3, p. 23, and volume 4, p. 101.

98. Martin Diamond argues that the usefulness of local governments in this respect recommends "decentralization" but does not necessarily require a federal system. See Diamond, "The Federalist's View of Federalism," pp. 56, 59.

99. See pp. 84–85 above and pp. 162–63 below.

100. This requires a *commercial* republic, according to Martin Diamond, "The Federalist," in *History of Political Philosophy*, edited by Leo Strauss and Joseph Cropsey, Rand McNally, Chicago (second edition), 1972, p. 648.

101. The suggestion of "physical" causes dimly echoes Montesquieu's remarks on the diversity among men introduced by diverse climates. See *De L'Esprit des Lois*, book 14 (pp. 474–89).

102. See Machiavelli, *The Discourses*, book 3, chapter 6 (edited by Bernard Crick, Penguin Books, Harmondsworth, England, 1970, pp. 405–9).

103. Douglass Adair, " 'That Politics May Be Reduced to a Science': David Hume, James Madison, and the Tenth Federalist," in *Fame and the Founding Fathers*, pp. 93–106; and Ketcham, "Notes on James Madison's Sources," pp. 23–24.

104. Hume, *Essays*, pp. 513–14.

105. Ibid., pp. 514–15.

106. Ibid., p. 508.

107. Adair, " 'That Politics May Be Reduced to a Science,' " p. 106.

108. Alpheus Thomas Mason introduces both of these absent elements in his account of *Federalist* 10 in "The Federalist—A Split Personality," p. 635.

109. See Diamond, "The Federalist's View of Federalism," pp. 56–60; and above, p. 98, and note 98.

110. Madison's prediction that the "changes of time" will introduce into the individual states "those branches of industry which give a variety and complexity to the affairs of a nation" (56, p. 349) suggests that the states will have a greater "variety of . . . interests" in the future. While factious impulses would then be less likely in a majority, the greater opportunity for concert in a small sphere would continue to be a defect of the individual states.

111. *Papers of Madison*, volume 8, p. 345. Locke made the more limited but related point that multiplicity of congregations is a security against revolutions inspired by religion. If the magistrate practices toleration, "all the several separate congregations, like so many guardians of the public peace, will watch one another, that nothing may be innovated or changed in the form of the government, because they can hope for nothing better than what they already enjoy— that is, an equal condition with their fellow subjects under a just and moderate government." John Locke, *A Letter Concerning Toleration*, Bobbs-Merrill, Indianapolis, 1955, p. 55.

112. *Papers of Madison*, volume 8, p. 106.

113. Ibid.

114. *Papers of Madison*, volume 10, p. 214. This point anticipated the concern Madison expressed in the 1790s that an extended country may result in "the impossibility of acting together," which leads to "universal silence and insensi-

bility" and a "self directed" government. "Consolidation," an essay in the *National Gazette,* December 19, 1791, in Hunt, *Writings of Madison,* volume 6, p. 67.

115. Farrand, *Records of the Federal Convention,* volume 1, p. 486.

116. This problem is stated by Daniel Boorstin, *The Genius of American Politics,* University of Chicago Press, Chicago, 1953, pp. 101–6; and by Gerald Stourzh, *Hamilton and Republican Government,* pp. 114–15.

117. Perhaps the slaves are among the "persons of other descriptions whose fortunes have been interesting to the human passions."

118. Farrand, *Records of the Federal Convention,* volume 1, p. 135.

119. *Papers of Madison,* volume 8, p. 404.

120. Hunt, *Writings of Madison,* volume 5, p. 209.

121. *Papers of Madison,* volume 9, p. 350 (Madison's memorandum, "Vices of the Political System of the United States," April 1787); the argument is restated in *Federalist* 43, pp. 276–77.

122. *Papers of Madison,* volume 9, p. 351.

123. Hunt, *Writings of Madison,* volume 9, p. 85.

124. Ibid., volume 8, p. 445.

125. While Madison believed slavery to be unjust, slaveholders violate the rights of other men but not of other "citizens," thus escaping part of the definition of faction; but slaves may be included in the "community."

126. Patriotism and love of justice are both "virtuous sentiments."

127. This may be why Madison defines "a pure democracy" as "a *society*" whose people govern it, while he defines "a republic" as "a *government*" of a certain kind (10, p. 81, emphasis added). In democracy, society is government; in a republic the two are more distinct.

128. Charles Beard, *An Economic Interpretation of the Constitution of the United States,* Macmillan, New York, 1913, pp. 156–57.

129. Albert O. Hirschman, *The Passions and the Interests,* Princeton University Press, Princeton, N.J., 1977.

130. See ibid., pp. 111–13. Adam Smith's formulations are said to manifest the newly dominant importance of "interest" in thinking about human motives. The eclipse of past concerns with aristocratic "passions" is related by Hirschman to society's democratization.

131. See below, pp. 163–65.

132. The fact that rights are more fundamental does not decide the question of priority in "emergencies" between an absolutely necessary means and the more fundamental end which depends on it. See no. 36, p. 223; note 135 below; and pp. 86–87 above.

133. Robert J. Morgan, "Madison's Theory of Representation in the Tenth *Federalist,*" *Journal of Politics,* volume 36, number 4, November 1974, p. 861.

134. See *Federalist* 56: "Taking each State by itself, . . . its interests [are] but little diversified" (p. 348). Compare note 110 above.

135. In *Federalist* 22 Hamilton suggests that the "goodness" of the government, i.e., its ability to serve "the public good," is "of the greatest importance" in certain "emergencies" (p. 148).

Chapter Four

1. Hobbes, *Leviathan*, chapter 13 (p. 186); Locke, *Second Treatise*, chapter 9, section 123 (p. 395).

2. Montesquieu, *De L'Esprit des Lois*, book 11, chapter 6 (p. 397); see also book 12, chapter 2 (p. 431).

3. Witherspoon, *Lectures on Moral Philosophy*, pp. 5, 6, 10.

4. For example, George Mason's speech of June 4, in Farrand, *Records of the Federal Convention*, volume 4, p. 19.

5. The Declaration's list of grievances does give some guidance about forms of government. For example, it calls representation in the legislature an "inestimable" right, and condemns taxation without "Consent." Whether the right of representation is "inestimable" as a means of securing other, inalienable rights, or is regarded as fundamental in itself, the Declaration of Independence certainly recommends a government at least partly popular, but does not condemn the English government for not being wholly popular.

6. Compare the "predetermined" friends and foes of the proposed Constitution whom *The Federalist* does not wish to address (37, p. 225).

7. See above, pp. 107 and 15–16.

8. England's free, mixed government includes nonrepublican branches which contribute the energy of a monarch (see below, pp. 171–72) as well as a security (but a "precarious" one) for minority rights (see below, p. 143). In addition, its "one republican branch" insures that laws cannot be made without the people's consent and will be made for the public good (see below, pp. 147–48). On the other hand, there may be a danger if the nonrepublican branches possess impressive "means . . . for seducing" the republican branch (52, p. 330). A prevalent "corruption" (see 8, p. 70; 41, pp. 259–60) could undermine a free, mixed government by in effect depriving the people of the republican branch which protects them. Perhaps this possibility explains a remark in Hamilton's *Federalist* 28 suggesting that a partly popular government might not protect the people. A "full answer" to men's concerns about standing armies is "to say that the *whole power* of the proposed government is to be in the hands of the representatives of the people. This is the essential, and, after all, the only efficacious security for the rights and privileges of the people which is attainable in civil society" (p. 180, emphasis added). If a free, mixed government is corrupted away from its balance of republican and nonrepublican elements, it is not only dishonorable but dangerous to the people in a way that a wholly popular government is not. But *The Federalist* suggests that a more likely result of a free, mixed government is that its popular element will triumph—tending to neutralize both the advantages and dangers of its nonpopular branches. In that case, England's government can be praised according to *Federalist* 28's apparently rigid standard because its "whole power" is in effect in the people's hands. See no. 58, p. 359; and below, chapter 6, note 2.

9. Farrand, *Records of the Federal Convention*, volume 1, pp. 291–93.

10. A life term gives the people a choice only on the "chance" event of the death of an incumbent; see 52, p. 328.

11. Montesquieu, *De L'Esprit des Lois*, book 3, chapters 1–4 (pp. 250–54), and book 5, chapters 2–3 (pp. 274–75). In Montesquieu's usage, both democracy

and aristocracy are republics; democracy requires a strict virtue, while "moderation" is virtue enough in an aristocracy. Ibid., book 3, chapter 4 (p. 254).

12. Aristotle, *Politics*, book 1, chapter 1, 1253a (pp. 11, 13); see book 3, chapter 2, 1277b (pp. 193, 195). The variety of regimes and partisan claims makes clear the difference between speech and instinctive harmony. Speech allows men to share *and* to dispute opinions. Ibid., book 3, passim.

13. Wood, *Creation of the American Republic*, p. 612. Wood does not equate *The Federalist's* view with "interest group" theories of politics, but locates the difference in the hoped-for qualities of leaders and not also in the people's political impulses. Ibid., p. 505, and Gordon S. Wood, "Framing the Republic," in Bernard Bailyn et al., *The Great Republic: A History of the American People*, D. C. Heath, Lexington, Massachusetts, 1977, p. 338.

14. The activity of republican government appears as an end in itself to political men, distinct from the (other) ends to which good government is an instrument.

Chapter Five

1. Madison's emphasis. Quoted from Montesquieu, *De L'Esprit des Lois*, book 11, chapter 6 (p. 397).

2. Montesquieu, *De L'Esprit des Lois*, book 11, chapter 6 (p. 397). This definition differs from *The Federalist's* usual use of the word "liberty" to refer to the people's share in rule; see p. 148 below.

3. Montesquieu, *De L'Esprit des Lois*, book 11, chapter 6 (p. 398).

4. Locke, *Second Treatise*, chapter 11, section 136 (p. 405).

5. Ibid., sections 137, 136 (pp. 406, 404).

6. Ibid., section 137 (p. 406).

7. Montesquieu, *De L'Esprit des Lois*, book 11, chapter 4 (p. 395).

8. Locke, *Second Treatise*, chapter 12, section 143 (p. 410).

9. Montesquieu, *De L'Esprit des Lois*, book 11, chapter 6 (p. 398).

10. W. B. Gwyn, *The Meaning of the Separation of Powers*, Tulane Studies in Political Science, volume 9, Tulane University, New Orleans, 1965, pp. 108, 128.

11. Locke, *Second Treatise*, chapter 14 (pp. 421–27).

12. See, respectively, Montesquieu, *De L'Esprit des Lois*, book 11, chapter 6 (p. 403); ibid. (pp. 397–98); ibid. (p. 405) ("Ces trois puissances . . ."); and ibid., chapter 7 (p. 408), chapter 20 (p. 430), and chapter 18 (pp. 425–26), which makes clear that Rome's powers were distributed, but not separated according to type of power.

13. Montesquieu, *De L'Esprit des Lois*, book 11, chapter 6 (p. 398).

14. See ibid. (p. 401): "Des trois puissances dont nous avons parlé, celle de juger est en quelque façon nulle."

15. Montesquieu, *De L'Esprit des Lois*, book 11, chapter 6 (p. 402).

16. George W. Carey, "Separation of Powers and the Madisonian Model: A Reply to the Critics," *American Political Science Review*, volume 72, number 1, March 1978, pp. 151–64.

17. "Draught of a Fundamental Constitution," Appendix 2 of Jefferson, *Notes on the State of Virginia* (p. 221).

18. Montesquieu, *De L'Esprit des Lois*, book 11, chapter 6 (p. 398).

19. Hamilton later emphasizes the importance of this power: "The [House of Representatives] will be the umpire in all elections of the President which do not unite the suffrages of a majority of the whole number of electors; a case

which it cannot be doubted will sometimes, if not frequently, happen. The constant possibility of the thing must be a fruitful source of influence to that body. The more it is contemplated, the more important will appear this ultimate though contingent power of deciding the competitions of the most illustrious citizens of the Union, for the first office in it" (66, p. 404). An important effect of the later appearance of the two-party system was to narrow the field of candidates in advance of the Constitution's electoral mechanism, and greatly reduce the "constant possibility" of this contingent power for the House of Representatives.

20. Ann S. Diamond emphasizes the importance of giving branches "constitutional means" of resistance to avert their resorting to unconstitutional means of resistance which could destroy the government. "The Zenith of Separation of Powers Theory: The Federal Convention of 1787," *Publius*, volume 8, number 3, Summer 1978, p. 63.

21. For example, Hofstadter, *American Political Tradition*, pp. 8, 16.

22. According to Hobbes, the fact that some men, "taking pleasure in contemplating their own power in the acts of conquest" are not (like others) "glad to be at ease within modest bounds" causes quarrels in the state of nature—although there are other causes of quarrel as well. *Leviathan*, chapter 13 (pp. 184–85).

23. See note 14 above.

24. Montesquieu, *De L'Esprit des Lois*, book 11, chapter 6. Compare p. 405 ("Ces trois puissances . . .") with p. 401. While the House of Lords acts as the judicial power in certain (important) instances (p. 404), it is the House of Lords' share in the legislative power which makes it a suitable replacement for the "nulle" judicial power as one of the "three powers" (pp. 401, 405).

25. Montesquieu, *De L'Esprit des Lois*, book 11, chapter 6 (pp. 400–401).

26. See *Federalist* 52, where a portion of liberty is said to inspire "a zeal for its proper enlargement" (p. 329); and *Federalist* 58's account of the continual triumph of the House of Commons in Great Britain (p. 359).

27. Locke, *Second Treatise*, chapter 7, section 90 (p. 369).

28. I say "perhaps" because while a power "altogether independent" of the people would seem to go beyond a mixed government such as Britain's where the permanent branches are influenced by the Commons, Madison's formulation that "some" such "power" would be "called for" leaves unclear whether that power would be part or all of the government. The earlier reference to "liberty" being "lost" is consistent with but does not prove the suggested interpretation of "altogether independent" because it might refer to inadvertent loss of liberty.

29. While the American revolutionaries "nobly established their general liberty" (2, p. 38), this was surely aided by the fact that they already enjoyed a "portion" of liberty (52, p. 329). In practice, the people can best exercise their right of revolution if they already have representatives to lead the fight (28, p. 180).

30. Madison's use of "wish" here is consistent with my suggestion regarding *Federalist* 10 (see p. 67 above). While the political faculty of choosing is peculiar to man, man resembles other animals in wishing for those things which men desire in common with other animals (e.g., in *Federalist* 10, air; in *Federalist* 51, protection).

31. The sentence quoted could also mean that men will come to wish for a government like the proposed Constitution which makes impartial protection more likely.

32. Men use elections to prevent oppressive government, but the distribution of power is an auxiliary precaution (51, p. 322). The extended sphere inhibits oppressive majorities, but a stable senate is an auxiliary precaution (63, p. 385). In each case, the auxiliary precaution is less simply popular than the primary precaution.

Chapter Six

1. Montesquieu, *De L'Esprit des Lois*, book 11, chapter 2 (p. 394). See Hobbes, *Leviathan*, chapter 21 (pp. 266–68); and Jean Louis de Lolme, *The Constitution of England* (a book quoted and cited in *Federalist* 70, p. 430), book 2, chapter 5 (Preface and Notes by William Hughes Hughes, J. Hatchard and Son, London, 1834, pp. 208–12), and chapter 14 (p. 279).

2. See above, chapter 3, note 7. "[O]ne republican branch only" can provide the safeguard of consent unless the popular branch is under the control of an unpopular branch (see chapter 4, note 8). But in England, the House of Commons has tended to triumph over the other branches (58, p. 359; 71, p. 435), reflecting the "irresistible force possessed by that branch of a free government, which has the people on its side" (63, p. 389). Because liberty inspires a taste for its expansion (52, p. 329), free, mixed government appears to be an impermanent arrangement. Unless the unpopular elements can awe or corrupt the republican branch, and effectively extinguish free government, the confidence of the popular branch tends to turn free government into a wholly popular government. This may be why *The Federalist* refers to majority rule as "the fundamental principle" not only of republican government but of "free government" (58, p. 361). *The Federalist* recommends competing ambitious branches with a popular foundation, but does not try to balance the pride of free men with the independent authority (based on "arrogant pretensions") of one or a few.

3. Aristotle, *Politics*, book 3, chapters 4–5, 1279a (pp. 205, 207). Because free government is not the same thing as wholly popular government, my suggestion here that free government is expected to secure the people's interest does not contradict my earlier suggestion that the justification for a *wholly* popular government goes beyond matters of "interest." See pp. 121–22 above.

4. Whether or not this "ambition" is grounds for "esteem" as well as for "confidence," the possible virtues and gratitude mentioned above would presumably be estimable human qualities.

5. The "restraint of frequent elections" cannot, of course, prevent a usurpation which cancels those elections. But it prevents lesser abuses, and may inhibit the accumulation of the spirit of independence which would dare to cancel an election.

6. Locke, *Second Treatise*, chapter 12, section 143 (p. 410)—quoted above, p. 129.

7. Thus while human selfishness can obstruct the public good, human sympathy does not guarantee the public good because sympathetic passions often attach themselves to only part of the public. See also chapter 1, note 17, and chapter 7, p. 168 and note 4.

8. Madison calls this "unbounded jealousy" a "passion," not a rational calculation about human passions. Skepticism of human motives, like confidence in human motives, faces the obstacles to reasoning discussed in *Federalist* 37.

9. Madison initially states the question regarding the length of term as whether biennial elections are "necessary or useful" (52, p. 327, and 53, p. 332); his concluding formula (53, p. 336) tacitly concedes that a two-year term is not "necessary."

10. The mercantile representatives' promotion of manufacturers' interests might be moderated by a mild conflict of interest. The merchants are considered a "natural patron and friend" of the manufacturers (35, p. 214), in that they are interested in selling manufactures; but they may be willing to sell imported manufactures and thus from their own interest will not favor a "premature monopoly" for domestic industry (35, p. 212).

11. Madison's *Federalist* 10 would seem to predict or hope that in an extended sphere the landed interest, contrary to Hamilton's remark in *Federalist* 35, would not be "perfectly united from the wealthiest landlord to the poorest tenant" (p. 215).

12. For similarly self-interested reasons, men should elect those wise enough to be equal to contests with leaders of other nations (see 4, p. 47, and 62, pp. 380–81).

13. "Nations in general, even under governments of the more popular kind, usually commit the administration of their finances to single men or to boards composed of a few individuals, who digest and prepare, in the first instance, the plans of taxation, which are afterwards passed into law by the authority of the sovereign or legislature.

"Inquisitive and enlightened statesmen are everywhere deemed best qualified to make a judicious selection of the objects proper for revenue. . . ." (36, pp. 218–19).

14. Note especially the context of Hamilton's reassurances in *Federalist* 60; he is arguing that the landed interest will likely refrain from attempting to completely exclude the mercantile interest from the legislature. Men who appreciate the value of commerce might devise "bias[ed]" policies short of that.

Chapter Seven

1. Locke, *Second Treatise*, chapter 8, sections 95–96 (p. 375).

2. See *Federalist* 57: "The aim of every political constitution is, or ought to be, first to obtain for rulers men who possess most wisdom to discern, and most virtue to *pursue*, the *common good* of the society . . ." (p. 350, emphasis added).

3. I adopt this word from *Federalist* 73 (p. 443), where Hamilton speaks of the diverse "situations" of the men of the different branches; and from *Federalist* 72, where Hamilton speaks of the president as "[s]uch a man, in such a situation" (newspaper edition only—in Jacob Cooke, editor, *The Federalist*, p. 489).

4. While David Hume implies that all men have at least a glimmer of benevolence, the "degrees of these sentiments may be the subject of controversy," and their influence varies among different men. See *Enquiry Concerning Morals*, section 5, part 2 (pp. 225–26).

5. Ibid. (p. 225n, p. 227).

6. Locke, *Second Treatise*, chapter 9, section 124 (p. 396).

7. For "tides" in the "affairs of men," see Shakespeare, *Julius Caesar*, Act 4, scene 3, line 218. Jay is also responsible for the other Shakespearean quotation of *The Federalist* (2, p. 41): "FAREWELL! A LONG FAREWELL TO ALL MY GREATNESS." See *Henry VIII*, Act 3, scene 2, line 351 (spoken by Cardinal Wolsey).

8. Locke, *Second Treatise,* chapter 12, section 147 (p. 411).

9. Except in the fact that a two-thirds vote by the other branches can override his veto.

10. George W. Carey, "Separation of Powers and the Madisonian Model," focuses too narrowly on nos. 47–51, treating the equally "Madisonian" nos. 62–63 as secondary. While Carey's argument might seem in the spirit of Martin Diamond's emphasis on "democracy" in *The Federalist,* compare the quite different account of separation of powers in Diamond, "The Federalist," in *History of Political Philosophy,* p. 643.

11. Hamilton refers to the executive here as one of the "guardians" of the people's interests (71, p. 432), just as Madison in *Federalist* 10 hoped for representatives who would be "proper guardians of the public weal" (p. 82). *Federalist* 63 refers both to a "blow meditated by the people against themselves," and to "unjust measures" (pp. 384, 385). The example given—Athens' condemnation of Socrates—appears to have been both.

12. Jay also spoke in *Federalist* 3 (p. 43) of the national government's being able to call upon the "best men," a phrase he echoes in *Federalist* 64 but which Hamilton and Madison do not use. Compare Madison's lukewarm remarks about indirect election of senators preceding his suggestion that it will favor a "select appointment": "Among the various modes which might have been devised for constituting this branch of the government, that which has been proposed by the convention is probably the most congenial with the public opinion" (62, p. 377). And Hamilton's argument for presidential nomination of subordinate officers reflects badly on the constitutional scheme by which state legislatures choose senators. One man chooses better than a "select body or assembly," but Hamilton says his argument on this point does not apply to the people at large. "The people collectively, from their number and from their dispersed situation, cannot be regulated in their movements by that systematic spirit of cabal and intrigue which will be urged as the chief objections to reposing the power in question in a body of men" (76, p. 455). The Constitution arranged the electoral college to prevent such "cabal" by requiring that the electors not meet in one place but rather "in their respective States" (Article II, section 1).

13. Adair, "The Federalist Papers," in *Fame and the Founding Fathers,* p. 257.

14. Although, Madison says, this is not easy when the representative body is numerous (see below).

15. See Hume, *A Treatise of Human Nature,* book 2, part 3, section 3 (edited by Ernest C. Mossner, Penguin Books, Harmondsworth, England, 1969, p. 462): "Reason is, and ought only to be the slave of the passions, and can never pretend to any other office than to serve and obey them." See also chapter 1, note 17, above.

16. This statement would need to be qualified if the rulers looked to the unbiased part of mankind (i.e., foreigners) for praise or fame.

17. Locke, *Second Treatise,* chapter 12, section 143 (p. 410).

18. The provisions are contained in Article I, section 9, of the Constitution.

19. Like the "silent and unperceived" effect of the existence of the executive veto, this judicial power may be useful by its possibility without even being exercised. The legislature's "bare apprehension of opposition" might be enough to stop them (73, p. 446).

Conclusion

1. I owe this suggestion to Professor Harvey C. Mansfield, Jr.

2. Compare De Lolme's praise of England's constitution for leaving the people out of the government entirely; this unites them as "one body" with "one opinion" "on the subject of their liberty." They can keep the government in awe, but are not partisan. De Lolme, *Constitution of England*, book 2, chapter 14 (pp. 279–81).

3. Maynard Smith, "Reason, Passion, and Political Freedom in *The Federalist*," *Journal of Politics*, volume 22, number 3, August 1960, p. 530.

4. *Federalist* 61 (p. 373) calls voting "so invaluable a privilege."

5. "Speech to One Hundred Sixty-sixth Ohio Regiment," August 22, 1864, in *The Collected Works of Abraham Lincoln*, edited by Roy P. Basler, Rutgers University Press, New Brunswick, New Jersey, 1953, volume 7, p. 512:

> I happen temporarily to occupy this big White House. I am a living witness that any one of your children may look to come here as my father's child has. It is in order that each of you may have through this free government which we have enjoyed, an open field and a fair chance for your industry, enterprise and intelligence; that you may all have equal privileges in the race of life, with all its desirable human aspirations. It is for this the struggle should be maintained, that we may not lose our birthright—not only for one, but for two or three years. The nation is worth fighting for, to secure such an inestimable jewel.

Index